Swords Into Dow Shares

Swords Into Dow Shares

Governing the Decline of the Military-Industrial Complex

Rachel Weber

URBAN PLANNING AND POLICY PROGRAM

UNIVERSITY OF ILLINOIS AT CHICAGO

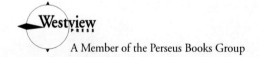

A Member of the Perseus Books Group

Copyright © 2001 by Westview Press, A Member of the Perseus Books Group

Published in 2001 in the United States of America by Westview Press, 5500 Central Avenue, Boulder, Colorado 80301-2877, and in the United Kingdom by Westview Press, 12 Hid's Copse Road, Cumnor Hill, Oxford OX2 9JJ

Find us on the World Wide Web at www.westviewpress.com

Library of Congress Cataloging-in-Publication Data

Weber, Rachel Nicole, 1967–
    Swords into Dow shares : governing the decline of the military-industrial complex / Rachel Weber.
        p.   cm.
    Includes bibliographical references.
    ISBN 0-8133-9790-1 (pbk. : alk. paper)
    1. Economic conversion—United States.   2. Disarmament—Economic aspects—United States   3. United States—Defenses—Economic aspects.   4. Military-industrial complex—United States.   I. Title.

HC110.D4 W35   2000
338.4'7355'00973—dc21   00-046225

PERSEUS
POD
ON DEMAND

10   9   8   7   6   5   4   3   2   1

Contents

List of Acronyms

ARPA	Advanced Research Projects Agency
AIA	Aerospace Industries Association
AUC	Alternative Use Committee
CICA	Competition in Contracting Act of 1984
CBIA	Connecticut Business and Industry Association
DARPA	Defense Advanced Research Projects Agency
DCAA	Defense Contract Audit Agency
DCMC	Defense Contract Management Command
DOD	Department of Defense
EDA	Economic Development Administration
EDWAA	Economic Dislocation and Worker Adjustment Assistance Act
ERISA	Employee Retirement Income Security Act
FAR	Federal Acquisitions Regulations
GAO	General Accounting Office
GFE	Government-furnished equipment
GFP	Government-furnished property
MCLR	Midwest Center for Labor Research
NIST	National Institute for Standards and Technology
NLRA	National Labor Relations Act
OEA	Office of Economic Adjustment
OTA	U.S. Congress Office of Technology Assessment
OTCA	Omnibus Trade and Competitiveness Act
PIC	Private Industry Council
SEC	Securities and Exchange Commission
TECHCONN	Technology for Connecticut
TRP	Technology Reinvestment Project
WARN	Worker Adjustment and Retraining Notification Act

Preface

Scholarship in the social sciences aspires to the highest level of objectivity and value neutrality. Positivists invoke Max Weber's distinction between the vocations of science and politics to support the assertion that truth claims require an obedience to an impersonal, objective system of analysis. We must adopt scientific methods so that our values do not dictate the results of our research. To betray some personal connection to one's subject matter is to elicit suspicions about the soundness and rigor of one's methods. "What are the checks you use to control your biases?" people will ask. "Don't you need some distance from a problem in order to fully understand it?"

In the following book, I do not reveal my personal attachments to the subject matter, but they are nevertheless very present. I grew up in the region that is a focus of this study—New London County, Connecticut—and imbibed some of the bitterness and anger of my interview subjects. My parents and friends bore the brunt of the dislocative restructuring decisions I describe. Many lost their jobs and left the area. Stories circulated about laid-off Electric Boat employees who squandered their severance pay at the new casinos. The involuntarily retired engineers on my block, antsy with skills and know-how, took to making endless home improvements. Their wives still held jobs outside the home and could be seen commuting to work in the family car. Such was the changing demographic of the suburban military-industrial complex in the early 1990s.

When asked why I did not choose a more distant subject matter or a more value-neutral method, I respond in a few ways. First, all problem definitions, methods, and research questions involve interpretations and decisions about value. Why are only those who reveal their attachments suspect? Much of neoclassical economics, for example, betrays value judgments about the primacy of efficiency over equity, markets over states, and choice over control. In his recent book about doing documentary work, Robert Coles reminds us that "a search for the factual, the palpable, the real, a determined effort to observe and authenticate, and afterwards, to report, has to contend, often enough, with a range of seemingly irrelevant or distracting emotions—the search for objectivity way-laid by a stubborn subjectivity" (1997, 5).

Second, the dualism that distinguishes so clearly between distance and proximity, experiential knowledge and detached, objective knowledge offers a false choice. My judgments and values do not simply come from the experience of having lived close to the situation I study. Many, if not most, of the residents of the region would interpret the actions of Electric Boat in a much different light from mine. I make judgments about the justness of the corporate strategies based on my readings of political, le-gal, and economic theory, my interpretations of empirical data, and his-torical and ethnographic research. Any research project involves the blending of the objective and the subjective; indeed, it is what makes so-cial science scholarship so interesting and challenging. We must always question just "what blend of the two is proper, and at what point we [should] begin to cry 'foul'" (Coles 1997, 8).

Third, academics have misread Max Weber, whose goal of value-neu-trality had a very specific and confined meaning. What is dangerous is not the presence of value judgments per se but only "those judgments that remain beyond the reach of critical reflection and are not subject to revision in light of experience" (Bellah 1977, xi). My status as a local and quasi-insider provided me with access, but this access does not blind as much as it produces an intense self-scrutiny. The following book is the outcome of years of reflection and academic inquiry into the legal-institu-tional roots of American capitalism. It is my hope that it will help steer the discussion of corporate restructuring and corporate obligations in a new and productive direction.

Acknowledgments

I would like to express my sincere thanks and gratitude to the host of people and institutions who supported me through the process of writing this book. In acknowledging them, I confess that the following product is not my own but the result of collaboration, friendships, and continuous interaction with a supportive and intellectually vibrant group of people.

In particular, I would like to thank the following individuals at Cornell University. Susan Christopherson was always inspiring. Her bold insights, free-flowing advice, and charisma serve as a model for all of us mentors-in-training. Judith Reppy shared her wisdom and her home with me and displayed a generosity of spirit that I will strive to emulate. John Forester teased out ideas when I thought I had none and asked the hard questions, forcing me to put my ear to the ground (or, at least to my interview transcripts) and listen more closely. Greg Alexander welcomed me into the world of legal theory and shared the clarity of his analysis with me. Along with these four individuals, I would like to thank Donna Wiernicki in the Department of City and Regional Planning, and Elaine Scott in the Peace Studies Program.

I benefited from the financial support of several organizations, namely, the Urban Planning and Policy Program at the University of Illinois–Chicago, the Graduate School, Peace Studies Program, and Department of City and Regional Planning at Cornell University, the Institute for the Study of World Politics, and the President's Council of Cornell Women. The Center for International Security and Arms Control at Stanford University provided me with a predoctoral fellowship and the opportunity to spend a year in a warm and intellectually challenging environment.

I want to express my appreciation to Dave McBride and the staff at Westview for turning my manuscript into a published volume. Dave's detailed editing, constant feedback, and intellectual support for interdisciplinary work sustained me through the process. I took the extensive comments of three anonymous reviewers to heart as I reorganized and refined the manuscript.

Special thanks are owed to the individuals who agreed to be interviewed for this project. The following colleagues and friends offered invaluable suggestions on my work-in-progress: Gerald Frug, Jerrold Kayden, Ann Markusen, Harvey Sapolsky, Jessica Pitt, Sara Hymowitz, Richard Clayton, Joe Persky, Wim Wiewel, David Perry, Dan McGrath, Barry Bluestone, Karen Polenske, Merritt Roe Smith, Gordon Clark, John Lovering, Therese McGuire, Charlie Hoch, Janet Smith, Cynthia Ward, Ken Delacruz, Joanne Sheehan, Jim Benn, Domenick Bertelli, Ernie Sternberg, Don Goldstein, Evalyn Tennant, Don Peppard, Lynn Eden, Judith Sedaitis, David Holloway, Bill Simon, Aaron Belkin, Charlie Glaser, and Erika Weinthal. I am lucky to have a widely dispersed and infinitely generous network of friends and cousins who offered me free food and lodging. Joshua Steinhauer, Marilyn Webb, Beatrice Gottfried, Frieda Stolzberg, Judith Lurie, and Sharon Jacobs provided great comfort in my travels.

My greatest thanks goes to my immediate family, Corinne, David, Ben, and Lauren, and my husband, John Slocum, who have supported me through the many strange phases of my life and who have always encouraged me to live fully and thoughtfully.

Introduction

The public be damned! I work for my stockholders.
—William Vanderbilt, 1879

In 1991 the chairman of the General Dynamics Corporation, William Anders, announced that he was going to transform his corporation, one of the largest prime defense contractors in the nation, into a shareholder-driven enterprise. Management embarked on an explicit strategy of creating shareholder value through divestiture, downsizing, and an executive compensation plan that linked executive pay to stock price. General Dynamics realized a 440 percent return between 1991 and 1993, compared to the industry average of approximately 110 percent, and upper-level management received record bonuses (Dial and Murphy 1995). During this same period, the corporation reduced its workforce by 64 percent, laying off thousands at its few remaining plants. General Dynamics cut its capital expenditures by half while steadfastly refusing to explore opportunities for commercial production.

In response to accusations of peacetime profiteering at the public's expense, Anders replied:

> I do not see that we have a special obligation to our employees. This is an issue of excess human capacity that had to leave the defense industry. We trained our people to have specific skills and paid for that training. What are we to do when those skills are no longer required? . . . We are not going to start to build bridges. That's not our business and not our obligation. (Dial and Murphy 1995, 303)

What are corporate directors obligated to do, and to whom are they obligated? Who among the various participants in the corporate enterprise owns and controls what, and who makes which decisions? Who has responsibility for, and legitimate claims against, the revenues and assets of

1

a corporation? How does management prioritize the claims of different stakeholders with potentially conflicting interests?

The answers to these questions comprise a subfield of business, economics, and law referred to as "corporate governance." Corporate governance describes the relations between actors in publicly traded corporations, especially the rights and obligations of the board of directors, managers, and shareholders. The prevailing paradigm of corporate governance in the United States asserts that corporations are the property of shareholders alone. Shareholders "assign" directors/managers as their proxies, entrusting them with the task of managing the firm on behalf of the true owners. Senior management has obligations, first and foremost, to satisfy the short-term profit maximization goals of the company's shareholders. This doctrine is based on the assumption that shareholders alone bear the financial risks and contribute the equity necessary for production. Institutionally, changes in the regulation of financial markets, the increasing strength of pension and mutual funds, and new systems of executive compensation enforce management's obligations to shareholders.

With a legal-institutional method and a programmatic intention, I examine the post–Cold War restructuring of the defense industry as an example that challenges and confounds many of the assumptions underlying our current understanding of how and in whose interests corporations should act. The primacy of shareholders in the investment decisions of corporations is unjustified, I argue, when other constituents (i.e., the state, workers, customers) enable corporate activity and shelter shareholders from financial risks. A wide array of corporations receive tax breaks, regulatory relief, and free property from the government, yet management, in collusion with investors, has extraordinary and unchecked control to dispose of its subsidized assets. Defense contractors are particularly notable in this regard. Pentagon capitalism is the most visible example of a long-standing tradition of granting monopoly power, special privileges, subsidies, and legal immunities to corporations that perform public tasks. The government and its suppliers negotiate a system of contracting and pricing whereby the federal government and taxpayers assume many of the risks associated with operating a business. Despite the public's enormous contribution, corporate investment decisions are made exclusively by private managers. Managers are less beholden to the state than they are to the stock market, and, in their shareholders' interests, they have pursued restructuring strategies in the last decade that jeopardized other public interests, such as fiscal austerity and national security.

The restructuring of the military-industrial base in the 1990s clearly illustrates the failures and abuses inherent in the American model of corporate governance.[1] Prompted by the financial sector, defense firms disinvested in their productive capacities, engaging in mergers and divestitures, spin-offs and split-ups, stock repurchases and leveraged buy-outs. While their stock prices soared, these companies left a trail of pink slips, empty plants, and devastated local economies in their wake. During this time, the stewardship of public moneys passed from government officials to private shareholders and senior management of defense firms. Investment bankers and financial intermediaries were attracted by large cash reserves, opportunities for liquidation and downsizing, and assured government markets of defense contractors, without respect for or interest in their military-industrial missions or the fact that the federal government had provided the bulk of their assets. Defense firms had successfully resisted financial pressures in the 1980s, due to the profits they had extracted during the Reagan buildup, but in the early 1990s, they began aggressively courting the stock market. Contractors experienced enormous financial gains, even as their government markets shrank and their workforces dwindled. Their phenomenal returns derived not from increased efficiency or entrepreneurialism but from complex financial machinations, mass layoffs, risk-shifting, and the exploitation of the federal government's largesse. I argue that defense budget cutbacks could have been achieved without redirecting billions of dollars to shareholders and their financial advisors.

The normative thrust of this book is that corporations should be held accountable not only to their shareholders but also to nonshareholder constituents—workers, customers, and communities. I suggest an alternative model of power sharing within the corporation, one that more accurately reflects the degree to which other stakeholders have made risky, firm-specific investments there. I distinguish my approach from the tomes of work on "corporate social responsibility," for I am not concerned with the *voluntary* sacrifice of corporate profits for some third party gain. These tracts assume that being a responsible corporate citizen requires an efficiency-for-equity trade-off and a loss of profits that only the corporation rightly "owns." In this literature, the rights of nonshareholder constituencies are summarily reduced to just another set of economic costs that constrain the natural profit-making desire of private firms (Council on Economic Priorities 1986; Drucker 1993; Reder 1994). In contrast, I am arguing that those corporations that have availed themselves of public resources possess diluted control claims on the use of their profits because, through this process, the state becomes a corporate risk-bearer and bona fide stakeholder. The complicity of the state in defense procurement politicizes production decisions and undermines the legitimacy of "private" managerial prerogatives.[2] The profits and assets of defense contractors are not management's alone to distribute as it sees fit; the state and, by association, other stakeholders should have a larger, legally enforceable voice in decisions governing the future of the defense-industrial base.

The Realm of Law

This book focuses on the law as an object of analysis, because corporate strategies take place within a legal-institutional framework. Markets do not regulate themselves, for the law is deeply rooted in American life (Commons 1957; Polanyi 1944; Block 1987; Sklar 1988; Horwitz 1992; Berk 1994). The market itself is a social and political construct, "a realm of contracts and property rights, that is, a realm of law" (Sklar 1988, 6).[3] Institutional scholars have challenged many of the assumptions underlying neoclassical economic interpretations of corporate behavior, primarily the idea that external market stimuli—the price of inputs, changing customer demands, the cost of capital—alone determine management strategies. Management makes decisions about capital structure, geographic expansion, product diversification, and workforce organization within an incentive-and-penalty structure framed by the law.

One of the ways in which the law influences corporate strategy is by validating or invalidating the claims of certain stakeholders to corporate resources. Corporate law, for example, allocates rights and obligations to management and shareholders. Shareholders have the right to elect the board of directors, and management is obligated to take shareholders' best interests into account when deciding corporate strategy. The law defines, often loosely, what is within the range and what is beyond the pale of acceptable managerial behavior and therefore influences the motivations, design, and implementation of corporate strategies (Etzioni 1988). The law determines how different stakeholders conceive of their interests in the corporation and how the distribution of bargaining power among these actors will be determined. Other factors certainly contribute to this distribution; for example, union membership rates influence management's perceptions of the relative power of workers' claims. However, corporate actors rarely articulate their claims and motivations in the abstract language of power or autonomy. Instead, they make concrete claims cast in the vocabulary of specific legal rights and duties (Dan-Cohen 1986, 189).

Understanding how market pressures are mediated by law requires a closer examination of "corporate governance"—the rules and norms that govern the relationships within the firm. In recent years many neoclassical economists have become fascinated with the subject. This interest can be read as "an implicit admission that markets do not regulate themselves as perfectly as we're told. . . . That means that capital is admitting that corporations must be subject to some kind of outside oversight. If that's the case, then the question becomes oversight by whom, in what form, and in whose interest" (Henwood 1997, 247).

Corporate governance "rules" prescribe the internal structure and functioning of publicly traded corporations, especially the rights and obligations of the board of directors, managers, and shareholders. No single authoritative source for the rules exists; corporate governance is a body of legal practice and custom culled from case law, legal texts (e.g., corporate charters and bylaws), and boardroom practices. These basic ground rules—some legal, some customary—influence the allocation of rights and responsibilities within the corporation and justify the actions of management.

The so-called "contractarian" paradigm has been the dominant theoretical orientation in corporate law since the late 1970s (Jensen and Meckling 1976; Butler 1989; Easterbrook and Fischel 1991). Rooted firmly in neoclassical economics, scholars advocating this model view the corporation as a legal fiction, a "nexus" of voluntary contracting relations among individual input owners. In 1819 Chief Justice Marshall set the stage for this model when he called the corporation "an artificial being, invisible, intangible, existing only in the contemplation of law. Being the mere creation of law, it possesses only those properties which the charter of its creation confers upon it either expressly or as incidental to its existence."[4]

The corporation is disposable, instrumental only in facilitating the contracting interactions of different corporate actors. Management raises funds to acquire physical capital and to finance operations through contracting with creditors (i.e., debt) and contracting with shareholders (i.e., equity). The proceeds of the corporation's activities are then divided among its employees, suppliers, and creditors based on contracts that are assumed to be set in advance, and drafted on terms independent of the success of the enterprise as a whole (Blair 1995). Wages and loan payments are fixed liabilities, not contingent on whether the firm is thriving or performing poorly. Only shareholders contract for a variable share of net proceeds, once all previously contracted-for obligations have been paid to the firm's employees, suppliers, and creditors. Because payments to shareholders are paid last and because these payments vary depending on the profitability of the business, shareholders are said to have a "residual" claim on the corporation's profits.

The nexus of contracts model is guided by the notion that the corporation should be structured in the best interests of its shareholders, because shareholders are perceived to be the only owners and residual risk-bearers of the corporation. The central problem of corporate governance, then, is the relationship between shareholders and management. Corporate law seeks to make executives accountable to shareholders, while at the same time giving managers the freedom and control over resources they need in order to take advantage of investment opportunities. Thus, corporate law includes a standardized provision that directors owe shareholders "fiduciary duties" to maximize the value of shareholders' investments. Fiduciary duties are legal-institutional mechanisms for ensuring corporate accountability; they include the duties of loyalty, care, and concern. They oblige management to work for the exclusive benefit and in the best interest of the shareholders.

Privileging shareholders is not simply an ideological position. The courts enforce management's duties to shareholders. Financial market institutions, pension and mutual funds, and executive compensation incentives enforce management's obligations to shareholders. The hostile takeover bids and leveraged buyouts of the 1980s and 1990s pressured management into improving corporate financial performance by increasing dividends and stock prices. "Creating shareholder value" became the slogan of this era.

I argue that legal doctrine and institutional pressures offer up a compelling but distorted image of the internal governance of corporations. They justify management's authority to undertake corporate restructuring for the sake of satisfying fiduciary obligations to shareholders. Corporate law's preoccupation with rationality, contracts, and free will, no matter how compromised in practice, justifies management's autonomy from external interventions or nonshareholder claims on investment decisions. What may look like greed and opportunism—shareholders and senior management making record returns in a declining market—falls squarely within the bounds of laws governing corporate obligations, because the laws themselves favor profit-making and financial imperatives. As Clark (1993) points out in his excellent study of pension fund regulations, the courts rarely take into account a corporation's social obligations when examining the impact of industrial restructuring. They tend to support corporate behavior based on profit maximization ("business considerations," in legal parlance) without regard for the source of the profits or the contributions of other stakeholders. The courts perpetuate the idea that to serve other stakeholders (e.g., aiding customers by lowering prices charged for products), corporations would have to act irrationally and betray their obligations to maximize shareholder value.

Corporate restructuring involves judgments about equity: Who is deserving, who is next deserving, and so on. Contemporary corporate governance assumes that shareholders have the largest claim to the residual returns of the corporation because they take on the greatest risk of economic loss. Following this logic, corporate law treats shareholders as the most deserving of management's devotion, fidelity, and accountability. In this study, I question the normative content of these justifications. My concern is not whether there are reasons for corporate restructuring or whether managers' strategies are consistent with the law. Rather, I show how the legal justifications that managers rely on to support their restructuring strategies are undermined by the contributions and risk-bearing of other corporate stakeholders.

The Case of Defense Adjustment

The behavior of defense contractors in the 1990s brings the contradictions inherent in the American system of corporate governance to the forefront. Prime contractors are publicly traded companies, owned by individual and institutional investors. They have legal obligations to satisfy the short-term profit maximization demands of their shareholders, who have placed their investments at risk and in the hands of management. When their product market changed after the Cold War, defense contractors responded to market uncertainty as their civilian counterparts did in the 1980s: by shedding excess capacity, pursuing more flexible forms of work organization, and restructuring at a rapid pace. Defense firms pursued a plurality of strategies: divesting noncore divisions (General Dynamics); acquiring a larger stake in key defense sectors (Lockheed Martin); intra-firm consolidation (Northrop-Grumman); subcontracting out routinized activities (McDonnell Douglas, now owned by Boeing); pursuing foreign military markets (Lockheed Martin); and developing civilian markets (Hughes; now owned by Raytheon) (Ettlinger 1992; Oden 1999; Markusen 1997b). Encouraged by Wall Street intermediaries seeking rents in shrinking government markets, prime defense contractors undertook bold transformations that were rewarded by the stock market but cursed by the laid-off workers, communities, and state and local governments debilitated by their actions.

The case of the General Dynamics Corporation most clearly illustrates this point. In 1989, General Dynamics was the second largest contractor in the United States and was heavily diversified, supplying each branch of the armed services with products as diverse as tactical missiles, tanks, and aircraft. In response to defense budget cuts, the contractor decided to divest and specialize, not in commercializable high technology, but in the two stagnant military sectors where it had near monopoly power (tanks and submarines). It initiated a controversial strategy of divestment in the early 1990s, cashing in on its sold-off divisions and concentrating on the two segments where its market power was high and the risks low. After the sale of its discontinued businesses and massive layoffs at its remaining divisions during the early 1990s, senior executives at General Dynamics adhered to their stated priorities in allocating the company's new cash. They retired some of its outstanding debt, but then proceeded to return $4.63 billion to shareholders between 1991 and 1993 alone (Dial and Murphy 1995). Stock prices shot up, and nineteen top executives made $22.3 million in one year. The press dubbed the company "Generous" Dynamics, and financial analysts hailed it as a trendsetter in the industry for its explicit shareholder orientation.

Restructuring in the defense industry, as in civilian firms, has involved the rationalization of productive capacity, wage and price discounting, and increasing the flexibility of labor-management relations (Bluestone and Harrison 1982; Clark 1993; Harrison 1995). Instead of responding to the decline of military Keynesianism by searching for new markets or investing in new technologies, General Dynamics and other contractors pursued quick-fix strategies, reducing labor costs and shifting capital interregionally into more profitable investment opportunities. As a result, shareholders saw their profits rise dramatically, and senior management received record bonuses and compensation because their pay was tied to share prices. The accompanying labor reorganization and lack of investment in process technologies and new product lines produced severe casualties in the form of unemployed workers, declining investments in research and development, obsolete skills and knowledge, and overburdened, revenue-poor local governments.

In restructuring for shareholder value, defense contractors like General Dynamics discounted their explicit and implicit contracts with the federal government, organized labor, communities, local governments, and taxpayers. Over one and a half million private-sector defense workers lost their jobs between 1989 and 1996 (U.S. Department of Defense 1996). The remaining workers had to accept wage and benefit concessions. The military-industrial complex was hollowed out, spurring fiscal crises in states as diverse as California, Maine, and Mississippi during the early 1990s. The goal of the private enterprise, profit maximization, obviously did not benefit everyone who contributed to the firm. Defense restructuring involved a wealth transfer from employees to shareholders, corporate raiders, and upper management, in a sense denying nonshareholder constituencies their claims on the firm's future cash flows.

These strategies were viewed by many as rational responses to shrinking federal defense outlays and procurement contract cancellations in the post–Cold War era. Defense contractors were simply managing their market decline, responding to the stimuli transmitted to management from the internal and external environment in the form of the price mechanism (i.e., stock prices). After all, private firms are expected to be accountable to "the market" and are highly responsive to information derived from it. Contractarian scholars argue that the defining characteristics of the private firm are its financial autonomy, limited membership rights, and broad discretion to use its resources in any legal manner that maximizes profits (Easterbrook and Fischel 1991; Jensen and Meckling 1976). No more should be expected from firms than that they operate within the purview of the law, and when issues of internal governance arise, the law should accordingly protect managerial authority and firms' "rationality of enterprise" (Selznick 1992, 345).

Social theorists from Max Weber to Michel Foucault have pointed out that instrumentally rational organizations, although oriented to meet their intended objectives, may substantively ignore broader human purposes and subvert other social ends. Rational behavior, after all, involves the relationship of means to ends, connecting clear criteria of cost and performance to definite purposes. Rational behavior does not specify what the ends are, nor does it question whether ends are appropriate or socially beneficial. It only tries to make us aware of the congruence or dissonance between means and ends (Arrow 1974).

In contrast, I ask if the postulated goals of profit maximization and shareholder value are justified given the role of other stakeholders in defense procurement. The ends pursued by defense contractors during this period were clearly oriented toward the interests of shareholders. Contractors suppressed their obligations to other stakeholders and focused on narrow, private ends: short-term financial returns and shareholder satisfaction. Under the Clinton administration, segments of the Pentagon actually encouraged this behavior, whereas other federal agencies and nonstate actors, such as the Department of Labor, community conversion coalitions, and organized labor, were unable to compete with stockholder demands in influencing managerial behavior. These nonshareholder constituencies appear to have born the brunt of the post–Cold War adjustment.

This is inequitable, given that shareholders of defense contractors are not the only residual risk-bearers; the state and, indirectly, the taxpayers make unrecoverable investments in contractors and assume many of the risks of defense production through a complex system of contracting and pricing. The Pentagon has provided risk-minimizing contracts for billions of dollars, as well as specialized components, machinery, land, and facilities for arms manufacture. The federal government has underwritten the cost of production with subsidies, generous tax laws, and unique accounting practices, improving contractors' financial health. The liabilities that shareholders avoid fall heavily on the state and its public purse as the ultimate residual risk-bearer. In a way, defense procurement can be thought of as a form of state capitalism in which the Secretary of Defense acts as a CEO of a network of corporations that are capitalized annually at the taxpayer's expense (Melman 1971).

Contractors alone cannot be blamed for privileging the interests of shareholders. Under William Perry, a secretary of defense (1994–1997) with his roots in high finance, the state sided with its contractors and socialized the risks and costs of production while allowing profits and control over investment decisions to remain in private hands. The Department of Defense had an overriding interest in maintaining capacity at lower cost. It encouraged contractors to consolidate by subsidizing restructuring costs and quickly approving mergers and acquisitions. It encouraged foreign arms sales by removing regulatory barriers to trade and offering price offsets. In sponsoring restructuring, the federal government behaved like an impatient customer; it wanted to see the industrial base rationalized fast and was willing to pay a premium to shareholders and managers to achieve this objective (Oden 1999). This supportive behavior also points to the degree of collusion between the private interests of key suppliers and certain segments of the state. Pentagon capitalism has nurtured groups of political, economic, and military elites, mutually dependent "iron triangles" that have historically made wasteful expenditures, invited corruption, and enlarged the national deficit. These rent-seeking triangles made it difficult to actually eliminate excess capacity, leading many to question whether or not the shareholder-oriented strategies of the 1990s had achieved their goal and provided cost savings to the government and taxpayers.

In its post–Cold War adjustment policies, the Pentagon acted primarily as a customer—and not a particularly shrewd one at that. As a unique, corporate risk-bearer, one funded by public dollars, the state could have played a more representative role, seeking to make a place for other affected stakeholders at the table. It could have tried to soften the blow of defense adjustment for workers and communities by requiring firms to use some of their profits for retraining and reinvestment into commercial product lines. It could have tried to salvage the investments taxpayers had made into the defense industrial base, instead of promoting a policy that allowed shareholders and executives to extract windfalls from its remains. Although the Clinton administration did appropriate additional funds for dislocated worker assistance and dual-use technology development, its primary goal was lowering procurement costs. This goal could have been achieved without the redistribution of rents to shareholders and senior management.

The state's shouldering of investment risks and its contribution to the asset base of defense contractors justify a more actively interventionist role on the part of the federal government and other stakeholders in the discretionary investment decisions of management. By extending the contractarian logic of risk bearing, management of defense contractors should owe the public fiduciary duties to act in its interests. In other words, defense contractors should have legally recognized obligations to the state to either create public benefits besides expensive weaponry or, at least, to refrain from behavior that negatively affects large groups of people. This logic also expands the range and effectiveness of account-ability mechanisms that the state should use to protect those non-shareholder constituencies that are adversely affected by the defense drawdown, yet who have little legal protection against the effects of fun-damental corporate changes.

Making Government Contractors More Accountable

In this book, I do not necessarily question the ethics of continued state fi-nancing for expensive and destructive weapons of war. Instead, I assume that, given the ideology and rhetoric of national security, the strong ties between contractors, legislators, and the Pentagon, and the bureaucratic stasis that infects policymakers, the levels of defense spending will not drop dramatically in the coming years. If we accept that the nation will not stop arming itself, we need to focus our attention and activism on ex-tending the accountability of defense contractors and their government procurement markets.

Accountability is part of the fundamental problem of mutual responsi-bility in our society: We must rely on others whom we can influence to a degree but cannot completely control. Accordingly, every act of delega-tion involves constructing mechanisms by which the agent has an incen-tive to take into account the interests and welfare of the principal (Don-ahue 1989). Defense contractors, however, are the agents of dual principals, shareholders and the state, and each principal possesses dif-ferent mechanisms through which it controls the agent's behavior. Share-holders, for example, can bring derivative suits against management. They can vote for the contractor's board members and pressure manage-ment to maximize share value and increase dividends. They can sell their shares if they are unhappy with the firm's performance.

Although the Pentagon operates a huge regulatory and oversight ap-paratus, the federal government confronts several structural barriers to enforcing contractor accountability. The federal government has an inter-est in retaining financial control over defense contractors and curtailing contractor opportunism. However, it cannot tell its suppliers what to do with their profits once they have fulfilled their contractual and regula-tory obligations. In many ways, the government supports the discretion and financial independence of private contractors because of the prospects for increased efficiency and cost savings. It has also devised a system that compensates contractors for the uncertainty of defense spending with unique, cost-minimizing contracts and cheap property.

The Pentagon's close-knit, long-term relations with a few suppliers in leading-edge technologies has made it vulnerable to regulatory "capture" by powerful coalitions of contractors and legislators (Stigler 1971).

During the 1990s, shareholder interests were allowed to define contractors' goals. To keep the goals of these enterprises consistent with other public interests, the government fiduciaries overseeing contractor activity should be made accountable and answerable to the wider public. Given that need, the overarching delegation problem in defense adjustment is really the one between the state and its citizens, whose interests the state purports to represent. After the Cold War, a few legislators sought to represent localities and workers, proposing reforms that would decrease the cost of weaponry that the taxpayers bear, encourage defense diversification, and ease the trauma of job loss and economic adjustment in defense-dependent communities. Grassroots community groups, labor unions, and peace activists organized coalitions to press for alternative adjustment policies that would wean regions and firms out of their defense-dependency while minimizing the amount of job dislocation and fiscal crisis associated with drawdown. These coalitions backed a more comprehensive strategy of defense conversion, whereby existing facilities would produce new, socially useful products guided by more participatory processes.

Conversion coalitions urged state representatives to impose more external constraints on the investment decisions of defense contractors so that they would pursue ends broader than shareholder value. Because the government contract is the essential reference point for a contractor's actions, these activists demanded reform efforts that inserted opportunities for public governance into procurement contracts and into government regulations. Various kinds of diversification requirements and workplace reform provisions can be imposed on contractors as a condition of receiving a public procurement contract or diversification subsidy. In Connecticut, as a result of one such coalition's efforts, all defense contractors that receive subsidies from the state and over $1 million per year in federal defense contracts must establish a labor-management committee to explore diversification possibilities.

In addition to these external constraints, the internal legal core of "private" corporations and the financial market institutions in which corporations are embedded must also be transformed if contractors are to become more accountable to public interests. Because of their quasi-public nature, I suggest that *federal* charters establish general principles to which prime defense contractors must adhere and for which they can be held accountable by legislatures and courts. Financial market institutions can be reformed to encourage longer-term, relational investing and allow for partial ownership rights by the state. Regulation through some form of modified public ownership would grant the state more leverage to plan the future of the private arsenal system. It would also decrease the transaction costs associated with writing cumbersome, yet habitually incomplete, procurement contracts. Only by some combination of internal corporate reform and public control over such socially consequential decisions will the benefits and burdens of defense adjustment be more equitably distributed.

Implications

In this book, I ask provocative questions: Should the shares of government contractors be publicly traded? Should the behavior of weapons suppliers be dictated by the stock market or by public fiat? In order to answer these questions I examine the basis for shareholder primacy in corporate governance: the claim that shareholders alone bear the financial risks and contribute the equity necessary for production. I find the ideological justification lacking and the institutional pressures inappropriate in the case of creatures of the state, such as defense contractors.

In challenging the conventional wisdom that vesting power in shareholders and management leads to the most efficient allocation of capital, this book questions many of the arguments for privatization in general. Scholars and policymakers typically view the shareholder-oriented corporate enterprise as the model of instrumental or formal rationality (M. Weber 1978). Private corporations have one overarching objective: the maximization of profits. In theory, their profit motive guarantees that corporate resources are used as efficiently as possible. Because any waste or misuse cuts into their profits, managers, as rational actors, will do everything in their power to avoid such behavior and will choose the best means of achieving corporate objectives.

Private equity ownership creates an incentive structure that ensures fidelity to this purpose. As owners, shareholders trade and transfer their individual property rights to determine the true value of the firm and to control the behavior of management (Alchian and Demsetz 1972; Furubotn 1974; Jensen and Meckling 1976). Shareholders respond to inefficient management decisions by "voting with their feet," selling their stock, and forcing the value of shares down. Bottom-line results, whether reflected in stock prices or some other measure of economic rents, are the indicators of organizational success. Accordingly, privately owned corporations are believed to provide the correct incentives and information to management so that their assets are used efficiently.

Private corporations are considered preferable to government agencies in allocating capital not only because of the power and singularity of their ends, but because of the bounded nature of their jurisdiction. A system of rules defines and delimits corporate membership and rights (M. Weber 1978). Corporations, like the state with its citizenship requirements, are hierarchical governance structures, but they are subject to impersonal market forces, namely the shareholding transactions of private property owners, instead of the cumbersome, overtly "political" and representative authority of the government. Obligations extend only to designated members of the corporation and not wider, more diffuse interests of society or "the public." Recent developments in corporate law stipulate that the primary beneficiaries of corporate activity are the company's shareholders, on whose behalf directors and management are legally required to act (Jensen and Meckling 1976; Easterbrook and Fischel 1991). The need to maximize shareholder value is offered as a reason for excluding certain constituents' claims for membership and for violating other weakly protected claims. The internal structure and centralized control of corporations, unlike control of public agencies, is not oriented toward democratic participation but toward the rational pursuit of profit. If constituents other than shareholders wish to "join" the corporation, they must draft explicit contracts with management specifying the terms of their relationship.

For these reasons, many policymakers and scholars regard shareholder-oriented firms as the most optimal property configuration for the delivery of public goods (Butler 1985; Savas 1987; Fixer and Poole 1987). Hence, they have suggested that once "society" establishes the public nature of such a good, the government should retain collective financing but delegate the production of such goods to the private sector. The mechanism they suggest for privatizing the production of public goods is the procurement contract. Procurement contracts transfer control rights to private, profit-seeking agents and, it is believed, offer the government competition and choice in quality and price. These contracts preserve the sovereign identities and private property of contractors, upon which their financial freedom and decisionmaking autonomy are based. Instead of the flexible membership requirements, inalienable property rights, and muddled objectives associated with public production, contracts allow the state to reap the efficiency gains that inhere in the private corporation.

In opposition to this logic, I argue that a shareholder-oriented contractor is not the most optimal property configuration for producing public goods like national defense. Contracting out strengthens the financial position of select private firms by creating a guaranteed market, but it also weakens the government's control over the agents to whom it has delegated the task of producing public goods. When a public function is contractually assigned to a private entity, "there is an inevitable weakening in the lines of political accountability" (Moe 1987, 453). This lack of accountability allows contractors the freedom to engage in unethical and inefficient behavior in the name of fiduciary duties to their shareholders. One needs to look no further than the countless billing scandals of the 1980s to see how profit-seeking defense contractors wasted public moneys. Again in the 1990s, the restructuring decisions of monopolist contractors placed the government in a compromised position—dependent on the continued manufacture of public goods but relatively impotent to control the distribution of profits within the firm.

The case of General Dynamics clearly illustrates these points. General Dynamics is one of the largest and oldest contractors in the nation. Its tumultuous history—involving spectacular cost overruns, fraudulent billing, and lengthy litigation with the United States government—has been widely documented. During the 1980s, General Dynamics' behavior prompted calls for contracting reform and other major procurement policy changes. The company then instituted the most controversial shareholder-oriented restructuring strategy in the wake of the Cold War—divesting, downsizing, specializing in mature, low-risk products, and returning record profits to management and owners. This strategy was so successful—the General Dynamics' increases in share price outpaced the stock market in the 1990s—that financial analysts urged other prime contractors to emulate its actions.

The importance of other corporate stakeholders to General Dynamics makes it painfully obvious that shareholders are not the only residual risk-bearers. General Dynamics is a first-tier prime contractor, in that it acts as a final systems integrator and assembler, not as a subcontractor or component manufacturer.[5] Since the company's inception, it has been the recipient of generous contracts, bailouts, tax concessions, and below market rate property. Local governments and workers have made firm-specific contributions to its divisions and have depended on their continued operation. New London County, Connecticut, home of General Dynamics' Electric Boat division, was the most defense-dependent region of the country in 1989. At that time, it received the most prime contracts per capita in the nation at $9,785, followed by Fort Worth, Texas, home to General Dynamics' aerospace division (Arthur D. Little 1992). As such, these were also regions most hard hit by cuts in the defense budget and General Dynamics' subsequent restructuring strategy.

Over a period of two years (1994–1996), I conducted structured interviews with members of the various constituencies involved in and affected by restructuring at General Dynamics, primarily at one of the company's two remaining divisions: the Electric Boat shipyard in Groton, Connecticut. I interviewed senior management, laid-off and retained employees, conversion activists, state and local policymakers, labor organizers, and federal contract managers and procurement officials at the ship-yard. These interviews provided insights into how different groups interpreted the patterns and adequacy of relations between the Department of Defense and its primary supplier of nuclear submarines and tanks. Obviously, participants offer accounts that are biased and self-interested, but these biases and self-interests were important to my analysis in and of themselves. The information I requested was of a sensitive nature, and I ensure the subjects' anonymity by not citing their names or formal titles in the text. The interviews were given with the understanding that they would not be made publicly available.

I focused on Electric Boat for several reasons. Before 1989, General Dynamics built tactical missiles, fixed-wing aircraft, space launch vehicles, satellites, tanks, and submarines. The company decided to retain the Electric Boat shipyard and its tank-producing facilities in the Midwest but demanded that these divisions meet more stringent financial criteria. Accordingly, Electric Boat offers a glimpse into the long-lasting *impact* of General Dynamics' adjustment strategy. Electric Boat is also the oldest of the conglomerate's remaining divisions and has historically been its core operation. In 1952 the president of then Electric Boat, John Jay Hopkins, renamed the corporation "General Dynamics" to reflect its major expansion and diversification into new defense activities (Goodwin 1985). General Dynamics became one of the largest prime contractors in the country and the only defense contractor to supply major weapons systems to all three branches of military—until the present-day consolidation of the industry.

My interviews were supplemented with quantitative data reflecting socioeconomic conditions in the regions in which General Dynamics has operated, newspaper accounts, and other empirical studies of the changing political economy of defense contracting. I also reviewed the annual reports and proxy statements to General Dynamics' shareholders between 1985 and 1997, market appraisals prepared by management consultants, and publications for institutional investors. Because I analyzed corporate behavior with respect to the law and public policy, much of the book is legal in nature. I conducted textual analyses of relevant case law and legislation regarding both military procurement and corporate governance, and secondary research using law review articles and legal theory. In addition, my analysis relies upon a theoretical framework composed of insights culled from a variety of disciplines, namely, comparative political economy, economic geography, institutional economics, and planning theory.

Although General Dynamics' billing scandals and exorbitant returns provide the most persuasive evidence of the failure of corporate governance of public contractors, in many ways the company is quite unique.

One powerful family, the Crowns, has owned the majority of its stock and has historically demanded that management focus on shareholder value. Management at other defense contractors, such as Raytheon, Rockwell, and Hughes, was less beholden to shareholder pressures, at least until it capitulated to Wall Street pressures in the 1990s. Moreover, General Dynamics' antiquated asset base was especially difficult to convert to commercial uses. A platform builder, the company did not have the capacity to build avionics, electronics, or guidance systems. Specialization in these more high-tech fields might have allowed the contractor to pursue alternative adjustment strategies.

But General Dynamics should not be dismissed as an outlier. Nor should defense contracting be dismissed as a subset of "more" typical industrial behavior; the problems faced by General Dynamics and other defense contractors at the end of the Cold War strongly parallel those problems faced by civilian companies. Commercial firms, especially in sectors such as agriculture, pharmaceuticals, and utilities, are also heavily subsidized by the federal government and have also engaged in intensive restructuring over the last two decades. Archers Daniel Midland (ADM) Company, for example, has received $10 billion in subsidies from the federal government (mostly for ethanol) since 1980 (Bandow 1997). At least 43 percent of ADM's profits come from products subsidized by the taxpayers. Pentagon capitalism is just the most visible example of the state granting monopoly power, special privileges, subsidies, and legal immunities to corporations that perform public tasks. In this way, it reflects a more general trend, differing only in degree and magnitude from the situation found in other companies and industrial sectors. Local policy analysts interested in the obligations of firms that receive location incentives from cities and states and public administration scholars interested in the contracting out of public tasks will all find the analysis of risk-bearing in defense contractors useful for their own purposes. Similarly, the power of defense contractors in crafting regulation is, perhaps, the most extreme example of business influence on public policy. "To question the legitimacy of corporate power in the Pentagon, therefore, is to question the legitimacy of all manifestations of corporate rule in government" (Bowman 1996, 282).

Policymakers can learn from the lessons of post–Cold War defense restructuring to adopt a more activist stance on corporate adjustment when public moneys are at stake. The key to transforming the general legal terrain of corporate change is the recognition that any corporation that has availed itself of public resources has reciprocal obligations to the public that supports and finances its operations. These obligations constrain the rights of managers to unilaterally make restructuring decisions oriented only toward short-term shareholder returns. Corporations owe the public these obligations because they are part of the implicit quid pro quo of public financing. If management owes shareholders fiduciary obligations because of equity financing, management should owe the public similar obligations because of public financing.

As one of the most expensive and well-documented experiments in government reliance on private suppliers, defense procurement is a fertile source of lessons and cautionary tales for other types of public-private partnerships (Donahue 1989). An examination of the contours of these relationships is particularly relevant to professionals in the field of city and regional planning who stand at the juncture of the public/private divide. Planners are often responsible for balancing "economically necessary" measures that can maintain the viability of a corporation and the "collective good" of a particular community. Economic development policies stress the significance of public-private partnering to retain existing businesses and lure new ones, to provide the physical infrastructure necessary for the incubation of new start-ups, and to foster an innovative high-tech milieu. For example, states and cities currently offer incentives for urban "brownfield" development—loans, fees, equity participation schemes, financial and liability assurances—to improve the investor's rate of return and reduce some of the risks associated with contaminated industrial sites. The public sector subsidizes and absorbs the risks that accrue to private businesses with the implicit understanding that some public benefit will be created (e.g., a decrease in vacant city space, job or revenue creation) and that the developer will refrain from behavior that negatively affects the public.

My examination of defense procurement provides a valuable analytic framework for understanding the distribution of ownership and control rights in these kinds of public-private partnerships. Privately owned property in corporations usually entails the right to absolute and exclusive control over all decisions affecting investment and production. As governments subsidize and embark on intimate collaborations with private businesses, however, there is less basis for assigning exclusive private property rights and managerial autonomy. Capital that was jointly produced and financed by the government may be more subject to the limited control rights of the state. Thus, in the case of public-private hybrids, such as those created by a heavily subsidized business retention scheme, the state may have legally protectable interests in previously "private" realms to regulate profit levels, curtail downsizing, and suggest investment strategies that are less injurious to dependent stakeholders. Defense production, as this nation's largest experiment with centralized economic planning, could be a laboratory in which to rethink the reciprocal nature of other economic development subsidies, even at the state and local levels.

In essence, this study is designed to bring to bear a wide range of social science, philosophical, and policy literature on the very material topic of corporate governance and industrial restructuring. Because it operates at both the practical and academic level, one of my loftier objectives is to bridge the perceived gap between theory and practice and contribute to a dialogue that can be mutually beneficial to those on either side of this imagined divide. On a theoretical level, I ask questions about obligations, legal justifications, and the nature of the corporation. On a more practical level, I am ultimately concerned about how we as a society can do better: how we can make private firms more accountable to wider public interests and less responsive to the short-term interests of private shareholders. I subject our recent policies and practices to reevaluation and demonstrate how the state could use the law and its regulatory powers to shift the governance of defense contractors from the stock market to the state and other stakeholders.

The first two chapters introduce the reader to the field of corporate governance. Chapter 1 explores the dominant rationale and institutional pressures for management to privilege the interests of private shareholders above all other corporate stakeholders. Chapter 2 is the crux of my argument and my contribution to the corporate governance debate. Here, I demonstrate how even the popular contractarian paradigm can advance a view of an industrial sector where actors other than shareholders and managers have legitimate control over corporate resources. In the case of defense contractors, the federal government absorbs most of the risks and costs of production, becoming the structural equivalent of shareholders. I describe the different contractual and regulatory mechanisms through which the state bears these risks and costs.

The next three chapters focus primarily on the case of General Dynamics and the regulatory regime in which it has operated. Chapter 3 describes the shareholder-oriented adjustment strategies that defense contractors adopted in response to declining defense procurement budgets, in particular General Dynamics' strategies from 1989 to 1995. Chapter 4 moves back in time to examine how, particularly in the case of nuclear submarine production, the federal government buffered General Dynamics' shareholders from real financial losses through a variety of subsidies and risk-sharing agreements. Chapter 5 explores the government's problematic role in supporting the restructuring of defense contractors to the detriment of other public interests.

Chapter 6, the conclusion, more fully addresses the normative issues raised in previous chapters, namely the nature of obligation that defense contractor managers should owe to the public sector. I suggest that local stakeholder activism is a means of democratizing corporate welfare by pressuring state actors to enforce their claims on defense contractors. I also recommend contractual and regulatory reforms to tie the receipt of public funds to public obligations and benefits. Finally, I outline prescriptions for expanding fiduciary obligations to the state, through corporate charters and partial public ownership.

Notes

1. Restructuring is a strategy of corporate change that materially alters, sometimes with minor modifications and at other times with fundamental transformations, the composition of the firm's asset portfolio and the claims against those assets.

2. The extension of the state into this area of economic life renders the political, economic, and legal bases of corporate legitimacy more visible and therefore more vulnerable to interrogation and resistance (Habermas 1973; M. Weber 1978).

3. Such an approach is in keeping with the work of institutional economists, economic sociologists, and legal realists, starting from the first half of the twentieth century, who believe that economic outcomes (e.g., regional economic development, unemployment) cannot be understood, even in the aggregate, without an adequate theory of economic organizations and legal institutions. Underlying the simplest transaction is a complex structure of property rights, contracts, and social relationships (Hale 1923; Cohen 1927; Polanyi 1944; Commons 1957; Simon 1958; North 1981; Granovetter 1985; Hodgson 1988).

4. *Trustees of Dartmouth College v. Woodward,* 4 Wheaton 518, 627 (1819).

5. Roughly 40–60 percent of procurement funds for any given weapons system remain with the prime contractor (U.S. Congress Office of Technology Assessment [OTA] 1991, 39–57).

1

The Crisis of Corporate Governance

Corporate governance "rules," culled from case law, corporate charters and bylaws, and customary workplace practices, provide guidance to managers in allocating power and resources within the corporation. The legal structure of the corporation, therefore, is critical to the process of restructuring and regional economic decline because it provides incentives and disincentives for stakeholders to engage in wealth-creating activities at the local level. Along with other factors, such as competitive pressures within individual product markets, the cost of capital, and the relative strength of unions, corporate governance rules condition the investment decisions of management. They are the filters through which management views and chooses corporate strategies.

Despite their significance, corporate governance rules are rarely invoked in current debates about industrial restructuring, technological development, or the viability of regional economies (for exceptions, see Christopherson 1993; Appelbaum and Berg 1996; Clark 1992).[1] In explanations of firm behavior, the structure of corporations is overshadowed by the actions of individual CEOs as "highly effective people" and by macroeconomic shifts in comparative advantage. If they are mentioned at all, the complex interactions within the black box of the corporation are boiled down to the simplest of maxims: Management must maximize the value of shareholders' investments.

In this book, I adopt an approach that goes beyond the decisions of individual managers to examine the enduring patterns of relationships within which these decisions are embedded. Accordingly, this chapter explores the legal principles and institutions that reinforce the notion of shareholder primacy. In the first section, I introduce the dominant paradigm of corporate governance, the nexus of contracts model, which maintains that shareholders are the only residual risk-bearers of the firm and therefore deserve special legal protections from corporate change. In the second section, I explore the institutional pressures on management to privilege the interests of shareholders above all other corporate stake-holders. In the third section, I question the hegemony of these institutions and their philosophical underpinnings. Theoretical and empirical weaknesses in contemporary corporate governance doctrine destabilize the conventional wisdom about whose interests corporations should serve. These weaknesses provide an opportunity for the development of a new "multifiduciary" conception of the corporation, one grounded in actual business practice and not simply in the glorification of private property.

The Contractarian Paradigm: Shareholder Primacy in a Nexus of Contracts

Corporations are complex organizations whose workings have fascinated scholars and social critics since their inception as legitimate legal configurations.[2] Tracing the evolution of the corporation, historians and sociologists have noted not only the diversity of organizational forms but also the diversity of theoretical approaches to understanding the corporation (Frug 1980; Hartog 1983; Sklar 1988; Fligstein 1990; Horwitz 1992; Bowman 1996). No objective "theory of the firm" has ever come to dominate the legal-intellectual terrain because, at any historical moment, corporations mean different things to different people (Bratton 1989). Nevertheless, every era has its dominant paradigm, a model that is both popular with academics and operationalized by the legal and managerial professions. Corporate law doctrine presupposes some theoretical orientation, as judges weave theory into doctrine and justify doctrine with theory.

The evolution of corporate law, although uneven and complex, proceeded from the notion of a "concession" granted by the state to businesses as a special privilege. In the first half of the nineteenth century, the corporate entity represented a state-created juridical structure with a social role that extended beyond the confines of private property or contract. Under concession doctrine, the corporation is viewed as coming into existence only as a result of a special grant made by the government (Butler and Ribstein 1989). This doctrine treats incorporation as a special privilege conferred by the state for public purposes and therefore justifies the public regulation of corporate property (Horwitz 1992; Hurst 1970). During this period, many judges believed that unrestricted exchange threatened the solvency of local communities and the autonomy of small businesses, most of which were headed by a single owner-manager.

Moreover, private and public corporations were not yet fully differentiated as entities with different individual rights and amounts of state power (Frug 1980). The critical *Dartmouth College* opinion decided in 1819 established the grounds for dividing corporations on the basis of property rights. Private corporations, the judge argued, were those founded by individual contributions of property, whereas public corporations were founded by the government without such contributions.[3] As incorporation became more readily available in the middle of the nineteenth century, many viewed corporations as just another contractual arrangement between private parties, much like a simple partnership. Special state chartering, whereby corporations were created by legislative acts, yielded to private formation under general corporation laws (Butler and Ribstein 1989). Concession theory began to lose ground to the more decidedly liberal notion of private and voluntary contract. The notion of private contracting implied "lessened public concern with the impact of the new entreprenuerial giants on consumers, employers, suppliers and the public generally. And denying that the enterprise originated in a state grant of authority to exist for only limited purposes implied that there was less state power to impose limits and restraints on the scope and character of the corporation" (Brudney 1985, 1409).

Another landmark case, *Santa Clara v. Southern Pacific Railroad*,[4] held that a corporation is a person under the Fourteenth Amendment and can enjoy constitutional protections. This ruling chipped away at the basis for state regulation of corporations (Horwitz 1992; Hovenkamp 1991; Dewey 1926). *Santa Clara* introduced the idea that a corporation is an entity separate from its shareholders yet able to possess all of the rights that individuals enjoy. What came to be known as "entity theory" focused attention away from the equity contributors, the shareholders, who were seen as mere "investors." Entity theory focused more on the managers and directors, who were believed to personify the corporation as an entity. By the early 1900s, the doctrine of shareholders' limited liability was firmly established, an event that coincided with the birth of the national stock market and the growing concentration of capital.[5] By this time, much corporate property was capitalized in the form of negotiable securities, which were widely dispersed in ownership (Sklar 1988). Stockholders were able to distance themselves from the daily operations of the corporation and create new responsibilities for managers as their fiduciaries.

In the early twentieth century, the courts asserted that directors were "the primary possessors of all the powers which the charter confers."[6] This perspective came to be known as the "managerialist" conception of the firm, best articulated by Adolph Berle and Gardner Means in 1932. In their landmark work, the authors point out the contradiction between shareholders' passive ownership position and management's almost absolute control of property. The will of the shareholders is subservient to the power of managers whose expertise, they argued, legitimates their authority to organize resources and control the processes of production (Bratton 1989). Shareholders were regarded not as owners but as victimized buyers of investments from crafty issuers, promoters, and financiers.

The managerialist position came to be displaced by the nexus of contracts approach in the 1970s, the beginning of the current era of finance or "paper" capitalism. This model of enterprise governance is an outgrowth of basic assumptions from contract and property law. The model rests on the idea that a corporation is simply an amalgamation or "nexus" of different contracting relations among individual input owners.[7] Adherents believe that corporations are nothing but contracts arising out of the willful and voluntary interaction of actors who trade rights and obligations among themselves. These actors, it is assumed, take into account their respective skills and abilities as well as the corporation's best interests (Easterbrook and Fischel 1991; Jensen and Meckling 1976). The contractarian firm is comprised of both transactions that take place within an internal system of hierarchical governance (in this case, a firm) as well as those that take place across a market interface (Coase 1937; Williamson 1975; 1985). Contracts may be formal and discrete or implied and informal, but parties' respective rights and responsibilities are always defined by the twin themes of commerce: consent and ownership.

The nexus of contracts model of the corporation flows from this assumption of freely contracting input owners and private asset ownership. Management raises funds to acquire physical capital and finance operations by contracting with creditors (for debt) and shareholders (for equity).[8] The proceeds of the corporation's activities are divided amongst its employees, suppliers, and creditors based on contracts that are assumed to be clear, set in advance, and drafted on terms independent of the success of the enterprise as a whole (Blair 1994, 20–25). In other words, wages and loan payments are fixed liabilities; they are negotiated in advance of performance and are not contingent on whether the firm is thriving or performing poorly. *Only shareholders contract for a variable share of net proceeds,* after all previously contracted-for obligations have been paid to the firm's employees, suppliers, and creditors. Because payments to shareholders are paid last and because these payments vary depending on the profitability of the business, shareholders are said to have a "residual" claim on the corporation's profits.[9]

Shareholders' status as "residual claimants" is the most significant organizing principle of the contractarian corporation. Shareholders are thought to have the most at stake in management's ability to generate profits because they subject themselves to the risk that they will earn no return on their investments (Macey 1989). Their status as residual claimants entitles shareholders to act as the principals of the firm, who then "hire" agents—the corporation's directors and senior officers—to act on their behalf. Agency is a common-law concept that establishes a relationship in which a principal delegates certain rights to a proxy who is bound by a formal or informal contract to represent the principal's interest in exchange for some benefit (Moe 1984; Pratt and Zeckhauser 1991; Eggertsson 1990).

Contractarian scholars insist that the agency relationship is embodied in explicit contracts (e.g., those found in corporate bylaws and charters). Shareholders, creditors, and others enter into contracts when they invest in, lend to, or otherwise transact with the corporation. Under the contractual theory of the corporation, state corporation statutes—such as the Uniform Partnership Act and the Uniform Commercial Code—enforce corporate contracts, reduce the costs of private contracting by creating standard corporate forms into which parties can opt, and provide central notice to potential creditors that the firm has adopted limited liability (Butler and Ribstein 1989).

Because shareholders bear the residual risk of corporate activity, management is expected to devote its energies to advancing shareholders' interests by maximizing their return on investment. The nexus of contracts model of governance is guided by the notion that the corporation should be structured in the best interests of its shareholder-principals.[10] In other words, shareholders bear the residual risk of corporate activity in return for the promise that directors will maximize the value of their investments. Profit is the reward for residual risk-taking.

The separation of ownership from control creates wide "information asymmetries" between management and shareholders; each has access to relevant information to which the other is not privy (Pratt and Zeckhauser 1991; Williamson 1985). Although shareholders may be the corporation's most important residual claimants, they are a dispersed and disorganized lot. The effective control of corporate property actually lies in the hands of a few managers instead of the multitude of individual investors (Berle and Means 1932). Given the separation of ownership and control and the decentralization of owners, shareholders find it extremely difficult to monitor management to make sure management is using corporate assets to generate profits. Shareholders must prevent managers from abusing their power, shirking their responsibilities, and acting in their own interests. Although shareholders bear the residual risk, they cannot devise contractual restrictions to fully control managers, because they are incapable of predicting and handling the various contingencies that arise in long-term relationships.

Likewise, managers have few means of intuiting shareholders' preferences because of the sheer number of shareholders in a single corporation and the rather passive nature of shareholding. Managers also need the discretion to respond quickly to unexpected events and the authority to take advantage of time-sensitive investment opportunities. These dilemmas, caused by the separation of ownership from control, reflect serious "principal-agent problems" that corporate law has sought to rectify.

Because the principals cannot effectively police or evaluate the agents' every action and because a shortage of information keeps the agents from drawing conclusions about the principals' preferences, a special type of arrangement is required to govern transactions between shareholders and management. Corporate law has responded by providing a special, standardized provision that directors owe shareholders "fiduciary duties" to maximize the value of shareholders' assets. In theory, managers are able to act as de facto owners in exchange for their vows to uphold their fiduciary duties to shareholders (Clark 1985; Demott 1988).

Fiduciary principles originated in the law of trusts. Fiduciary obligations are legal-institutional mechanisms for ensuring corporate accountability to shareholders, obligations (of loyalty, care, and concern) that the agents work for the "exclusive benefit" and in the best interest of the principal (Pratt and Zeckhauser 1991; Easterbrook and Fischel 1993). Courts have applied this term to relationships as diverse as guardian-ward, attorney-client, and manager-stockholders. Fiduciary duties are treated differently from mere contracts; they are imbued with a distinctly moral character and applied judiciously to express the highest standard of accountability. Clark argues that fiduciary law is stricter than contract law in four respects: the fiduciary's affirmative duty to disclose information that the principal would find relevant, his open-ended duty to act in ways that further the principal's interest, his promise not to take advantage of his position for personal gain, and the distinctively moral rhetoric in which all of these duties are couched (1985, 71–79). Fiduciary relations rely expressly on trust, a trust that may extend beyond the terms of the actual contract (Bratton 1995).[11]

Compared to shareholders, the other constituencies involved in the enterprise are of little concern to corporate law. Because employees, customers, suppliers, and creditors do not own property in the corporation, they are not believed to risk as much as shareholders (Macey 1989).[12] Because these stakeholders do not own equity in the corporation, management does not owe them fiduciary duties and is not obligated to further their interests at the expense of the "real" owners. Loyalty is assumed to be a scarce good: The more that goes to propertyless stakeholders, the less that is available for stockholders. Within the contractarian paradigm, managers are accountable only to those stakeholders whose assets they are "borrowing." Other constituencies serve exclusively at the managers' pleasure.

Only explicit contracts and regulatory statutes, rather than fiduciary duties or other internal accountability mechanisms, determine management's obligations to nonshareholder constituencies. Managers, for example, are legally obligated to adhere to individual collective bargaining agreements and the National Labor Relations Act, but beyond these and other civil rights–type regulation, corporate law vests managers with the authority to act in shareholders' interests.[13] Managers may allocate investment capital, select production techniques, and initiate layoffs in any way they see fit, unless their behavior is prohibited by contracts or regulations. If there is no express private agreement to the contrary, nonshareholder constituents have no common-law property right in a corporation, and thus managers do not owe them any duties of loyalty, care, or concern beyond those articulated in their contracts (Friedman 1970).

The contractarian approach holds that management is not accountable to these groups beyond the terms of their contracts and views any judicial or legislative attempts to further protect these stakeholders from corporate change (e.g., mergers and acquisitions) as anathema (Macey 1989). By this logic, state intervention should not be used to protect stakeholders and improve social welfare because in any such intervention the state would have to overrule the private contracts to which parties have already given their express consent. If stakeholders do not choose to protect themselves against the possibility of harms (e.g., due to a plant closing) in their individual contracts, then their consent signals a willingness to assume the risk of that harm. State intervention should not substitute for private ordering, and managers and corporate constituencies should be free to "establish systems of governance without substantive scrutiny from a regulator" (Easterbrook and Fischel 1991, 2).

Enabling Institutions

The nexus of contracts paradigm has an ideological naturalness to it, partly because corporate relationships *do* embódy a fair amount of voluntary exchange (Bratton 1989, 410). This paradigm also affirms the liberal current underlying much of our law and political theory; it resonates with deeply held convictions about the freedom of contract, the importance of consent, the value of private property, and the integrity of the person against outside interference.[14] In this model, explicit contracts specify rights and duties between two parties that are fixed by their own voluntary and actual agreement. Because obligations stem only from individuals' explicit promises, not from any paternalistic belief in distributive justice, enforcement of contracts is therefore consonant with individual freedom.[15]

The hegemony of this model, however, is based not only on the ideological strength of particular ideas but also on the degree to which these ideas are institutionalized. In other words, fiduciary duties are perceived as effective deterrents against managerial opportunism not simply because they reflect strongly held beliefs about choice and freedom, but because they are enforced through prevailing institutional arrangements. The nexus of contracts paradigm reflects and reinforces the way that large, publicly traded corporations raise capital in the United States: namely, through a reliance on dispersed, institutional shareholders, with share prices established in competitive capital markets (Roe 1994; Zysman 1983). Whereas firms in countries such as Germany and Japan depend on debt and long-term relations with banks to finance their operations, the American system is based on equity investments and short-term relations with shareholders. The institutional context privileges the interests of shareholders, as management's resource dependency on them allows shareholders a large degree of control over American corporations (Pfeffer and Salancick 1978).

In the decades following World War II, the control of corporate strategy rested primarily with a new professional managerial class (Chandler 1977). An oligopolistic market structure sheltered large corporations from product competition and the pursuit of profit maximization above all other goals (Appelbaum and Berg 1996). During the 1950s and 1960s, managers generally enjoyed a high degree of autonomy and chose to focus on increasing sales, revenues, and control over their markets. Equity investment was regarded as just another way to increase the productive capacity of the company's assets. During this period, other corporate stakeholders, such as organized labor, gained a cut of the economic rents generated by corporations.

In the late 1970s and early 1980s, financial deregulation, overvalued dollars, and foreign competition drastically changed the environment in which American firms operated. Japanese corporations, for example, challenged the American dominance in steel, automobiles, and consumer electronics. Domestic manufacturers were unable to achieve their desired sales and revenue growth. As banks raised their borrowing rates, corporations sought more equity from the stock market. This period also witnessed the rise to power of institutional investors, particularly pension and mutual funds and insurance companies. The specific purpose of these funds is to generate high yields for their multiple and dispersed members by giving them access to money managers who can buy and sell large blocks of stock (Lazonick 1992). Data compiled by Columbia University's Institutional Investor Project reveal that the percentage of equity in United States corporations held by institutional investors skyrocketed during the 1980s. In 1950, institutional investors owned 8 percent of the equity in American firms; by 1980, this level had risen to 33 percent; and by 1988, it had reached 45 percent (Coffee 1991).[16] Institutional investors, or at least their representatives, now exert a tremendous amount of power over management.

Institutional shareholders are able to challenge management's ability to set the firm's strategic agenda through a variety of control and enforcement mechanisms. They can enforce management's fiduciary duties through the threat of derivative suits in which a single shareholder can challenge a breach on behalf of the "corporation" (Blair 1995). Fiduciary duties are also enforced by voting rights, which enable shareholders to elect and remove directors (Brudney 1985). In companies where they hold large blocks of stock, institutional shareholders have been able to directly influence the actions of management. Institutional shareholders, particularly public pension funds and "cowboy" raiders like Warren Buffet and T. Boone Pickens, initiated rebellions in the 1980s by bullying management at underperforming companies. These groups and individuals pressed management to restructure and deliver more shareholder value, and if they were still not satisfied with the company's performance, they would sponsor resolutions to change governance structures.

Shareholders fully utilize their powers of voice and exit to appropriate the rents that companies may have previously shared with suppliers, consumers, and employees (Appelbaum and Berg 1996; Hirschman 1970). Managers are compelled to increase price/earnings ratios, repurchase their own stock, and provide higher dividends to shareholders. Wage reductions and downsizing have become a primary means of boosting profits, which were then distributed to shareholders. Pressures from money managers and Wall Street gurus have paid off for shareholders: Lazonick (1992, 459) found that the share of after-tax profits distributed as dividends grew from 40 percent in the 1960s to 85 percent in the early 1990s.

Shareholder groups periodically urge management to adopt incentives to align their respective interests: namely, rewarding managers with stock options and bringing on outside directors who have fewer attachments to the corporation and more sympathy for investors. Compensation systems that link managerial rewards to stock price (as opposed to total sales or revenue) are becoming increasingly popular: In 1982, 37 percent of senior management's compensation was based on stock incentives (and annual bonuses) but by 1993, 54 percent of their compensation derived from variable measures (Lorsch and MacIver 1991). Stock grants or options are intended to make management's goals more consonant with those of shareholders by further riveting managers' attention to fluctuations in stock price (Jensen and Murphy 1990). Shareholders also support bringing more outside directors onto boards in hopes that they will be less beholden to management. At the end of 1993, 86 percent of manufacturing companies and 91 percent of financial companies had a majority of outside directors (Wayne 1994).

Shareholder value was the justification for the hostile takeovers and leveraged buy-outs of the 1980s, as a liquid market for corporate control emerged. Advocates of takeovers believe that companies with low stock prices need to be disciplined by the threat or reality of buy-out activity (Manne 1965; Jensen 1989).[17] Indeed many financial economists interpreted the mergers and acquisitions frenzy of the 1980s as a mutiny of shareholders, angry that the balance of corporate priorities had tipped in favor of career management and that managers were not upholding their fiduciary duties. Shareholders of targeted companies supported takeover bids as a way of unlocking "hidden value," and they frequently reaped the benefits of windfall profits when their companies were purchased. Shareholders of firms simply *targeted* for takeovers saw their profits double and triple (Kleinman 1989; Hite, Owers, and Rogers 1987). Most takeovers have led to a change in managerial control, and for that reason even the threat of a takeover has been a powerful incentive for management to deliver higher stock prices. Companies increased their debt burden to acquire new companies or buy back their own stock to avoid takeovers, selling off assets in order to pay down debt. New high-risk debt instruments, such as junk bonds, were developed in the 1980s to finance these activities.

In addition to exercising "voice" to influence management, shareholders have another powerful and more commonly used control tool at their disposal: exit (Hirschman 1970). If shareholders are not pleased with management's performance, they will "vote with their feet," sell their stock, and force share values down. Institutional investors engage in short-term trading practices, sometimes holding shares for just days or weeks (Jacobs 1991). Note Baldwin and Clark, "If one can create personal wealth by shifting money around frequently from one stock, fund or asset manager to another, it's not only acceptable, it's a sign of financial acumen and brilliance for arbitrageurs, individuals and institutional investors alike" (1991, 7). Lorsch and MacIver reported that turnover rates for stock in the mid-1980s were the highest since the speculative 1920s and 1930s; shares were held, on average, for just 1.9 years in 1985, compared with an average rate of 7 years in 1960 (1991, 9–11). And the pace of turnover has sped up considerably since the 1980s.

Transient and diversified, shareholders have no stake in working with management on a day-to-day basis to transform an underperforming company into a more profitable enterprise (Alexander 1993). Expressing dissatisfaction through exit is easy and costless, and the threat of or actual exit can spur managers to attend to the short-term interests of investors. Other parties with long-term interests, such as banks, are forbidden by law from owning shares of the companies they finance (although this is changing due to financial modernization legislation passed in

1999) and are unable to exert much influence over investment decisions (Roe 1990).

The information barriers between owners and managers force shareholders to rely on index funds and short-term earnings data to monitor and evaluate managerial performance. Possessing limited technical knowledge about their agents' inputs, shareholders look to current stock price, rather than long-term shareholder value, as the basis for measuring whether or not managers are upholding their fiduciary duties. Passive investors also rely on the occasional bits of disclosed information—such as reductions in workforce—to buy or sell stocks. Executives are reluctant to share much information about their corporate strategies with shareholders for fear that the market will respond negatively to such disclosures. This creates a dilemma for investors, who increase their investment risks because they are unable to monitor corporations closely and who are then forced to judge the quality of management through blunt and often imperfect output measures, such as stock price. Shareholders habitually accuse management of incompetence, inefficiency, indifference, and self-dealing. Although Wall Street funds extensive research operations, shareholder groups often urge the Securities and Exchange Commission (SEC) to require more frequent financial reports and outside audits to acquire more meaningful information.

Similarly, managers interpret the behavior of shareholders to infer the market's preferences. Although information asymmetries keep dispersed shareholders from directly communicating their true preferences to managers (relying on fund managers or their ability to exit), managers depend on share appreciation to drive their strategy. Internal capital budgeting takes place "by the numbers," with management second-guessing how the market will respond to their (dis)investment decisions. Corporations have institutionalized the obsession with shareholder value by developing new systems of control over lower levels and different divisions of their organizations. Internal performance measures now form the basis of strategic decisions made within operating units; each unit is its own individual profit center, where every decision about human resources or industrial location is evaluated against its potential effect on share prices (Appelbaum and Berg 1996).

Proponents of this system claim that vesting power in shareholders leads to an overall efficient allocation of capital in our economy. To support the stock market's control of investment decisions is to believe that there is a high positive correlation between the true value of the firm and the market price of shares of that firm—the basic assumption of efficient markets theory (Fama 1990). According to this theory, the price set in financial markets for a company's shares fully reflects the true net value of the firm. Shareholders flock to emerging sectors, such as information technology and biotechnology, because they recognize their high net value. They flee from stagnating sectors, moving capital out of durable manufacturing and the like. This theory holds that shareholders distribute finance capital in a fluid and fast-paced manner that will lead, in the end, to sustained economic growth and development.

Challenging Models and Institutions

Ideas and institutions are mutually constitutive; ideas will not be adopted without political and legal institutions, and institutions rely on the strength of ideas for their own legitimacy. Max Weber (1978) recognized that the authority of law is two-sided: It relies on both inner justifications for legitimacy and external institutions for enforcement. Scholars in the 1970s who reconceptualized the corporation as a nexus of contracts and viewed shareholders as the only residual risk-bearers of the firm presaged the evolution of corporate law and financial institutions. Their contractarian explanations justified institutional changes that, in turn, increased and enforced the strength of shareholders groups in influencing managerial investment decisions. Other intervening factors—such as changes in global capital markets, currency valuation, and the cost of capital—buttressed the power and significance of shareholders.

Despite the hegemony of this paradigm, many criticisms have been leveled at it and the financial institutions that conform to its normative assumption of shareholder primacy. Taken together these criticisms represent a serious assault on the dominant model of corporate governance.

First, contractarian scholars and judges have never offered convincing justifications for shareholders' privileged status. Underlying the dominant paradigm and institutions of corporate governance is the concept of a fiduciary relationship; fiduciary relationships involve duties that impose the highest standards of conduct on the agent to serve the principal's interests. In the nexus of contracts model, management is the fiduciary of the shareholders, who entrust management to act in their behalf to maximize profits. But what is the basis of this corporate control? Is it shareholders' actual *ownership* of the equity of the corporation or their ability and authority to *contract* with management for their privileged role?

One of the main insights of the contractarian model is that being a principal is a contractual role, not a property right (Hart and Moore 1990; Ellerman 1992; Blair 1996; Rajan and Zingales 1996). The implicit and explicit contractual role of shareholders as residual risk-bearers provides the economic and moral rationale for their principal status. This role permits shareholders certain control rights and legally obligates management to work in their interests. Even the leading figures of the contractarian approach argue that ownership is not the basis of shareholder primacy within the corporation. Notes Fama: "The firm is just a set of contracts covering the way inputs are joined to create outputs and the way receipts from outputs are shared among inputs. In this 'nexus of contracts' perspective, ownership of the firm is an irrelevant concept" (1980, 289). Shareholders are contributors of resources and bearers of risks, and it is their risky investments that obligate management to reciprocate—in the form of variable dividends, maximized stock prices, and some vaguely defined notion of loyalty.

If shareholders' rights over the profits of the enterprise constitute simply another contractual claim, and not an exclusive ownership right, then it is possible that other propertyless stakeholders could receive similar treatment. Employees, customers, suppliers, and creditors are all "stakeholders" in that they make risky investments that are highly specialized to the enterprise and have direct interests in the survival of the organization (Blair 1995, 239). Accordingly, it is difficult to see managers as having one overriding duty as fiduciaries: profit maximization. When the firm is viewed "as a sort of coalition of human-resource holders," it is hard to imagine "such a thing as *the* single, well-defined objective of the firm" (Aoki 1990, 11).

If contracts, and not property, determine the identity of residual risk-bearers of the firm, then shareholders must have very strong contracts protecting their interests. They must have "better," more explicit contracts than other stakeholders possess. In reality, this is not the case. The privileged relationship between management and shareholders is not explicitly contractual (Brudney 1985). Corporate law derives from business corporation statutes adopted by legislatures and from fiduciary and other doctrines developed by courts. Both statutes and fiduciary doctrine are nebulous in terms of specifying responsibilities and are not meant to act as or supplement actual contracts (O'Connor 1991; Clark 1985). The exact duties of the fiduciary are rarely specified beyond a general obligation, so it is difficult to assume that anything approximating a contract exists between shareholders and management.

The contractarian model of the firm, despite its name, is a poor approximation of real-life contracting. This theory assumes that the "contract" negotiation process is cheap and fully competitive, which it is not (Crotty 1992; Aoki 1990; Brudney 1985). Empirical evidence demonstrates that dispersed shareholders do not see themselves as parties of discrete contracts, but instead simply expect managers to work "hard" (left undefined) for their salaries. There are no explicit limits on managerial discretion or specific performance requirements for maximized returns. The dispersed and detached position of shareholders allows them no opportunity to engage in direct bargaining or explicit contract negotiation with management or other constituents, such as employees. Moreover, shareholders lack the volition and information characteristic of parties to contracts formed by individualized bargaining. Shareholders and management never really meet each other face-to-face to resolve the principal-agent problems in their relationships because the transaction costs are too high. Notes Clark, "Given this relationship, it is difficult to imagine how these actors 'bargain' over the terms of contract (even implicitly)" (1985, 64; see also Crotty 1992). Contract is more of a metaphor for the stockholder-manager relationship.

Shareholders do not even act like real principals. Lawyers spot an agency relationship when a principal retains power to control and direct the activities of an agent and sets out the objectives and strategies for the agent to pursue. In reality, Clark claims, stockholders do not direct the activities of the firm nor do they delegate their authority. Institutional shareholders themselves do not engage in active monitoring of the corporation (Alexander 1993). Their powers are limited to derivative lawsuits (on behalf of the "corporation"), the hiring and firing of directors, and the inspection of corporate books and records. Investors in large, publicly held corporations have little or no ability to choose or negotiate the terms of their relations, holding only loose, undocumented understandings about managerial obligations.

Second, shareholders and financial markets are myopic, blinded to good investment opportunities that may only pay off in the future. Prominent scholars of economic and industrial policy have made normative arguments regarding the American corporate governance and financial market system based on the nexus of contracts paradigm and the notion of shareholder primacy (Hayes and Abernathy 1980; Block 1992; Baldwin and Clark 1991; Porter 1992; Christopherson 1993; Goldstein 1995; Blair 1996). They argue that both the legal structure of American corporations and the financial markets upon which they are dependent are poorly suited for sustained economic growth, productivity, technological innovation, and competitiveness. This is so because the system encourages managers to focus myopically on short-term performance to the detriment of long-term market share and productivity growth. In an effort to show their dispersed shareholders that they are doing a good job, managers concentrate on measurable, tangible quantities—such as quarterly earnings—in the short term. They neglect variables that are important but are nonetheless difficult to document or observe—such as investments in research and development (R&D) or training. Zeckhauser and Pound refer to this practice as "performance tilting" (1990, 150), whereby managers intent on demonstrating to shareholders that they are performing ably foster those aspects of firm performance that can be readily monitored by shareholders (such as sales levels) at the expense of those investments that will affect the balance sheet or income statement only after many years. Risky, long-term investments with high fixed-costs, such as R&D, are likely to be misunderstood and undervalued by the market.

Those who are most likely to know the true value of such intangible and risky investments—the scientists, workers, management, and engineers most familiar with particular projects—are often ignored in favor of outside directors and dispersed shareholders. Labor practices that do not value this kind of tacit knowledge are part of American companies' "adaptive" adjustment strategies that cut costs and provide short-term returns, as opposed to "innovative" strategies, which build long-term capacity by investing in new relations of workforce organization (Harrison and Bluestone 1988; Lazonick 1990; Blair 1993; Appelbaum and Berg 1996). Until quite recently, this model stood in stark contrast with European companies, which focused on labor-centered innovation and productivity growth, investments in training and firm-based learning, and the substitution of quality-based competitive strategies for price/cost-based ones (Christopherson 1997). American companies lack institutionalized feedback mechanisms—such as the practice of co-determination in Germany—to evaluate long-term returns from alternative investment strategies.

Third, the American system of corporate governance may move capital around quickly and, possibly, efficiently, but at what cost? Many have noted that corporate governance rules inequitably distribute the *effects* of corporate change (Goldstein 1995; O'Connor 1991; Singer 1988b; Harrison and Bluestone 1988). Many stakeholders make investments in the firm, but the law protects only some of them. Shareholders, for example, possess many legal protections for their equity investments compared to employees, who, despite years of service and technical training, can be dismissed "at will." Contractarian scholars would argue that employees willingly agree to work without these legal protections; if they did not, they would negotiate for them in their individual employment contracts (Macey 1999).

The sanctity of the contract is predicated on the notion that if there is voluntary consent, both parties must be better off, thereby making society better off as a consequence. Critics point out that corporate actors often possess incomplete information about the future consequences of contracting, such that they are unable to include protections *ex ante* (beforehand) in the contracts they negotiate with management to protect against future harm (Bratton 1989; Daniels 1993; Stone 1993). More systematically, certain groups have unequal bargaining power in relation to others. Their lack of leverage forces them to accept unfair, suboptimal contracts. For instance, workers are forbidden by law from bargaining over issues that will determine their standing in the corporation, like at-will employment or investment decisions. Legal precedent and their "agreement" to submit to managerial authority once they are hired impair workers' capacity to bargain freely to their best advantage (Klare 1988; Bowles and Gintis 1988; Stone 1993).

As legally enforceable obligations, corporate governance rules influence how the costs of economic adjustment are allocated within the corporation. When faced with the growing internationalization of production and declining market shares, this system of corporate governance encourages firms to restructure in a manner that benefits shareholders and upper-level management but unfairly burdens employees, communities, and other stakeholders. Risk averse and legally bound, managers often take quick-fix strategies—such as sub-contracting, downsizing, or divestiture—that go straight to the bottom line and keep shareholders happy (Harrison and Bluestone 1988; Appelbaum and Berg 1996). Existing corporate and labor regulations often do not protect these stakeholders, denying them a voice in influencing the managerial decisions whose outcomes tend to adversely affect them (O'Connor 1991; Stone 1993).

The Need for a New Model

Propositions for new paradigms of corporate governance and reformed financial market institutions flow from these three categories of criticism. Most of the aforementioned critics assert that, as a starting point, directors and managers should be required to consider the interests of other corporate stakeholders.[18] Fiduciary duties, they contend, should be viewed not as discrete contracts between management and shareholders, stipulated by corporate charter or bylaws, but as broader obligations to represent all of the important stakeholders in the firm—whether shareholders, employees, consumers, creditors, or suppliers. Some believe that these obligations are owed on the basis of the social effects of managerial decisions (i.e., negative externalities) and that all corporations must be managed in the "public interest." Others believe that management has an obligation to protect those stakeholders who are disadvantaged at the bargaining table yet who have nonetheless relied on management's implicit promises (e.g., for job security) (Stone 1993; Singer 1988b). All suggest further loosening the legal constraints on managers to encourage them to consider the long-term effects on nonshareholder constituencies.

Although their suggestions to realign fiduciary duties are sound, these progressive critics of corporate governance do not answer a very important question: How can one define the *extent* of managers' responsiveness and legal obligations to different nonshareholder constituents? Should all stakeholders affected by corporate changes be involved in decisionmaking simply because they are affected? Selznick wisely notes, "Selectivity is the Achilles' heel of responsiveness" (1992, 338). Rather than searching for different groups, each of which could possibly be regarded as the beneficiary of a manager's fiduciary duties, scholars and judges need to develop better criteria for selecting and weighing various social and political interests. Without such criteria, managers and directors cannot set priorities and decide among competing uses of corporate resources. Without such criteria, managers and directors cannot determine the extent of reliance on the corporation and therefore the degree of legal protection that should be accorded to each different constituency. Without such criteria, policymakers cannot develop policies to provide enforcement mechanisms to ensure that corporations live up to their social obligations (Blair 1995). Too broad an expansion of fiduciary duties could render a potentially powerful mechanism for accountability meaningless and vacuous, because it would allow management to justify any action on the grounds that it benefits some group.

In the next chapters of this book, I set out such criteria by examining the kinds of firm-specific investments the federal government and other nontraditional corporate stakeholders have made and continue to make in defense contractors. Through an exploration of the property and contractual relations of government contractors, I propose a model of corporate governance that extends the nexus of contracts paradigm to include other corporate constituencies and that can serve as a guide for evaluating the extent to which management should be accountable to groups other than shareholders. My model is based not on the negative externalities of managerial decisions or the need to protect the most vulnerable stakeholders but rather on the degree to which a constituency makes risky, firm-specific investments in the corporation.

Notes

1. This absence is not surprising, given that the dominant neoclassical traditions within economics and business tend to neglect or downplay the institutional arrangements of the economy. Wisely noting this fact, Coase argued that "it makes little sense for economists to discuss the process of exchange without specifying the institutional setting, since this affects both the incentives to produce and the cost of transacting" (1994, 122).

2. Segments of this section and the next are revised from an earlier article on economic development incentives entitled "Why Economic Development Subsidies Don't Create Jobs: A Legal Analysis of Corporate Incentive Structures" (Weber 2000).

3. *Trustees of Dartmouth College v. Woodward*, 4 Wheaton 518 (1819).

4. 18 F. 385 (C.C.D. Cal. 1883).

5. Limited liability means that if a company's net assets become negative, investors stand to lose only their initial investments—not the rest of their assets.

6. *Manson v. Curtis*, 223 N.Y. 313, 322, 119 N.E. 558, 562 (1918).

7. This theory of the firm, often referred to as the neoinstitutional theory of the firm, the finance view of the firm, or simply as the nexus of contracts firm, is actually a conflation of its neoclassical and institutional variants. The neoclassical variant, developed by Alchian and Demsetz (1972), Easterbrook and Fischel (1991), and Jensen and Meckling (1976), applies microeconomic assumptions to the nexus of contracts. Its actors are rational, self-interested maximizers who make complete choices and negotiate long-term contracts. As a result, the firm is always in a state of equilibrium, having optimally allocated risk, costs, and benefits. In contrast, the institutional variant described by Williamson (1975) acknowledges that the firm is more than just the aggregate of transactions among individuals; it constitutes a hierarchically ordered governance structure fundamentally different from market contracting. Firm actors engage in satisfying behavior, behaving opportunistically in an uncertain environment (Cyert and March 1963).

8. It is commonly accepted that a board of directors does not manage the corporation's business, but rather vests that function in its corporate officers and managers. In this study, I use the term "managers" when referring to corporate officers and senior managers (Eisenberg 1976, 139–141).

9. Black and Kraakman define "residual claim" as applying in those situations in which "the expected value of a contracting party's future dealings with the corporation increases as the firm's value increases, and decreases as the firm's value decreases" (1996, 4).

10. Most adherents of the shareholder primacy argument point to the famous *Dodge v. Ford Motor Co.* case, in which the Dodge brothers sued Ford Motor Co., asserting that Henry Ford had chosen to forgo dividend payments in order to lower the price of his cars and expand the business. The Michigan Supreme Court agreed, stating that "(a) business corporation is organized and carried on primarily for the profit of the stockholders. The powers of the directors are to be employed for that end. The discretion of directors is to be exercised in the choice of means to attain that end, and does not extend to a change in the end itself, to the reduction of profits, or to the nondistribution of profits among stockholders in order to devote them to other purposes" 204 Mich. 459, 170 N.W. 668 (1919).

11. Despite the moral weight of fiduciary duties, some neoclassical theorists view them as explicitly contractual, a relationship articulated in corporate charters, state corporate law codes, and bylaws. This off-the-rack contract includes a collection of terms that benefit shareholders and standardly affirm management's obligation to act in their best interests. In this vein, Easterbrook and Fischel state that "these duties have no moral footing. They are the same sort of obligations, derived and enforced in the same way as other contractual undertakings. Actual contracts prevail over implied ones" (1993, 427).

12. Because of its notion that the assets of the firm are the property of shareholders, the contractarian model is sometimes referred to as the "property conception of the firm" (Allen 1992, cited in Blair 1995, 210). See *Charland v. Norge Div., Borg-Warner Corp.*, 407 F. 2d 1062, 1065 (6th Cir.), *cert. denied*, 395 U.S. 927

(1969) (in this case, the employer's decision to relocate did not infringe on the employee's rights, since the employee had no property interest in the job).

13. Collective bargaining agreements have also preserved management's ability to make important corporate decisions without the interference of labor by including what is known as a "management's rights" clause. These clauses are tightly worded and provide that management retains the decisionmaking authority over all issues not explicitly delineated in the contract or precluded by federal, state, or local law (Bluestone and Bluestone 1992).

14. These traits are all characteristic of what is known as "classical liberalism," evident in the works of Locke, Rousseau, and Kant (McConnell 1967; Lowi 1969; Rawls 1971; Scheppele and Waldron 1991; Trebilcock 1993). The liberal orientation of contract theory is often contrasted to a more communitarian conception of the firm, which values the more relational attributes of the firm and downplays the idea of rational actors maximizing their individual interests (Pateman 1988; Selznick 1992; Sandel 1996).

15. Horwitz notes that legal doctrine has a difficult time assimilating the concept of a collectivity, as it is so used to assigning liability and determining will. As a result the social side of corporations is downplayed, despite the fact that corporations have been viewed at certain points in history as quasi-public entities (1992). See also Frug 1980; Simon 1990.

16. Among some of the largest corporations, the percentage of institutional ownership was extremely high in the early 1990s; for example, General Motors Corp. (82 percent), Mobil Corp. (74 percent), Citicorp (70 percent), Amoco (86 percent), and Eli Lilly & Co. (71 percent) (Coffee 1991).

17. Empirical studies have found that this conventional explanation for takeovers—disciplining underperformance—is unfounded. In reality, those companies with high cash flows and low debt were most vulnerable to takeovers (see, for example, Davis and Stout 1992).

18. In keeping with these assertions, a wave of state stakeholder statutes—instituted during the 1980s takeover era—were enacted to allow management to consider the interests of these nonshareholder constituencies during potentially damaging events such as hostile takeovers.

2

Governing Defense Contractors

We do have a unique type of business with the Department of Defense. It's not typical of a commercial business. It is different. I have called it a quasi-fiduciary responsibility. At General Dynamics, we are spending the taxpayers' money, and that means that we must have higher standards of performance and responsibility than maybe a normal commercial-type of manufacturer.

Stanley Pace, CEO of General Dynamics,
on the MacNeil/Lehrer Newshour, *February 17, 1986*

We need to reevaluate the notion of corporate responsibility. Contemporary legal doctrine asserts that beyond contracts and regulation, corporations are responsible only to shareholders, because shareholders have the greatest stake in the outcomes of corporate decisionmaking. Shareholders enjoy many institutional privileges, such as superior legal protections for their equity investments. Moreover, their ability to exit easily from corporations whose performance they find unsatisfactory gives them important control rights. But clearly, shareholders are not the only residual risk-bearers of the firm. Other parties—creditors, customers, employees—make risky investments in corporations and have substantial interests in protecting those investments.

The same contractarian arguments used to justify assigning control rights to shareholders can provide an equally legitimate rationale for assigning these important rights to other parties in the corporate enterprise. In other words, the logic behind the nexus of contracts model can be applied to other types of relations in the firm because "the stockholder-manager relation is but a special case of a more general relation between those who have a 'right' to control an organization (ordinarily, residual risk-bearers) and those decision makers (managers) who, in fact, make most of the important organizational decisions" (Moe 1984, 753). If the current allocation of rewards and risks in the corporation is an artifact of contractual design, and not an inherent correlate of ownership, this allocation could be altered. It could be calibrated to better reflect the reality of risk-bearing and resource contribution in different kinds of firms (Blair 1996).

In this chapter, I demonstrate how even the nexus of contracts paradigm—with its microeconomic underpinnings, contractual understanding of organizational relationships, and decidedly liberal bias—can advance a view of corporations in which actors other than shareholders and managers have legitimate control over corporate resources. I focus on the defense industry to develop this argument. In this industry, the federal government and taxpayers absorb most of the costs of defense production and therefore take on many of the same risks as the firms' shareholders. In a convoluted web of procurement agreements, federally owned property, and direct subsidies for research and development, the public sector commissions private corporations to provide the textbook example of a public good: national defense. In defense production, the state goes far beyond its normal role as regulator and redistributor, assuming the function of investor, consumer, and active market participant. The hybrid status of defense contractors directly challenges the theoretical basis for shareholder primacy.

The first section of the chapter introduces readers to the defense industry, an industry protected, subsidized, and generally enabled by the state. I examine the organizational structure of large defense contractors that has evolved through years of government procurement. In particular, I focus on the problems associated with setting specifications and assigning costs in uncertain technological, political, and military environments, as well as the lack of real competition among bidders. In response to these problems, the federal government has made large and risky investments in a small group of prime defense contractors. I describe the multifiduciary nature of publicly traded government contractors, who must satisfy the conflicting goals and time horizons of shareholders and the public sector. In the concluding section, I point out how the law fails to react to defense contractors' multifiduciary structure and, more normatively, why the law *should* recognize that managers of defense contractors have responsibilities to other important corporate stakeholders.

The Organization of the U.S. Defense Industry

In liberal market economies, governments supposedly lack the legal means, administrative power, and popular support to directly intervene in the economy. By enforcing contracts and property rights, the state is expected only to ensure the legal conditions under which individuals may carry out productive activity and to correct for market failures through regulation, redistribution, and compensatory welfare policies (Hartz 1955; McConnell 1967; Lindblom 1977; North 1981). The state is not expected to control private production and investment decisions, although it can encourage desired behavior (e.g., through subsidies) or penalize undesired behavior (e.g., through taxes and fines). In the United States, the courts have held that decisions regarding technology investment, product strategy, and internal governance fall near the "core of entrepreneurial control" and, therefore, should not be infringed upon by the government.[1] Even if it should want to intervene in these kinds of decisions, the state is often regarded as too weak and underdeveloped bureaucratically to do so in an effective manner (Skowroneck 1982). These beliefs advance an idealized free market conception of the economy, with its emphasis on bounded, diametrically opposed private and public domains.

The public/private distinction itself is a rather arbitrary construct. In reality, there exist multiple public/private distinctions; the economist, for example, defines private and public differently from the abortion rights activist. For the purposes of this study, however, I use "public" to connote those actors and functions associated with the government and the wider citizenry it purports to represent, whereas "private" refers to those acts and actors enabled primarily by firms and commercial exchange. As many noted authors have pointed out, the public/private distinction is more an exercise in classification than a reflection of any true status (see Polanyi 1944; Klare 1982; Kennedy 1982; Walzer 1983; Offe 1984; Fraser 1989). The distinction is a convenient fiction, yet when codified in law it legitimates one of the basic contradictions of capitalism: that production is publicly enabled but privately owned and controlled.

Even the staunchest free marketer, however, will admit that defense contracting is an expensive (and often embarrassing) exception to the notion of separate public and private spheres.[2] Since the Revolutionary War, the federal government of the United States has acted as a market participant in the defense industry. It has actively promoted firm-based research and development and created a huge market for advanced military technologies (Melman 1971; 1974; Lindblom 1977). Even in the post–Cold War era, annual discretionary spending for the military totaled almost $259 billion (fiscal year 1996), which was 16 percent of the federal budget and 3 percent of the gross domestic product in that year (Kosiak 1997). Of all government contracting, military procurement is by far the largest category of public purchases from the private sector.

The simple fact that the federal government finances the research for and production of military hardware has not caused much controversy, due to the state's constitutionally mandated role in "providing for the common defense." All nation-states support their militaries collectively with funds raised through taxation. Economists explain this phenomenon by arguing that national security is the textbook example of a "public good," which, according to neoclassical theory, is a collectively valued good or service that is both nonexcludable and nonrival (Schultze 1968. See note for meaning of terms).[3] Governments, the logic goes, need to pay for these goods because simple consumer demand will not supply them in adequate quantities or quality. Property rights will be difficult to define and assign due to the inalienable qualities of the goods, and they will be underfinanced by the private sector. Noneconomists argue that states happily finance defense production because of the military's role in state formation and legitimation. Tilly (1990), for example, demonstrates how "wars make states." Historically, the drive for military modernization has required a stable bureaucratic apparatus and administrative mechanisms for collecting tax revenues. Moreover, norms construct global standards of prudent, appropriate behavior for state bureaucracies, one of which is the maintenance of armed forces (Katzenstein 1996; Scott and Meyer 1994).

Assigning defense financing to the public sector, however, by no means eliminates controversy; the levels at which defense is collectively funded and the distribution of the so-called public benefits of defense spending are perennially contested. An equally contested issue is the *manner* in which these military products are produced and delivered: Either the government can produce and deliver the defense products itself through the use and control of its own property (i.e., through a nationalized industry, a publicly owned facility, or at least government employees), or it can enter into contractual arrangements with privately owned firms to perform the same tasks. Individual countries have structured state-market relations in the defense industry using different combinations of state regulation and private ownership to foster innovation and oversee the production of military technologies (Ergas 1986; Nelson 1988; Mowery and Rosenberg 1993). In France, for example, the state owns and manages most defense enterprises. The Japanese state, fueled by widespread "technonationalist" sentiment, has nurtured elaborate networks and market regulations to fortify the position of its defense firms (Samuels 1994). Other more decentralized states, like the United States and Great Britain, engage a cadre of privately owned suppliers but provide a procurement environment in which contractors are assured high profits and few financial risks. In these countries, the division between public and private authority and obligations in military production has been a source of contention since military procurement began.

One might expect that all nations would assign the task of producing weapons for the national defense entirely to the public sector. After all, weapons production involves high levels of technological uncertainty, financial risk, and the manufacture of complex systems comprised of millions of individual components. Far from the routine provision of standardized goods, weapons production creates systems based on initially vague requirements that get worked through over the production process. The government cares very much about every step of the process as well as the quality of the final product. Moreover, profit-seeking contractors have many opportunities for opportunism and fraud given the large budget appropriations for defense. Accordingly, defense production would seem like an obvious candidate for state ownership.[4]

In striking contrast, the United States, in the overwhelming majority of cases, has contracted out the research, production, and delivery of weapons systems to the private sector. The United States government has retained collective financing for defense technologies but has delegated the production of weaponry to private firms. The federal government exercises centralized authority over resource allocation in this sector, but it does so through the medium of contracting rather than by requisitioning goods and services internally through command (Melman 1974; 1983).

What explains this seemingly irrational arrangement? The historical details have hinged on political decisions about the efficiency of production and importance of technological innovation, the responsiveness of profit-seekers as opposed to civil servants to government demands, and the accountability of military suppliers to the public interest.[5] Before World War II, with the exception of the fledgling aircraft industry, there was almost no private capacity for the manufacture of arms (Peck and Scherer 1962; Baldwin 1967). The Ordnance Departments of the Army and Navy were each responsible for their own weapons production. Either the Ordnance Departments would decide to produce their own equipment in publicly owned arsenals and laboratories, or they would draft impersonal, "arm's-length" contracts with commercial firms for products that, for the most part, had been previously developed in civilian markets. Popular hostility toward private arms-makers during World War I and the Congressional desire to "take the profits out of war" combined to impede relationships with industry and concentrate peacetime research and production in federally owned facilities (McNaugher 1989; Friedberg 1992; Kaufman 1996).

Weapons production shifted dramatically from publicly owned arsenals to privately owned firms during the huge expansion of production in World War II. In the interim period between the two World Wars, advances in aircraft technology—particularly sophisticated aircraft engines—forced the Army's Ordnance Department to reexamine its strategies for obtaining the highest quality products. Finding their established procurement agencies and arsenals too slow and procedural to keep apace of innovations within the burgeoning aircraft industry, the services sought commercial firms to take over the entire delivery process, from design through production and deployment.[6] Coalitions of business leaders and commercial aviation firms pushed the privatization process along by criticizing the entrenched military bureaucracy for its lack of flexibility and low quality production processes. They lobbied Congress aggressively for greater funding, in part because it was becoming increasingly difficult for aviation firms to finance R&D from their commercial sales alone (Holley 1964). Joining potential contractors were the investment banking, accounting, and law firms that would create the technical support infrastructure to negotiate increasingly complex transactions between the government and its contractors (Kaufman 1996). In choosing a profit-seeking agent over a bureaucrat, the public sector was expected to gain the cost discipline of competition and the benefits of innovation by agents motivated to discover better, cheaper ways of delivering value. Private firms could also afford to pay higher salaries and thus attract higher quality workers, scientists, and engineers. In 1940, President Roosevelt asked Congress to appropriate funds for 50,000 aircraft, and the Army and Navy Air Corps implemented this order by procuring these craft directly from industry. There was relatively little opposition from the service procurement agencies because their arsenals could not compete with industry in the field of aviation.

Congress approved greater federal funding for corporations, not only because it agreed that higher quality products could be manufactured in privately owned firms, but also because it saw procurement contracting as a means of extending industry-state relations without disrupting the fragile political consensus regarding the state's limited role in the economy (Friedberg 1992). Through procurement contracts, the federal government was able to engage in centralized economic planning while supporting the liberal capitalist ideology that makes ownership of the means of production, control over the production process, and the appropriation of surplus the responsibility of private individuals. Firms took over the technical management and integration of defense technologies, while the military focused on coordination and some basic research. "In this way," McNaugher notes, "commercial firms became the equivalent of aeronautical arsenals" (1989, 23).

The process of shifting production to private firms was made easier by the pressures of war. War, by creating pervasive concern for national security, protected economic planning from potential protests emanating from different segments of society (Kaufman 1996). When World War II erupted, normal peacetime procurement strictures were overlooked, and the services were able to award contracts to commercial firms noncompetitively as demand for production increased. Contractors initially were fearful of the risks involved in defense production, but the services assuaged their fears by lobbying for regulatory reforms that offered risk-minimizing contracts and free real estate to contractors. Even in the years following World War II, military leaders continued to fund peacetime research, development, and production of weaponry. Desirable military innovations, such as proximity fuses for bombs and microwave radar, as well as increasingly adversarial relations with the Soviet Union, provided reasons to sustain the funding.

While more funds were allocated toward privately performed research, development, and production during the Korean War, the publicly owned arsenals were left to decline. The famous Springfield Armory, for example, was shut down in the 1950s, diminishing the Army's ability to monitor and control small firearms manufacturers (Smith 1985). Receptive to arguments about public ineptness and private efficiency, Secretary of Defense McNamara hastened the demise of the arsenal network during his tenure (McNaugher 1989). Most of the naval shipyards and depots were closed in the 1960s, when studies demonstrated that private yards could produce ships at lower costs because of lower labor and material costs and higher worker productivity. The remaining public shipyards focused primarily on refuelings and overhaul work, while the private yards were awarded lucrative contracts for new vessel construction. Technical bureaus in the Navy that once managed the manufacture of ships in government yards became contract managers, writing, negotiating, and overseeing contracts (Sapolsky 1990). While the arsenal system languished, procurement contracting expanded the government markets in which particular industrial sectors and corporations flourished.

Since World War II, the defense procurement system has evolved into a system of contractual governance whereby the federal government and defense firms work together to produce complex military technologies. The system is intended to progress through the following phases:

1. Concept formulation phase: One of the branches of the armed forces will promulgate loose operational requirements after establishing the need for a particular system. Pentagon staffers prepare detailed estimates of costs, schedule, and technical risk.
2. Concept demonstration and validation phase: The service solicits bids from industry, so that potential contractors compete to fulfill the requirements at the lowest cost. If the concept is flawed or unfeasible, it is assumed that no contractors will bid on the project. Contracts are awarded to the company that will be responsible for the engineering development of the preliminary design or awards are made to a few firms that will compete for the chance to develop the system.

3. Full-scale development phase: Final design, engineering, and manufacturing specifications are drafted, and every aspect of the weapon, from final prototypes to the design of spare parts, is completed and tested. The contractor chosen to perform the development is guaranteed the production contract if the weapon in ultimately built.

4. Final production and deployment phase: The contractor will first build a small number of units and then accelerate into mass production. (McNaugher 1989; Mayer 1991)

When the government signs a contract to procure a major weapons system, it agrees to pay for the technical procedures in each phase, as much as it agrees to purchase the actual weapons system (Goodman 1988, 409).

Managing Uncertainty

The smooth functioning of this system is undermined by the uncertainty inherent in the weapons procurement process. This uncertainty takes many forms, above all technological uncertainty associated with operating at the frontier of the unknown, political uncertainty associated with the fluctuating demand for defense systems due to changing geopolitical strategies and military missions, and budgetary uncertainty arising from changing Congressional preferences about funding levels for particular programs (McNaugher 1989).

Private contractors produce the technical knowledge and hardware of national security. These products, however, are not standardized, off-the-shelf commodities. Cold War rivalry created a political environment that supported a system of radical and rapid innovation aimed at the highest level of performance: the flexibility, maneuverability, invisibility, undetectability, and infallibility of lethal weapons and their delivery systems (Melman 1971; Kaldor 1981; Markusen 1985a). Such goals require massive investments in computing, electronics, communications, and instrumentation. They also require a reserve of highly specialized skilled labor and scientific personnel. Prime contractors create elaborate weapons systems and subsystems comprised of millions of components, many of which are fabricated by elaborate webs of sub-contractors (Walker, Graham, and Harbor 1988). Contractors are geared toward producing at low volumes while meeting the exacting demands for technological performance. They abide by rigid, detailed specifications (called "milspecs"), not only for the actual product but also for the entire process of manufacture.

When one is operating at the technological frontier, uncertainty—about both cost and performance—makes it is difficult, if not impossible, to specify in advance precisely what is required of particular systems and how much such systems are likely to cost (Greer and Liao 1986; Donahue 1989; McNaugher 1989; Markusen and Yudken 1992; Oden 1994). Overall defense demand as well as demand for particular systems is highly unstable, because of political, security, and budgetary factors (Oden 1994). The Pentagon, for example, spent $700 million on the Snark surface-to-surface missile, only to cancel the Snark before full deployment when ballistic missiles made it obsolete (Peck and Scherer 1962, 43–47).

This kind of uncertainty creates a relationship of extreme mutual dependence between the government and its contractors. The contractor may initiate contract changes, incur schedule delays and cost overruns, and manufacture products of suboptimal quality, which will impede the government's ability to procure weapons. The government may unilaterally impose changes, terminate work, order work stoppages, or take other action that in commercial contracting would be considered a breach of contract. Scherer observes that "buyer and seller are locked together in a relationship analogous to a bilateral monopoly for the life of the program, and they must deal with each other on a bargaining basis" (1964, 2).

Agency relations become strained in highly uncertain situations because principal and agent cannot exchange necessary information. On one hand, because of the high degree of uncertainty, most specifications and performance requirements must be worked out through the course of the contract. Defense products are often entirely new products, bearing little resemblance to commercial items. They exist only because they have been imagined by the services and produced jointly with contractors (Greer and Liao 1986, 1259). On the other hand, Pentagon program managers are required to draft highly specific requirements to set the terms for competitive bidding and codify the obligations of the winning bidder. No "market price" exists for weapons systems; all prices are negotiated throughout the process. Thus, the contracting officers need to know enough about the desired product to select suppliers before the technical requirements are fully worked out. Moreover, contractors need the discretion to initiate changes and respond to technical contingencies; at the same time, the public sector must prevent the abuse of public funds.

Defense contracts bear the burden of taking this great uncertainty into account, as they cannot define and allocate all possible risks in advance. Contracts must govern future, not present, exchanges and long-term, not short-term, relations (Goldberg 1976, 426).[7] Orlans summarizes this problem succinctly:

> In a hands-off buyer-seller relationship, all of the terms that are necessary to the satisfactory completion of a contractual obligation may, perhaps, be put

down on paper: the exact goods to be delivered, at a given time and place for a stated sum. But the most significant aspects of the contracts are precisely those that cannot be satisfactorily reduced to writing for they involve the quality of effort made to reach, not a precise target, but goals that must be continually readjusted by mutual agreement, and—beyond gross and obvious limits—the balance of initiative and responsibility, of freedom and control, that should lie in public and private hands is also a shifting one that must be worked out individually for each major contract. (1967, 128)

During World War II, unique types of contracts were developed to facilitate the procurement of complex military systems. When Congress passed the National Defense Expediting Act in 1940, it allowed for new contractual arrangements to increase collaboration with private firms in research, design, and production (Peck and Scherer 1962; Kaufman 1996). The military was urged to buy through "negotiated contracts" that required the services to work closely with contractors, in contrast to the previous system where the services wrote clear specifications that described existing products. Research and development contracts provided the legal basis for agencies to purchase the products and basic science that they could not define in adequate detail in advance.

The act also acknowledged that new forms of pricing were necessary to encourage such collaborations. In the 1950s, the services shifted from using fixed-price contracts, where suppliers agree to produce a certain quantity at a preset price, to cost-reimbursement contracts, in which contractors are paid for the costs they incur—plus a negotiated amount of profit. This kind of "cost-plus" pricing is a way of shifting the risks involved in technological uncertainty from the contractor to the state (Peck and Scherer 1962; McNaugher 1989; Kaufman 1996). Even most fixed-price defense contracts come with price adjustment mechanisms—such as change proposals—that allow principals and agents room to redefine the project specifications and adjust for additional compensation. Because prices are negotiated, not set by the market, there are additional incentives for contractor opportunism. Negotiated contracts give the contractor few reasons to control costs, and they require that both parties devote more resources to monitoring and oversight.

Cost-plus pricing was intended to make contractors invest in defense-specific assets. Defense products are built to exacting engineering specifications with specialized equipment, facilities, and labor. Contractors must install expensive equipment and train labor to compete successfully for contracts that they may only potentially win (Markusen and Yudken 1994; McNaugher 1989).[8] Perhaps more so than in any other industry, the technological and economic obsolescence of facilities is a constant and serious problem due to the rapid rate of technological change in products, plants, and equipment employed in defense production. Defense firms must also invest in political capital, which they "assiduously buil[d] up over the decades by working with Congress, government agencies and the military, often amplified by hiring former military officers in marketing and management positions" (Markusen 1997a, 3).

The firm's physical, human, and political capital stock may not have any market value because it has no use other than military production.[9] Once investments in such specialized capital have been made, they cannot be easily recovered or redeployed without a significant loss of economic value. Because the development of weapons systems is subject to extremely long product cycles, these assets become even more arcane, illiquid, and specific to the firm and to its routines over time (Oden 1994). In this sense, most physical, human, and political capital costs in defense production are considered "sunk costs," in that they are irrevocably committed to a particular use.

Sunk costs do not have an entirely negative effect on the finances of defense contractors; significant competitive advantages can accrue from having distinctive, firm-specific labor and capital stock (Clark and Wrigley 1995).[10] Sunk costs are a means of guarding against competition because they create barriers to entry for rival contractors that do not possess the same technological know-how, facilities, and political savvy. Sunk costs are essential for developing the defense-specific expertise and processes that make particular defense firms so indispensable to the government. The specialization that comes with sunk costs has increased contractors' dependence on the government market (because there is no alternative market for their assets) and concurrently increased the government's dependence on these few firms.

By keeping potential rivals out, sunk costs influence the market structure of the defense sector. Defense production has always had a competitive structure unlike that of other sectors producing for commercial markets. The market for defense products is the weapons acquisition process, a highly regulated process administered by the huge planning apparatus of the Department of Defense (Peck and Scherer 1962; Fox 1974; Gansler 1980; McNaugher 1989). The Pentagon acts as a monopsonist, a solitary customer. But this customer does not have a fixed identity, and its demand for military products cannot be determined by a singular utility function. This public agency's demand is determined through an extensive political process in which legislators represent the special interests of defense-dependent regions and firms.[11] Moreover, the Pentagon's demand is highly inelastic (e.g., the Navy is not likely to purchase fewer submarines if their price increases); oligopolistic contractors therefore can raise their prices considerably above costs without losing business (Markusen 1985b; Gansler 1980).[12]

Congress and the executive branch have made periodic attempts to create a competitive supplier base, even though perfect competition is not possible in this market.[13] The architects of the post–World War II acquisition system insisted that contracts be awarded to a large pool of suppliers, moving away from the practice of "sole-sourcing" that had become standard practice before the war (Pilling 1989). In 1965 Secretary of Defense Robert McNamara testified to Congress that a savings of 25 percent could result from the conversion of sole-source procurement to competitive bidding (McNaugher 1989). Although competition may force the cost of weaponry down, the uncertain technological environment undermines the potential for competition. After all, how can the services choose among bids to create the unknown? It is impossible to fully specify the nature of desired product in advance, and engineering specifications are constantly renegotiated. The Pentagon works with a few contractors to devise the technical criteria for which they will subsequently be evaluated. Maintaining multiple production lines with the kind of defense-specific facilities and knowledge necessary to production would be too expensive.

The collusion between principal and agent "destroys the arm's-length contracting relation between buyer and seller that makes for a competitive market" (Kettl 1993, 136). It creates a closed system of bureaucratic actors and a few select contractors who collaborate in designing the artifacts of national security. Sophisticated alliances with legislators and regulators have allowed defense contractors to create so-called "iron triangles" to protect and perpetuate their interests.

Thus, rather than encouraging competition between a multitude of equally competent, rival contractors, the weapons acquisition system has created an oligopoly comprised of a few cost-maximizing conglomerates, primarily in the aerospace, communications, and electronics sectors (Melman 1974; Markusen 1985a; McNaugher 1989; Gansler 1989). (See Table 2.1.) Only a handful of large defense corporations are qualified to submit bids for prime contracts and possess the technological capacity, research capabilities, and political ties to ensure the possibility of winning a contract. These enterprises also tend to be vertically integrated, having developed huge in-house capabilities. Smaller firms confront barriers to entry and get weeded out by the sheer volume and complexity of regulatory controls. The defense industry is more concentrated than most other industrial sectors. In 1992, for example, the top thirty-five contractors received fifty percent of all defense contracts in the United States (U.S. Department of Defense 1993, Table 2).

These prime contractors enjoy privileged access to capital, tax exemptions, government-furnished property, and the "follow-on imperative" (the practice of receiving successive orders to ensure that contractors

TABLE 2.1   Top Ten Military Contractors by Rank Based on
Prime Contract Awards

1986	1990	1996
General Dynamics	McDonnell Douglas	Lockheed Martin
General Electric	General Dynamics	McDonnell Douglas
McDonnell Douglas	General Electric	General Motors
Rockwell	General Motors	Raytheon
General Motors	Raytheon	General Dynamics
Lockheed	Lockheed	Northrop Grumman
Raytheon	Martin Marietta	United Technologies
Boeing	United Technologies	Boeing
United Technologies	Grumman	Litton
Grumman	Tenneco	General Electric

SOURCE: U.S. Department of Defense, Directorate for Information, Operations and Reports, "100 Companies Receiving Largest Dollar Volume of Prime Contract Awards," 1986, 1990, and 1996. Washington, D.C.

keep their productive capacities "hot") (Kurth 1973). The recent wave of mergers and consolidations in the industry underscores the trend toward vertical integration and concentration.

Multiple Principals, Multiple Goals

It is in the context of these high levels of uncertainty and sunk costs that the corporate governance of defense contractors gets worked through. Defense contractors, as government *agents*, are supposed to be accountable to the public sector. They must abide by the Pentagon's engineering specifications and timetables, among other things. But contractors are not actual government *agencies*; they are private, profit-seeking corporations that are legally bound to act in the interests of their shareholders, after all of their other contractual obligations have been fulfilled. As such, managers of defense contractors are beholden to (at least) two different masters: the federal government and their shareholders (Mayer and Khademian 1996).

This would not present a problem were it not for the fact that the interests of shareholders and the state are often fundamentally in conflict over production risks, the allocation of the costs of investment, and planning horizons (see Figure 2.1). As Donahue succinctly notes:

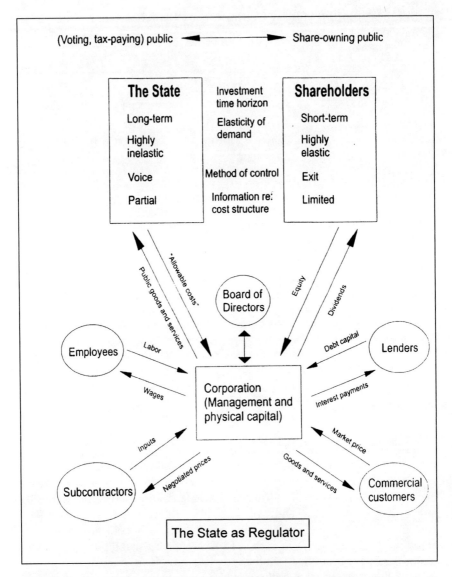

FIGURE 2.1   The Corporate Government of Defense Contractors
Based on Margaret Blair, *Ownership and Control*. Washington, D.C.:
Brookings Institution (1995), p. 21.

The government would like to pay as little as possible for each weapon it needs, while suppliers (and their shareholders) would like to earn as much as possible. Each party prefers stability and would prefer to shift risk to the other. Each wants the other to fulfill commitments precisely, while retaining flexibility for itself. (1989, 115)

Managers of defense contractors are situated in the precarious position of having to balance the interests of shareholders and the federal government. If one party is favored over the other, the thwarted party will threaten management's decisionmaking autonomy. For example, if managers devote extra resources to product improvement beyond what is called for in the contract, shareholders may respond to lower earnings by selling their stock or voting the directors out. If the contractor cuts overhead costs in order to please shareholders but skimps on quality, the federal government may withhold future contracts or seek some sort of legal recourse. Managers of defense contractors engage in complex negotiations over the allocation of profits, risks, and costs of production as their shareholders wield ownership rights (i.e., the ability to sell with ease) and the federal government wields regulatory authority in an attempt to control contractor behavior. The tension between shareholders and the state over the problems of risk, asymmetrical information, and oversight inherent in defense production forms, to quote Coffee, a "strain in the corporate web" (1988, 77).

Government officials and shareholders also have different tolerances for the risks inherent in defense production. These tolerances are determined by the size of their respective economic stakes in the firm, their ability to diversify their investments, and their potential for personal liability. Shareholders, especially institutional investors, hold diversified portfolios. Their liabilities are limited by definition to what they have paid for their shares, they can always sell their shares in a troubled firm, and they can handle an occasional wipeout with few repercussions (Henwood 1997). Shareholders seek higher capital gains and dividends than they would receive if they had invested their money elsewhere. Shareholders are less interested in the quality of the contractor's product, the treatment of its employees, or the legality of its accounting practices than they are in the price of the stock and the dividends they hope to receive. Because they receive corporations' residual returns and have diversified portfolios, shareholders may prefer a higher degree of risk-taking than the government in pursuit of potentially higher returns. However, stockholders are also impatient; they seek short-term returns and prefer that management not dedicate firm resources to projects that *might* benefit them, if at all, in the distant future. Market myopic, shareholders are extremely sensitive to short-term fluctuations in stock price and often buy and sell on a day-to-day basis (Kester 1990; Baldwin and Clark 1991; Lorsch and MacIver 1991; Goldstein 1995). This temporal sensitivity effectively neutralizes some of shareholders' preference for risk (Hu 1990).

The owners of defense contractors face qualitatively different risks than owners of commercial firms, especially in those defense product markets where items have very high per-unit costs and are acquired in small quantities. In these markets, prime defense contractors commonly engage in a winner-take-all competition rather than a struggle for market share. The government purchases a few large systems, and winning a development contract frequently means that a contractor will also win the "follow-on" contract for production (McNaugher 1989; Kurth 1973). With these high stakes, shareholders may be that much more reluctant to invest in highly specific assets (e.g., new process technologies or labor retraining), given the uncertainty about the award of future contracts, the declining defense budgets, and the government's ability to cancel contracts without notice.

In theory, the federal government has different objectives and planning horizons than shareholders do: The state wants its contractors to produce the highest quality military technologies to serve particular national security goals. Since human lives are at stake in military conflicts, the Department of Defense can argue that any expense is justified in acquiring the latest and best technology (Rogerson 1990). Favoring quality over cost-efficiency, the state wants contractors to make long-term, "deep" investments in highly specialized labor, tools, and equipment in order to foster continuous innovation.[14] Military technologies take a long time to move from the drawing board to the final product (especially with frequent design changes), and although the state may emphasize the need to minimize development time, its planning horizons tend to be much longer than those of shareholders. Unlike commercial enterprises, which receive and fill sales orders with a short turnaround, a large portion of a government business extends over several years. The maintenance of the armed services' preparedness and technological edge as well as future industrial-base concerns demand planning over a longer term horizon than is implied by the short-run performance measures of shareholders.

Because of the oligopolistic structure of the industry, the procuring service cannot turn to a host of rival, equally competent producers if it is unhappy with a contractor's performance. The government faces a severe "small numbers" bind: Because there are so few prime suppliers, each contractor can use its near-monopoly position to inflate prices, reduce quality, and demand more public concessions. Such unbridled cost growth and bargaining power effectively neutralize any kind of market discipline for errant contractors. The federal government has a heightened interest in sustaining its relationships with them because of the sunk costs it has incurred with these firms. Accordingly, the state cannot view the potential for business failure with the same equanimity that a diversified shareholder can; it will favor lower-risk, lower-return strategies to ensure the stability and security of its investments.

Because of the lack of real competition, the state needs to rely on its "voice" rather than its ability to exit if it wants to influence the investment and revenue decisions of its contractors (Hirschman 1970). The Pentagon will express its dissatisfaction directly to management. Because of the state's dependence on contractors and the accumulated sunk costs, the state cannot simply exit from bad relationships with contractors. It is compelled to work out the kinks individually through the terms of each contract. The specific terms of weapons acquisition contracts and the brokering process allow government contracting officers to negotiate the allocation of the costs and risks of production, even after the product is delivered. The state and its contractors are continually readjusting the balance of benefit and responsibility that will lie in public and private hands.

Shareholders rely on both exit and voice as means of controlling management. Individual shareholders, especially those in pension or mutual funds, have no realistic means other than selling their stock to express their concerns about performance, because they own too small a share of the company to bring direct pressure for change on directors or managers (Hirschman 1970; Coffee 1988; Roe 1994; Alexander 1994). Shareholders are also relatively ignorant about the actual cost structure of the firm, relying on managers to follow loose Securities and Exchange Commission (SEC) disclosure guidelines (Hu 1990; Zeckhauser and Pound 1990). They have a less comprehensive picture about actual revenues than either managers or the federal government, so they find it difficult to make informed judgments about the operating environment and optimal competitive strategy of the firm. Nonetheless, shareholders have become much less passive and managers much less autonomous since the 1980s. Although individual shareholders in pension and mutual funds are relatively impotent, fund managers and large investors have been able to wield a substantial amount of power over management decisions.

The conflict between the interests of the state and of shareholders constitutes an underlying tension that runs through state-industry relations in most government contracting situations. This tension is seldom visible in its operation, because private shareholders and the state never actually come into contact with each other. They both rely on management as their proxy to mediate the conflict between their interests and negotiate deals that will be beneficial to them.

Managers, of course, also have their own interests. Managers of defense contractors tend to be engineers who have risen through the ranks. Their priorities, like those of commercial managers, generally stress reinvestment of returns in research and development, growth in sales, innovation, and empire building over short-term profits and stable earnings (Coffee 1988; Fligstein 1990; Useem 1990; Markusen 1997b). Managers are not as footloose as shareholders; they are more willing to shoulder the burden of sunk costs and the risks of long-term investment if that will ensure their employment tenure. Managers want to protect their jobs by avoiding courses of action that could threaten their autonomy, such as losing a large contract, doing something illegal, or lowering the value of the company's stock (Coffee 1988; Clark 1993). Managers want peaceful lives with high salaries and minimal external intrusion.

At the same time, because of the practice of stock options, shareholders' threat of exit, and the increasingly vocal power of institutional investors, managers' interests have come to more resemble those of shareholders (i.e., focusing on short-term performance measures). They are under pressure to make their quarterly earnings announcements more "upbeat" even if the actual numbers are not. Doing so can make stock prices jump. Only later "does a more accurate picture emerge in filings with regulators. By then, though, investors have been swayed by analysts' exhortations and are no longer paying close attention" (Morgenson 1999, A1).

Often the goals of the state, shareholders, and managers collide and conflict. High-risk strategies that might bring big gains to stockholders (e.g., accepting a takeover bid) may strike the state as putting its investments at risk. Shareholders may resent the conservative influence of the state on corporate strategies. Both shareholders and the state will resent managerial perks like large executive compensation packages. As the official party to the procurement contract, management must balance these competing obligations and placate the state and shareholders. It must also uphold its other contractual obligations to creditors, employees, and suppliers. Ideally, revenues need to be sufficient to deter corporate raiders, mass exit, and organized resistance from shareholders. They must also be sufficient to maintain adequate control over the production process so as to meet the government's exacting quality standards. If they can maximize the flow of net revenue over time, managers will be able to satisfy both principals and will have wider discretion in capital budgeting, larger individual earnings, and enhanced flexibility in decisionmaking.

Managing Uncertainty by Shifting Risks

One of the few ways available to maximize revenues in defense production is to shift responsibility for the costs, risks, and liabilities of production to other parties. This is in keeping with Peter Marris's assertion that controlling uncertain relationships frequently involves farming uncertainty out to other stakeholders (1996, 8; see also Beck 1992). Because of the negotiated nature of procurement and the inelasticity of the government's demand, managers can easily shift the burden of sunk costs and long-term investments in specialized, "idiosyncratic" assets *to the state and taxpayers* so that the financial capacity of the corporation is not harmed in the short-run. Managers will agree to make the quality-oriented investments the state seeks only if their companies can reduce the liability for these sunk costs and forestall their responsibility for maintaining these costs.[15]

The power to control uncertainty is unequally distributed: The more powerful parties (powerful in that they are better able to use their assets to enlarge their freedom of action) transfer risks to the weaker parties (Marris 1996). In the case of the shareholder-contractor-state relationship, who has greater bargaining strength, and who is the weaker party? It is unclear. On one hand, contractors and their industry associations lobby Congress and the Pentagon to take on more risks and costs, claiming they are unable to achieve even average returns.[16] Contractors threaten to leave defense work unless they are offered incentives from the state. On the other hand, contractors are not simply duping the state. Historically, the federal government has been willing to bear many of these risks, costs, and liabilities—and for some very good reasons. The Department of Defense has recognized that contractors have to manage swings in employment and output due to the uncertain nature of defense contracting. To sustain the defense industrial base, the federal government has made certain allowances: it guarantees defense contractors' profits and limits their risks. Franklin Roosevelt's secretary of war, Henry Stimson, noted in 1940 that "if you are going to try to go to war, or to prepare for war, in a capitalist country, you have got to let business make money out of the process or business won't work" (quoted in Koistinen 1980, 58). Because of the structure of the defense industry and the nature of the economy in which it is situated, the public sector has been, however grudgingly, an accomplice to defense contractors' risk-shifting schemes.

The allocation of risks and costs between the shareholders and the state is not static; within the life cycle of a contract, there are different opportunities to shift and shoulder, transfer and absorb these liabilities. In the initial source selection phase, for example, the government has the power to choose among a few competitors. Because of competitive pressures, these few contractors will try to minimize the price of their bids. But as the project evolves, "sunk costs increase, competitors are eliminated and the winning firm moves into a monopoly position from which it can deal with the government with increasing authority" (McNaugher

1989, 72). The contractor will try to recoup investments borne out of earlier optimism (in contracting jargon, to "get well") by externalizing those
sunk costs to the public sector that might otherwise be attributed to its
operations.

Whereas in traditional commercial contracts, the seller is responsible
for the bulk of costs and risks of production, weapons acquisition contracts and regulations create elaborate administrative mechanisms to allocate the costs and risks of production *between* the government and the
seller (MacNeil 1978; Williamson 1985). The state assumes many of the
risks and costs of production through a number of different mechanisms:
cost-reimbursement contracts, government-furnished property, and
other protection from financial risk and product liability.

Cost-reimbursement contracts are distinctive in that the government
does not contract for the performance of a specified amount of work at a
predetermined price, but instead agrees to pay the contractor's reasonable costs of performance whether or not the work is even completed.[17]
In addition, the contractor is paid a negotiated percentage of the total estimated or incurred costs as a fixed profit. As work on the system pro-
gresses, the contractor is paid for the costs it incurs (in what are called
"progress payments"). Although actual cost-reimbursement contracts fell
out favor in the 1980s, elements of cost-plus pricing, such as escalation
clauses and easily approved change proposals, are found today in fixed-
price and incentive contracts.

Through these negotiated contracts, the government insures the contractor by bearing the risks of foreseen and unforeseen technological, political, and budgetary problems. Because the contract concerns a complex
product that will be continuously redefined during the life of the contract, many agree that cost-plus contracts offer profit-seeking agents opportunities for manipulation (Baron and Besanko 1987). Prices are negotiated, not set by the market, and this fact creates incentives for contractor
opportunism. In such a relationship, management has access to relevant
information about its cost structure to which the government is not privy.
"Overhead loading" and other tricks allow contractors to take a liberal
interpretation of "allowable costs" in submitting their requests for government reimbursement (McNaugher 1989). The contractor also con-
tributes an unobservable effort. As the government cannot monitor how
much effort management is making to limit costs, contractors can claim
that any cost increase is unpredictable and unexpected. Therefore, they
argue, the government should bear full responsibility for the overrun.
When one calculates the fixed fee against the firm's capital investment,
rather than the project's total costs, it is apparent that contractors are able
to make excess profits on cost-plus contracts at the expense of the state,
above all because they invest such a limited amount of their own capital
(U.S. GAO 1986a; Kaufman 1996, 43).

In addition to providing risk-minimizing contracts, the government provides many of the specialized components and process machinery, land, and facilities peculiar to defense production (U.S. GAO 1988a; Tomanelli 1995). Called "government furnished property" (GFP) and "government furnished equipment" (GFE), these grants of property have been used since World War I to expand the private sector's industrial capacity. In the course of World War II, the federal government paid for approximately 65 percent of total investment in plant and equipment, and at the war's end, it owned approximately 40 percent of the nation's capital assets. The mix of private and public investments in established factories, especially in steel, "created a number of 'scrambled' facilities that were nearly impossible to disentangle at the war's end" (Hooks and Bloomquist 1992, 305).

The government's rationale for the provision of GFE and GFP is threefold: It seeks to mitigate the contractor's risk in using new process technologies or components, achieve economies of scale (i.e., by purchasing in bulk so there are lower per-unit costs), and facilitate consistent performance and achieve uniformity among different contractors. The government generally prefers that the contractor pay for its own contract-specific equipment, but if the services want to convince a contractor to sign a particularly risk-laden contract, they may offer to absorb some of those risks through the provision of property. At the end of fiscal year 1992, defense contractors possessed government property valued at over $83 billion (Tomanelli 1995, 243). This figure is a rough estimate, given the fact that the federal government has only begun keeping detailed records of its property. Senator John Glenn (D.-OH) observed: "In March 1988, we reviewed the Department of Defense's loss of control over tens of billions of dollars of property furnished to government contractors. There wasn't even an inventory kept of it" (U.S. Senate 1988).

What may start out as a per-unit cost savings to the government has the effect of bestowing a competitive advantage on the beneficiary before and after the contract award (Tomanelli 1993). GFP allows contractors to enjoy greater liquidity and a more favorable cash flow since they avoid the expense of purchasing the property. Contractors with GFP and GFE are able to bid lower than their competitors because they do not have to incur the direct costs of purchasing or leasing similar property.[18] Contractors who do not possess GFP and GFE must include the expected costs of such property in their bids, raising the value of the bid and potentially jeopardizing their chances of winning initial contracts.

Even after the contract award is made, government property confers a competitive advantage upon the recipient. Private property owners are generally responsible for the upkeep and maintenance of their assets; they assume the risk that it may break down and the costs of repair if it does. When the state acts as a co-owner of the defense industrial base, it

takes on the financial responsibility for much of the property maintenance. Accordingly, the downside risks of production—cost overruns,
technological malfunctions, and obsolescence—fall heavily on the state,
as opposed to the contractors' shareholders. As with procurement contracts, the state and contractor become embroiled in negotiations to allocate risks, bringing to light the procedures by which contractors' rights
and governmental power are continually adjusted. If they are operating
under fixed-price contracts, contractors with GFP and GFE will not have
to capitalize and allocate their acquisition costs to particular government
contracts, thereby increasing net revenues.[19]

In defense contracting, the state acts as the insurer of last resort by rescu-
ing those contractors in dire financial straits with lucrative contracts, loans,
and subsidies—what Kurth calls the "bailout imperative" (1973, 135).[20] In
the 1970s, Lockheed asked for a $350 million government loan guarantee
to help it stay in business after problems with its C-5A military transport
and commercial L-1011 jetliner projects. In 1992, the Pentagon changed accounting procedures to help McDonnell Douglas with cash flow difficulties on the C-17 cargo jet. The Lockheed and McDonnell Douglas bailouts
were high profile, but the government engages in less conspicuous
bailouts all the time (Schmitter and Lembruch 1979; Reich and Donahue
1985).[21] As the case of General Dynamics will make clear, defense firms experiencing major losses attempt to extort additional assistance from the
public coffers. The Pentagon is reluctant to let major suppliers go bankrupt; national security concerns create formidable pressures to allow costs
to increase, the terms of contracts to be extended indefinitely, and contracts
to be let to contractors who have shoddy past performance records. Former member of Congress William Moreland (D.-PA) aptly summarized
this situation, comparing the Lockheed bailout in the 1970s to "an 80-ton
dinosaur who comes to your door and says, 'If you don't feed me, I will
die.' And what are you going to do with 80 tons of dead, stinking dinosaur
meat in your yard?" (quoted in Rice 1971, 183).

The state also provides financial insurance to defense contractors and
their shareholders through a variety of tax laws and accounting practices.
In the 1970s, tax loopholes allowed defense contractors to avoid paying
federal income taxes. In the 1990s, the federal government agreed to reimburse contractors for their restructuring costs and subsidize foreign
military sales. Part of a company's initial development research is reimbursed, as are interest costs for capital borrowed to purchase equipment.
Moreover, the Supreme Court recently granted defense contractors generous tort immunity, shielding them from liability arising out of defec-
tively designed military equipment.[22]

In sum, government procurement regulations, policies, and practices
shift the weight of investment risks and costs from the contractors' share-

holders to the federal government and the taxpayers.[23] The government has become a capitalist entrepreneur, absorbing the risks of technological change and the losses that limited liability and tort immunity spare the shareholders (Sapolsky and Gholz 1996). Because their investments are underwritten and subsidized by the federal government, defense contractors have lower investment risks and higher returns on investment than commercial firms (Greer and Liao 1986). Shareholders of defense contractors enjoy a guaranteed cash flow from contract revenue because the government absorbs much of contractors' overhead burden. This made the return on the relatively small amount of invested capital from a contractor's own pocket a healthy 20 percent or more in the mid-1980s, according to a U.S. General Accounting Office study (1986a).[24]

Even though the state does not "own" defense contractors, it does assume many of the downside risks of production—of cost overruns, technological malfunctions, and obsolescence. In contrast, shareholders receive the upside return. Because they have diversified holdings and limited liability, shareholders can avoid the downside loss, except to the extent that their capital is invested in the firm.[25] Critics of the defense industry long ago noted one of the key paradoxes of defense contracting: The risks and costs of production are socialized, yet profits and control over investment decisions remain in private hands (Adams 1981; Melman 1971). The liabilities that shareholders avoid fall heavily on the state and its fisc as the ultimate residual risk-bearer.

Contractors' Fiduciary Obligations to the Public

The contractarian model of corporate governance views shareholders as the only residual risk-bearers because they are believed to risk the most, "own" the corporation, and hold variable claims to the corporation's income stream. Managers' fiduciary obligations to their shareholders, and their shareholders alone, are justified on the basis of their risk-bearer status. Clearly, other important stakeholders—like the federal government and taxpayers—also bear the risk that the corporation will perform poorly and makes investments in the firm that they will not be able to recover. The federal government hires contractors for more than just the manufacture of a simple product. Taxpayers make risky investments in contractors from which they can not extricate themselves. The public becomes, in a sense, the structural equivalent of shareholders.

The peculiar nature of defense contractors' customer, products, and industrial organization has prompted several scholars across the political spectrum to observe that defense contractors are not true private entities (Peck and Scherer 1962; Sapolsky, Gholz, and McKinney 1996). For example, McNaugher notes,

[Their] structure and behavior have been shaped by a sustained and necessary interaction with the political system that remains the principal market
these firms confront. . . . In short, defense contractors, especially those at the
top of the defense industrial hierarchy, constitute a unique quasi-private,
quasi-public sector of the nation's economy. (1989, 151)

These authors imply that the organizational structure of defense contractors is public because the state is their market.[26] With few controlling
statutes or precedents, the law is similarly confused about the hybrid nature of defense contractors. In the case of *Holodnak v. Avco Corporation,
Inc.,*[27] for example, the court treated a defense contractor like a public entity for the sake of pursuing the First Amendment claims of one of its employees. In other cases, however, the courts have not found sufficient
state action to treat defense contractors as anything other than private
enterprises.

Many reformers recognize, and decry, the fact that government contractors resemble and act like the government with their bureaucratic excess, inefficiency, and cost insensitivity (Fox 1974; Gansler 1980; Kovacic
1990a; Sapolsky, Gholz, and McKinney 1996). They often suggest changes
in the procurement process that might transform contractors back into
"real" commercial corporations. Others reluctantly accept the fate of
those firms that work closely with such rule-based, formal bureaucracies
as the Department of Defense (McNaugher 1989; Melman 1970).

The government, however, does not simply "infect" private businesses
with its bureaucratic pathologies through intimate and frequent contact;
administrative complexity inheres in performing public tasks, not simply
in relations with public organizations (Donahue 1989). The fact is, defense contractors are quasi-public entities, and not simply because their
market and main customer is the federal government. Defense contractors are agents of the federal government, hired by the Pentagon and delegated with the public task of producing weaponry for national security.

Contractors are proxies of the government principal, who ultimately is
the agent of a more generalized (tax-paying, voting) public.[28] The object
of state production stands on a claim to represent a broad public interest,
an interest that is, in theory, voiced through formal democratic practices
such as voting (Johnston 1988). Separate layers of accountability exist between Congress and procurement officers, between voters and Congress,
and between agencies and contractors, constituting a complex chain of
delegation and responsibility.

Despite its public nature, however, contractor management still does
not have the same legally recognized fiduciary obligations to these public
actors as it does to its shareholders. In classic contractarian style, the law
views the relationship between the state and its contractors as governed

only by procurement contracts and statutory regulations. Contractors are obligated to follow the terms of their individual procurement contracts, which stipulate that they must complete their particular projects in accordance with specifications within agreed upon limits of time, costs, and damages within the event of a breach. However, the procurement contract alone cannot resolve the problem of the private agent's accountability.

Because individual contracts imperfectly govern contractor behavior, the government has made periodic attempts at acquisition reform so that those who wield state power would be made more responsible to the democratic electorate (Kaufman 1996; Friedberg 1992; Kovacic 1990; Huntington 1967; Lasswell 1994). The federal government, for instance, has demanded contractors' adherence to the procedural standards outlined in federal acquisition regulations in hopes of curtailing their opportunism and containing their profits. With so few and such weak constraints on contractor discretion concerning pricing and quality, procurement regulatory controls are designed, in part, to ensure that contractor-agents faithfully execute the directions of government purchasing authorities.[29]

In addition, firms performing work under government contract have been subject to a variety of unique requirements: minimum wages, profit caps, drug testing of employees, patent-sharing agreements, export controls, targeting labor surplus areas, "Buy American," and women, minority, and small business set-asides. The history of government contracting involves periodic attempts to control the excessive profits of contractors through price controls, excess taxes, contract renegotiation, forced disclosure of cost and pricing data, and rights to audit contractors' books. Defense contractors are singled out from other private firms because, in the words of one scholar, "the government should be a model employer . . . concerned about the conditions under which goods are produced in fulfillment of federal supply contracts" (Morton 1965, 131). Adhering to the cumbersome auditing and reporting requirements can be quite costly, but the receipt of a government contract, contractors acknowledge, is accompanied by special burdens of accountability (Donahue 1989).

Unfortunately, these external mechanisms of governance—contracts and regulations—inadequately resolve the tension between the interests of shareholders and the state. The state cannot devise contractual restrictions to fully oversee or control managers, because neither party is capable of predicting and resolving the various contingencies that arise in such a long-term relationship. Likewise, regulation does not really *control* economic relationships; it simply offers vague standards of performance that must be enforced if they are to be effective. Thus, there is a high premium placed on simply monitoring private behavior *post facto* (Clark 1993). Since 1960, there have been fourteen major analyses of the acquisi-

tion process, including four commissioned by presidents. Each has acknowledged that the mechanisms for governing the procurement process
were suboptimal and in need of reform (Packard 1986; McNaugher 1989;
Donahue 1989; Sapolsky and Gholz 1996). Reformers recommended re-
fining existing contract instruments or developing additional regulations
to resolve governance problems. They have been quick to stress the need
for more trusting relationships in order to remove the politics from acquisition and to cut down on the regulatory morass.

These critics did not recognize that another governance mechanism,
one that is internal to the firm rather than external, may be more appropriate for structuring government-industry relations in weapons procurement: fiduciary obligations. At present, the law does not recognize a
fiduciary relationship between defense contractors and the federal government. Courts are wary of assigning fiduciary duties to management
in these situations because the fiduciary relationship has not arisen by
consent, gained through a process of bargaining and negotiation. In the
United States, commerce is primarily contract-dominated, and the courts
have been reluctant to recognize fiduciary relationships and duties in any
commercial, contractual relationship (Bean 1995, 47).

In this chapter I have argued that the corporate governance of defense contractors must be understood as an imperfect and contested
risk-sharing arrangement principally *between* shareholders and the
state. The state incurs sunk costs in defense contractors, sunk costs that
have become an enormous financial burden in the post–Cold War era.
The state acts as the structural equivalent of shareholders, in many
cases taking on risks that exceed those of the shareholders because of
the nondiversifiable nature of its investment. The pervasive government investment in defense contractors challenges our conventional
understanding of corporate governance. If the state is a risk-bearing
party to a contract, then, like shareholders, it should expect to receive
substantial privilege rights or returns on its investments. Private managers should have a common-law obligation to operate their companies
in the public's interest. Just as there are multiple principals of the firm,
there must also be multiple objectives—and only one of them should be
generating profits for shareholders. Management must give equal, if
not more, weight to the interests of the public sector and accommodate
the diversity of its demands.

Notes

1. See, for example, *First National Maintenance Corp. v. NLRB*, 452 U.S. 666, 69 L.
Ed. 2d 318, 101 S. Ct. 2573 (1981), which held that an employer's decision to close
a part of its business is not a mandatory subject of bargaining.

2. As I discussed in the Introduction, I do not mean to imply that defense contracting is the *only* exception to the model of bounded private and public spheres; it is, perhaps, the most overt and extreme example.

3. Nonexcludable implies that once a public good is provided, no one can be prevented from benefiting from it. Nonrival implies that one person's use or enjoyment of a public good does not lessen the benefit to anyone else. Although "national security" is always used as an example of a pure public good, it cannot be operationally defined; in other words, we do not know if the production of a *particular* weapons system will improve or impede national security. Moreover, the government cannot objectively define demand for these products (Oden 1994).

4. Williamson (1975; 1985) and other "transaction cost" economists argue that the more obstacles to free exchange, the less likely production will be contracted out to other organizations. This thinking draws on Coase's article, "The Problem of Social Costs" (1960), in which he suggests that if there are no barriers to exchanging legal entitlements, they will be allocated efficiently by private agreement. Obstacles like the inability to write complete contracts (because product requirements are so vague) and the lack of perfect information impose transaction costs on parties and therefore are incentives to keep production in-house. In these situations, "hierarchies" rather than "markets" are better at monitoring exchanges and minimizing uncertainty.

5. Efficiency criteria are those that measure the lowest-cost method of supplying a given quality and quantity of good or service. Accountability criteria are those that measure the degree to which agents adhere to the specifications of their delegated tasks.

6. For example, the Springfield Arsenal took seventeen years to develop, test, and produce the M-1 rifle (Hatcher 1948, quoted in McNaugher 1989, 20). The service procurement bureaucracies felt that their responsibility was not to develop new weapons per se but to organize their enterprise to be able to produce in mass quantities. Scholars frequently depict the service's ordnance departments as committed to obsolete, outmoded techniques that *necessitated* a shift to the private production of weaponry. However, other historians of technology have taken a less deterministic approach, demonstrating that the public agencies were actually quite successful in fostering innovations (Smith 1985; Mendelsohn, Smith, and Weingart 1988).

7. The defense contract is the epitome of MacNeil's "relational contract" (1978). Relational contracts emerge in the context of ongoing extended relationships where the future is indeterminate and the details of the relationship cannot be fully specified.

8. Defense production is heavily dependent on tacit knowledge, which is embodied in the workers themselves. Technology "is in the heads of scientists and engineers who do not or cannot write it down, and it is embedded in the organizations that design, manufacture, and market goods and services of all kinds" (Alic et al. 1992, 372).

9. Williamson defines asset specificity as the degree to which an asset can be redeployed to alternative uses without sacrificing the productive value. He describes six different kinds: (1) site (what economic geographers would call "ag-

glomeration economies"—the benefits of proximity); (2) physical asset (i.e., specialized equipment); (3) human asset (tacit knowledge that arises in learning-by-doing fashion); (4) dedicated asset (discrete investments in general purpose equipment or facilities that are made at the behest of a particular customer; (5) brand name capital; and (6) temporal (1985).

10. Markusen argues that defense contractors' real estate and property holdings, particularly research facilities in urban and suburban areas, are relatively marketable (1997a).

11. Gansler lists two pages of differences between defense and "free" markets (1980, 30–31), while Peck and Scherer note that no matter how much policymakers attempt to make the defense market act like commercial product markets, "a complete market system is an impossibility in the weapons acquisition process" (1962, 60).

12. Political climate, events abroad, executive and legislative initiatives—not variance in price—determine the demand for major weapons systems, thus making demand highly inelastic (Goodman 1988, 396).

13. Although members of Congress have used the rhetoric of the free market to support this goal, their underlying intentions have had little to do with efficiency gains and everything to do with constituency politics. Satisfying the demands of local business, Congress has sought to spread production around by insuring that the bidding process should be open to all those willing to submit bids. The obsession with competition culminated in the passage of the Competition in Contracting Act of 1984 (CICA), enacted to expand the universe of potential suppliers.

14. Peck and Scherer found that "maximizing quality was slightly more important than minimizing development time, which in turn was much more important than minimizing development cost" (1962, 293). The attitudes of defense contractors may have changed in recent years. Former president and CEO of General Dynamics James Mellor urged management to "break with past industry paradigms that defense is a low-risk, volume-oriented business in which the management of costs, risks, and liabilities is of secondary concern. . . . If we are to serve our customers, employees, and shareholders well in the face of rapidly shrinking markets, we must focus on affordability, productivity, and financial strength through tight controls on costs, risks, and liabilities" (General Dynamics Annual Report 1993).

15. Arrow and Lind argue that the public sector is better suited to shoulder such risks because "when the risks associated with a public investment are publicly borne, the total cost of risk-bearing is insignificant and the government should ignore uncertainty in evaluating public investments" (1970, 366). In other words, the state can better cope with uncertainty because it spreads the risks around to every individual taxpayer.

16. One Aerospace Industries Association report concluded, "If industry is to continue to invest its capital in competing for and performing Government contracts, while meeting its responsibility to provide a reasonable return to its shareholders, Congress and the procuring agencies must be persuaded to reduce Governmental control and regulation of contractors and to recognize considerations of risk and profit" (1970, 48).

17. 48 Code of Federal Regulations (CFR) 31 (1989). Reimbursable costs are determined by an elaborate scheme of "cost principles" that require costs to be (a) properly allocable to the contract; (b) allowable according to statutes and regulations banning inclusion of certain expenses; and (c) reasonable in amount.

18. Acquisition regulations have attempted to level the playing field by suggesting that contractors with GFP include a "rental equivalent" (roughly the amount that the same property would cost to rent) into their initial bids (Federal Acquisition Regulations [FAR] 45.201). This promulgation has led contractors to haggle over the real value of property, especially when similar commercial products rarely exist.

19. Contractors claim that the effect of GFP on their profitability is minimal because the cost of upkeep, repair, maintenance, and reporting is so cumbersome that it negates any suspected benefits.

20. Kurth found that the timing of defense contracts often corresponded with significant declines in contractors' sales, income, or employment (1973, 135–156).

21. Between 1958 and 1973, the government undertook around 3,650 rescue operations to help financially troubled defense firms (Yudken 1993, 49).

22. *Boyle v U.S.*, 108 S. Ct. 2510 (1988). In this case, the Court determined that defense contractors should not be held liable for design flaws that conformed to government specifications.

23. Contractors have also passed risks on to their less powerful, second tier subcontractors and to other constituencies of the firm (e.g., workers), as I will discuss in the following chapters.

24. Because of the practice of buying-in and subsidized overhead, actual profit rates tend to be much higher than the rates agreed upon in initial contracts.

25. The state's investments in contractors are even more at risk of losing economic value, because the state invests in assets that are legally "owned" by someone else: the shareholders. The state risks having its investments appropriated by the owners (Haddock, Macey, and McChesney 1987).

26. This line of thinking is in keeping with a vast literature within organization theory and public administration that views organizations and their environments in a symbiotic, mutually constitutive way (see, for example, Pfeffer and Salancick 1978; Meyer and Scott 1983). For example, the preferences of consumers and the resource dependency of vendors shape the organizational structure of vendors themselves.

27. 514 F.2d 285 (2nd Cir. 1975), *cert. denied*, 432 U.S. 892 (1977).

28. In any contractual relationship between the government and private business, one must ask: What are the public interests? Who is representing these interests? Some authors believe that defense contractors, citizens, and workers have a very narrow perspective on the national interest, whereas the military services represent the real "public" in defense contracting (Sapolsky and Gholz 1996). Other social compact theorists, ranging from Hobbes, Locke, and Rousseau to contemporary authors, such as Walzer (1982) and Beran (1987), believe that, expressly or implicitly, all citizens consent to be governed by the polity in exchange for the government's pursuit of broad public interests. I discuss the question of the government's interest in defense production in my conclusion.

29. Detailed provisions in the Federal Acquisition Regulations (FAR) and Defense Federal Acquisition Regulations (DFAR) provide the government with the administrative authority by which to review and certify various contractors' accounting, project management, subcontracting, inspection, safety, security, insurance, and handling of property. The Defense Contract Audit Agency (DCAA) and the Defense Contract Management Command (DCMC) audit contractors' books, reviewing expenditures involved in the performance of contracts.

3

Adjusting to the Drawdown

The 1990s were a period of great turmoil in the defense industry. Having just extricated themselves from the billing scandals of the 1980s, military contractors again came under scrutiny for reaping undue private gain from defense production. This time their behavior was not illegal per se, but rather highly inequitable. By privileging shareholders in their restructuring strategies, contractors rewarded those who had contributed the least to their asset base. Moreover they ignored the stakeholders who had borne the bulk of the production risks: taxpayers' workers, and the state. Although legal (and, in some instances, encouraged by the federal government), the behavior of American contractors in the post–Cold War period raises serious concerns about the private stewardship of public funds.

When procurement outlays fell after the Cold War, the defense industry was forced to adjust to a smaller and changed product market. After decades of protection from intense financial and product market pressures, contractors experienced a wave of sell-offs, mergers, and restructuring. Only a handful of defense-dependent companies emerged from the buying and selling frenzy: Lockheed Martin, Boeing–McDonnell Douglas, Raytheon, Northrop-Grumman, and General Dynamics. Even in their shrinking government markets, however, the surviving prime defense contractors were able to generate a phenomenal amount of excess cash, most of which they distributed to their increasingly demanding shareholders. While over a million private defense-related jobs disappeared, Wall Street analysts said industry balance sheets had never been stronger.

The Pentagon argued that the "pure play" strategies of contractors would quickly rid the defense industry of excess capacity—the shuttered production lines, the redundant employees, the expensive overhead. But after the dust cleared in the late 1990s, not nearly enough capacity had been rationalized to justify the amount of money redistributed to share-

holders and senior management as windfall profits. Moreover, the benefits and the burdens of defense contractors' restructuring strategies
clearly favored certain corporate stakeholders over others. Defense contractors managed their market decline in ways that served shareholders
and management, while the interests of other "public" actors (i.e., the
state, labor, taxpayers, local communities) faded into the background. A
large part of the promised "peace dividend" ended up in a few private
hands instead of benefiting the country at large.

The Downturn in Defense Spending

The United States has experienced several major swings in military
spending since the end of World War II, and each time defense contractors have adopted different adjustment strategies. Following World War
II, military spending fell from nearly 40 percent of the gross national
product to less than 4 percent in a two-year time span (Defense Conversion Commission 1992, 11). High levels of private investment and con-
sumption, however, spurred by forced business and personal savings
during the war, were able to create robust demand for new products
(Sandler and Hartley 1995; Dumas 1977). Retained wartime profits allowed defense contractors to return to their prewar markets and fulfill
growing demand with the manufacture of new consumer goods. The
contractors that survived the war were less specialized in military hardware than today's contractors and had experience marketing and manufacturing commercial products (Melman 1971). Moreover, the government had been planning for conversion since 1943 and had policies in
place to aid defense firms and workers when the war ended. The federal
government, for example, allowed private contractors to purchase government-owned plants and equipment at rates substantially below market value and funded individual retraining and home ownership
through the massive GI Bill.

    After both the Korean and Vietnam wars, American rivalry with the
Soviet Union and the increasing technological complexity of weapons
systems ensured a high level of peacetime military spending that supported a growing number of large, specialized defense firms (Oden and
Bischak 1995). These two postwar cutbacks were cyclical, followed by
sharp increases in defense spending. In contrast, the spending reductions
following the end of the Cold War, although less dramatic in terms of real
size, are viewed as more permanent and structural (U.S. GAO 1995, 3).
Noted one commentator: "Companies are not simply 'hunkering down'
in anticipation of future contracts; present trends will foster a permanent
change in the industry's structure" (Pages 1995, 137). New arms reduction agreements, diminished threats to national security, and domestic

pressures for budget austerity forced the Pentagon to forgo many strategic modernization and procurement plans and limit certain conventional weapons programs.

Although defense budgets remained high in the 1990s, they contained deep cuts in several areas. The United States defense budget peaked in 1985 at almost $405 billion (in 1997 dollars), which comprised 6.5 percent of the gross domestic product that year (U.S. Department of Defense 1996). In 1987, defense spending began a modest decline from the Reagan buildup, but it was only after the dissolution of the Soviet Union in 1991 that real cuts were implemented (see Figure 3.1). By 1995, defense outlays had dropped to 3.9 percent of the gross domestic product, at $271 billion (1997 dollars). Overall defense spending decreased by 35 percent between fiscal years 1985 and 1996 (Kosiak 1997). The most dramatic declines, and those that most directly affected contractors, were in the procurement accounts. Between their peak in 1987 and 1995, real outlays for new equipment and weapons fell by 52 percent, so that in 1995 procurement outlays totaled $55.1 billion (U.S. Department of Defense 1996). Total defense sales for the top 25 contractors fell by $33.6 billion, or 31 percent, from 1989. The change in post–Cold War procurement spending was not equal across all programs. The average reductions in spending for aircraft, for example, were quite small compared to reductions for missiles and ammunition (U.S. GAO 1997, 12). As procurement budgets were cut, a greater share of defense spending went to personnel and operations and maintenance activities.

Despite these changes, the Clinton administration still spent, in real terms, over 80 percent of the Cold War average annual military budget through the 1990s. The Pentagon's plan for the post–Cold War defense industry, the Bottom-Up Review of 1993, sought to maintain forces large enough in size to fight in two simultaneous major interventions. It also called for increased mobility, the integration of advanced information and communications technologies into existing platforms, and the maintenance of capability to build the next generation of several major weapons systems (Oden 1999). In the Bottom-Up Review, the administration backed away from broader demilitarization and disarmament plans. Likewise, efforts to dramatically cut the budget were tempered by political pressures to save particular systems and extend the life span of products (Korb 1996). Lobbying from contractors, organized labor, and defense-dependent communities prompted Congress to prepare budgets that allocated spending at levels higher than the Pentagon requested. For 1996 alone, Congress added $11 billion to the defense budget over President Clinton's objections (Green 1995). Nonetheless, procurement budget cuts precipitated serious responses from contractors, especially those specialized in mature defense products.

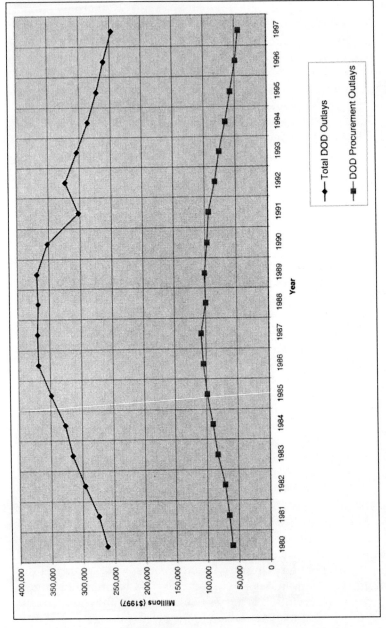

FIGURE 3.1 Total Department of Defense and Procurement Outlays, 1980–1996
SOURCE: U.S. Department of Defense, National Defense Budget Estimates. Washington, D.C.: Office of the Comptroller (1996), Tables 6–8.

Corporate Responses

Whereas commercial firms began experiencing intense restructuring after the 1970s profit squeeze, defense contractors were unfazed by the increasingly competitive and globalized economic environment until the late 1980s. Their subsidized market and guaranteed monopsony—the Pentagon—had concerns about the performance qualities of production, not costs. In the late 1980s, growing uncertainty in the defense product market and the decline in the number of major new weapons-acquisitions programs triggered a dramatic restructuring of the Pentagon's supplier base. In 1989 William Anders, chairman of General Dynamics, predicted, "It will be rag tag, rough and tumble, and dog-eat-dog. It's going to be a bloodletting, and the guy with the most blood will win" (Wayne 1989, 1). He was right. Declining market demand, the expectation of future trends, and the urging of financial market analysts prompted giant prime contractors and smaller component manufacturers alike to revamp their corporate strategies. With the encouragement of the Department of Defense, they restructured to cut costs, adjust the scale of their plants, and improve market share and profit margins.

In the first few years, management consultants warned that changes in product demand were structural and that those who did not adapt to the changes would be swept away by them. A widely cited article in the *Harvard Business Review* advised contractors that their only options were to "strip down, shut down, sell, swap or sink" in order to cope with shrinking defense budgets (Lundquist 1992, 74). Nonetheless some prime contractors, buoyed by their hefty production backlogs and cash reserves generated during the 1980s, moved at a slow pace. In some sectors, spending cuts did not begin to register until after 1992. Smaller contractors had less time to strategize; the loss of a major contract forced them to undertake a shutdown, rapid diversification, or high-risk survival effort.

In 1993, then Undersecretary of Defense William Perry sat down with CEOs of the major defense contractors in what was subsequently called "the last supper." There he informed the CEOs that the Pentagon could no longer support them all. Some would have to leave the industry. A wave of financial restructuring and business unit realignments within and among both large and small defense corporations ensued. During this period, prime contractors pursued three main adjustment strategies: specialization and consolidation in more limited segments of the defense product market, diversification through mergers and acquisitions, and active development of a world market for defense products (Christopherson and Weber 1994; U.S. GAO 1995a; Oden 1996; U.S. GAO 1997; Markusen 1997a). The majority of prime contractors adopted some combination of these three strategies, but the behavior common to all prime

defense contractors was their commitment to downsizing, rationalization, and creating shareholder wealth. Goyal, Lehn, and Racic (1993)
found that defense contractors began transferring resources from the industry as early as 1989 through increased leverage, dividends, share repurchases, and downsizing. Defense industry downsizing began in 1991,
while the defense merger movement started in late 1992 and culminated
in a rash of mega-mergers between 1994 and 1996 (see Table 3.1).

Many large prime contractors sold off their noncore businesses to specialize in product areas where they could enhance their competitive position in the defense marketplace. Most defense conglomerates owned a
mix of units in multiple sectors, which, in the past, had afforded them a
degree of flexibility in terms of product maturity and sector fluctuation.
In a more uncertain environment, contractors found it difficult to manage
unrelated business units with few synergies. When defense spending began to decline, some contractors focused on their positions in individual
product markets, which they saw as a strong determinant of profitability—even in weak sectors. Echoing this sentiment, industry strategists
urged contractors who could not be leaders in their individual markets to
exit or retrench. General Dynamics, for example, partially liquidated and
consolidated to focus on its core business niches in submarines and
tanks. Whereas seven American companies developed and produced
military aircraft in the late 1980s, by 1996, only two producers remained:
Boeing, which acquired McDonnell Douglas and Rockwell, and Lockheed, which acquired Grumman, Northrop, and parts of General Dynamics before merging with Martin Marietta (Markusen 1997a). The survivors who were able to dominate each product market were assured of
larger, sole-source contracts that could maintain their positions in specialized markets (Smith 1993; Oden 1996).

Although some contractors divested their noncore businesses if they
had little chance of becoming the dominant supplier, only a few deliber-
ately exited from the defense industry altogether. Some, like General Electric, sold off their main military divisions, but not before cutting jobs.
Unisys, IBM, Honeywell, and Westinghouse also sold their defense units.
A handful of contractors closed shop entirely; most chose to hold on to
vestiges of their previous capacity with a smaller number of workers, less
research and development, and fewer nonrecoverable investments.

Other prime contractors adjusted by merging and acquiring unrelated
divisions at a rapid pace (Morrison 1993; Meadows 1996; Oden 1996).
Mergers and acquisitions among commercial enterprises have occurred
throughout recent business history, heating up around 1900 and the late
1960s, but the pace, number, and value of acquisitions that began in the
1980s far outweigh those of previous years (Ravenscraft and Scherer
1987; Harrison and Bluestone 1988; Blair 1993). Among prime contrac-

TABLE 3.1   Merger and Acquisition Activity in the Defense Industry, 1990–1996

Year	Buyer	Unit Acquired
1990	Loral	Ford Aerospace
	Northrop	LTV Aircraft
1991	Textron	General Dynamics—Cessna
1992	Hughes	General Dynamics—Missile Systems
	Loral	LTV Missiles
	Martin Marietta	General Electric—Aerospace
	Lockheed	General Dynamics—Military Aircraft
1994	Northrop	Grumman
	Loral	IBM Federal Systems
	Martin Marietta	General Dynamics—Space Systems
	Martin Marietta	Lockheed
	Northrop	Vought Aircraft
1995	Loral	Unisys—Defense
	Litton	Teledyne—Electronics
	General Dynamics	Bath Iron Works
	Raytheon	E-Systems
	Hughes	Magnavox Electronic Systems
1996	Northrop-Grumman	Westinghouse—Defense Systems
	Lockheed Martin	Loral—Defense
	Boeing	Rockwell Aerospace and Defense
	Boeing	McDonnell Douglas

SOURCES: *Defense News*, January 8–14, 1996, cited in Michael Oden, "Cashing In, Cashing Out, and Converting: Restructuring of the Defense Industrial Base in the 1992," in A. Markusen and S. Costigan, eds., *Arming the Future*. New York: Council on Foreign Relations Press, 1999.

tors, Martin Marietta was one of the most aggressive: In a buying spree, the contractor doubled in size when it acquired General Electric's aerospace business, General Dynamic's space division, most of Loral, and aerospace giants Lockheed and Grumman. Its new incarnation, Lockheed Martin, currently manufactures a wide range of military hardware, including missiles, transport planes, fighter jets, and communications gear for satellites.

In the majority of mergers, contractors did not acquire similar productive capabilities, which would have helped them to achieve economies of scale and lower per unit costs (horizontal mergers). Nor did they acquire the producers of a major component, which would have allowed them to internalize part of the production process and achieve operating efficiencies (vertical mergers). Instead, the mergers and acquisitions extended the markets of contractors like Lockheed and Loral into new areas, increasing their revenue bases and their portfolio of offerings. The combinations during the 1994–1996 period helped to secure contractors' strongholds in several key product segments (Oden 1996; Sapolsky and Gholz 1996; Markusen 1997a). Active as they are in multiple product markets, it remains to be seen whether these conglomerates are simply too large and unwieldy to integrate assembly lines and management functions. If they are not successful, the savings from eliminating redundancies may never materialize.

A third post–Cold War strategy pursued by defense contractors was the internationalization of markets (U.S. Congress Office of Technology Assessment [OTA] 1991; Markusen and Costigan 1999; Hartung 1996, 1994). In order to augment declining domestic orders, defense contractors sought out foreign customers with the hope that foreign sales could account for more than a quarter of their business. American companies offered "offsets" to potential customers, in which they agreed to manufacture a portion of the final product in the purchasing countries and/or invest in other ventures in exchange for sales. An offset deal for Lockheed Martin, for example, stipulated that 2,000 Turkish workers would assemble F-16 fighter jets in Ankara. The American government subsidized this deal by providing $3.2 billion of the $4.3 billion purchase price through foreign military financing grants and loans (Sennott 1996, B11).

With the help of generous government subsidies (estimated to total anywhere from $5 to $7 billion per year) and cadres of marketing specialists, arms exports provided American firms with higher profit margins than domestic sales—due, in part, to the spurt of demand from the Gulf War and the fact that some unallowable costs were charged to foreign military sales. The Defense Security Assistance Agency noted that foreign military sales from the United States to other governments increased by 140 percent between 1986–1989 and 1990–1994, from $34.5 billion to $83.1 billion (Sennott 1996).[1] With the dissolution of the Soviet Union, it was estimated that the United States controlled over 64 percent of the global arms trade in 1993 (Federation of American Scientists 1993).

Some American contractors encountered difficulties winning business abroad. In many of the most lucrative markets, doors to American sales closed as European governments sheltered their own struggling "national champions" (e.g., British Aerospace PLC, the French firms Thomson-CSF and Aerospatiale SA, and Germany's Daimler-Benz AG). Similarly, the newly industrialized countries nurtured their own infant arms industry by erecting trade barriers (Lovering and Curran 1996). Ameri-

can contractors resorted to new teaming arrangements and subcontracting agreements with their competitors overseas. Contractors, such as
Boeing, followed in the path of major civilian industries that rely on foreign companies for components, conduct joint research, development,
and production, and enter into mergers with foreign firms. A larger problem for contractors, however, is that the international market may not be
big enough to make up for declining domestic demand.

Regardless of which adjustment strategy they pursued, all prime contractors engaged in massive downsizing. Like their commercially oriented
counterparts, defense contractors responded to market uncertainty by
laying off their employees and pursuing more flexible forms of work organization.[2] Contractors rationalized excess capacity by shedding capital
to become profitable at lower overall volumes of sales, curbing investment in research and development and facilities modernization. Whereas
Pentagon contracts once shielded firms from the intense price competition
that drove other industries to cost-cutting and interregional migration,
defense contractors began to aggressively shift costs and redeploy capital
across different industries, regions, and nations starting in the late 1980s.
Defense-dependent regions were held hostage to newly cost-conscious
contractors, who joined other commercial firms in pursuit of lower-cost
production sites. During this period Grumman, Lockheed, and Hughes
moved operations from Southern California and the Northeast to the
Southeast and Rocky Mountain regions in search of cheaper wages, fewer
unions, lower taxes, and less regulation (Uchitelle 1995, E1).

Contractors also refashioned labor and supplier relations in the military-industrial complex, as manifested in struggles over outsourcing,
compensation, unionization, and pension and insurance benefits (Harrison 1994; Clark 1993). All prime defense contractors initiated large-scale
layoffs and contracted out work to smaller firms. The remaining employees, like those at Pratt & Whitney in Connecticut, were forced to make
concessions so that their employers could reap higher productivity gains.
Even workers in low-wage states, like those at the Newport News Shipyard in Virginia, saw payrolls cut as their employers took steps to reduce
overhead. Newport News began a "total quality management"–style
reengineering in addition to paring layers of management, changing its
materials purchasing, and contracting out research and development operations. As prime contractors consolidated, they cut back on subcontractors, disrupting the agglomerations of firms that once comprised the military-industrial complex. For example, Pratt & Whitney eliminated
one-half of its suppliers as part of its restructuring between 1990 and
1993. The company also threatened to move its Connecticut production
facility to Maine or Georgia. In the end, the state of Connecticut and the
union developed a package that included property tax breaks, productiv-

ity improvements, and lower fringe benefits that convinced the company to stay put (Call to Action 1994, 21).

Restructuring stymied the transfer of defense technologies and other assets to the commercial sector, what is known as defense "conversion" or "diversification."[3] Both Grumman and Bath Iron Works, for example, halted their commercial projects when they were purchased by Northrop and General Dynamics respectively. Mergers further divorced contractors' military from their civilian capabilities, as in the case of Hughes and Rockwell, which were actively transferring technologies to their civilian automotive divisions before they sold off their defense units (Markusen 1997a). Acquiring companies, like Martin Marietta, increased their debt burden to purchase new companies. Squeezed by high debt service payments and disoriented from countless internal disruptions, restructuring companies were unable or unwilling to redirect funds toward new research and development. They were reluctant to undertake the high start-up costs to convert product lines or invest in marketing for new commercial products (Oden 1996).

Some defense contractors did enter commercial markets either through internal product development or acquisition (Oden 1999). Hughes, for example, applied its satellite technology to a commercial venture—satellite DirecTV—designed to compete with cable companies.[4] McDonnell Douglas had some success developing a medical testing company, which it subsequently sold off. Raytheon originally diversified its operations by acquiring appliance manufacturers, oil exploration firms, and a publishing house, although it recently divested its commercial operations. The contractor also took infrared imaging used in heat-seeking missiles and adapted it for fire rescue teams to use locating people in burning buildings. But these examples were exceptions rather than the norm. As opposed to small and medium-sized contractors, which had more success in penetrating commercial markets (Kelley and Watkins 1994), most large primes chose to ignore conversion or diversification opportunities (U.S. GAO 1994a; Markusen and Yudken 1992).[5] They opted instead for a strategy of "pure play," engaging in mergers, acquisitions, and downsizing.

Organizational, technical, and market barriers impeded the entry of defense contractors into alternative product markets (Melman 1971; Markusen 1991; Lundquist 1992; Markusen and Yudken 1992; U.S. GAO 1994a; Gansler 1995). Even if housed within the same private firm, military and commercial businesses are organizationally distinct; contractors traditionally maintain separate divisions, facilities, accounting procedures, and organizational hierarchies. In defense production, system performance is favored over costs, and defense workers work to a finer tolerance and higher precision than those in civil production. Defense management has adapted to the unique demands and arcane contracting arrangements of the military. The more specialized in defense work they are, the more difficult it is for contractors to traverse the "walls of separation" (Markusen and Yudken 1992). Because large prime contractors are "systems integrators" as opposed to individual component manufacturers, they are positioned at the end of the value chain and tend to carry the largest defense-specific overhead (Walker, Graham, and Harbor 1988).

Even when contractors had the capacity to finance and develop commercial product lines, the markets they confronted were uncertain, ultracompetitive, or nonexistent (Markusen and Yudken 1992). For example, the commercial shipbuilding business in the United States was so dominated by foreign competition that out of all the oceangoing civilian ships ordered worldwide in 1980s, only a handful were built in American shipyards (Todd 1991). Unable to compete with Japanese and Korean rivals in the manufacture of supertankers and bulk cargo carriers, the half-dozen major yards that remain in the United State depended almost exclusively on the Navy after subsidies for commercial shipbuilding were withdrawn in the early 1980s.

Although it may not have made sense for shipbuilders like General Dynamics to explore commercial shipbuilding, other product markets and clusters offered more promise. Telecommunications, commercial satellites, fiber optics, and medical imaging are all markets in which there was both strong commercial demand and existing technical expertise in the defense industry (Oden 1999).

Even those defense firms that diversified into commercial production experienced job losses. Acquisitions of commercial businesses, such as Raytheon's purchase of Amana, produced few employment crossovers from military to civilian production and thousands of layoffs (Hill et al. 1993, 204). The drop in defense employment was experienced throughout the decade: Total defense-related employment at its peak in 1987 was about 7 million and declined to 4.8 million in 1995 (U.S. Department of Defense 1996). Private industry employment accounted for more than half of these figures. Over one and a half million private-sector defense workers lost their jobs between 1987 and 1997. This figure approached the 1.7 million manufacturing job loss during the 1980s, when the automobile and steel industries contracted (U.S. GAO 1996). The top eight prime contractors alone reported over 150,000 employees voluntarily or involuntarily separated between 1989 and 1994 (U.S. GAO 1996; see Table 3.2). At McDonnell Douglas, for example, the workforce was cut in half between 1990 and 1994, from 133,000 to 66,000 employees. The largest layoffs took place in durable goods production, construction, and business services. Although skilled blue-collar workers were well represented in defense manufacturing, the shares of these occupations in the

TABLE 3.2 Employment at Top Eight Defense Contractors, 1989–1994

Company	1989	1990	1991	1992	1993	1994	Change in Employment 1989–1994
General Dynamics	102,200	98,100	80,600	56,800	30,500	24,200	-76%
McDonnell Douglas	127,900	121,200	109,100	87,400	70,000	65,800	-49%
Litton	50,800	50,600	52,300	49,600	46,400	42,000	-17%
Raytheon	77,600	76,700	71,600	63,900	63,800	60,200	-22%
Grumman	28,900	26,100	23,600	21,200	17,900	NA*	-38%
Loral	12,700	26,100**	24,400	26,500	24,200	32,400	160%
Northrop	41,000	32,800	36,200	33,600	29,800	42,400	3%
Martin Marietta	65,500	62,500	60,500	55,700	92,800***	90,300	40%

SOURCE: U.S. GAO, *Defense Downsizing: Selected Contractor Business Unit Reductions*, May 1995.

* Acquired by Northrop. Percent change reflects period between 1989 and 1993.

** Loral acquired by LTV Missiles and IBM Federal Systems.

*** Martin Marietta merged with Lockheed and acquired a General Dynamics division.

defense workforce declined steadily as budgets were cut and the remaining product lines became more high-tech.

These losses may be considered small on a national basis and are rather mild compared to prior postwar adjustments. In the most severely affected regions, however, defense job losses were more pronounced and problematic because of the general disappearance of manufacturing employment and preexisting labor surpluses. Defense spending has always served as a de facto regional development policy, dotting the landscape with specialized manufacturing enclaves and high-tech corridors and spurring growth in some regions while sapping the fiscal resources of others (Markusen et al. 1991). The Pentagon was not concerned about the potential for private profit maximization in allocating procurement awards across regions. Instead a premium was placed on awarding contracts to firms in areas where the Pentagon and contractors could maximize the quality, reliability, and timeliness of production. New defense complexes arose in locations without a history of industrial production, and the Pentagon underwrote the massive migration of skilled labor. Following World War II, contractors moved away from central cities and from the older industrial heartland of the Northeast and Midwest to suburban areas and Sunbelt states where land was inexpensive and labor unions less powerful (Saxenian 1995; Markusen et al. 1991). The Army and the Air Force showed a pronounced southern and western tilt, whereas the Navy, constrained by coastal geography, favored the Pacific coast and the Northeast corridor.

The geography of defense production remained relatively constant over the last four decades, until the recent cuts in defense expenditures. At the end of the Cold War just twelve states accounted for 64 percent of the country's 3.9 million private-sector defense jobs (Ellis 1991b). Unemployment in defense-dependent areas, such as Southern California and New England, shot up in the early 1990s as regional economies struggled to absorb laid-off defense workers.

By purely financial measures, however, prime contractors' adjustment strategies were highly successful (Dial and Murphy 1995; U.S. GAO 1997; Velocci 1996a, 1997). In the late 1980s, many defense company stocks were heavily discounted, suggesting the inevitable break-up and sell-off of some divisions. By the early 1990s, however, financial analysts and investment bankers targeted the industry, attracted by monopoly returns, and a heavily unionized labor force ripe for downsizing (Markusen 1997a). As financial restructuring took place in the industry, stock prices began to grow steadily, and, between 1991 and 1995, the stocks of major defense contractors were among the market's best performers.[6] Despite falling sales and backlogs in individual defense programs, contractors managed to not only stabilize but increase rates of return, share prices,

TABLE 3.3   Rates of Return at Top Nine Defense Contractors*

Company	1987–90	1991–93
General Dynamics	–59%	537%
McDonnell Douglas	–35%	197%
Northrop	–46%	147%
GM Hughes	0%	143%
Grumman	–2%	131%
Lockheed	–21%	130%
Martin Marietta	27%	118%
Raytheon	18%	103%
United Technologies	20%	44%

SOURCES: Jay Dial and Kevin Murphy, "Incentives, Downsizing and Value Creation at General Dynamics." *Journal of Financial Economics*, 1995, p. 286; Bloomberg Financial Services 1987–1993.
*Assumes dividends have been reinvested.

and dividends (Velocci 1994, 40; see Table 3.3). Surviving contractors won lucrative sole-source awards including follow-on contracts for current programs, maintenance on prior deliveries, and foreign military sales (Gansler 1995).

After the post–Cold War downturn in defense spending, CEOs and other senior management at defense contractors rewarded themselves with generous pay raises. Average executive compensation at six prime defense contractors tripled between 1989 and 1994, from $1.3 million to $4.0 million (U.S. GAO 1995a; see Table 3.4). Most of this increase was linked with share prices through some form of stock award. In 1993 alone, for example, the top five executives at General Dynamics exercised almost $26 million in stock options.

The recent wave of mergers and restructuring among defense contractors produced a small cadre of increasingly profitable corporations in a few key product markets. The Pentagon rewarded the survivors with increasingly lucrative contracts and more sole-source awards. Despite these more intimate relations, the surviving prime contractors appear no more efficient or innovative (Markusen 1997a; 1997b; Gansler 1995). More empirical research is needed to document the extent of cost savings due to new scale economies, but the merger activity does not seem to have resulted in the elimination of much excess capacity. Now that there is less competition for developing new products and upgrading existing ones, the remaining players are able to exercise their near monopoly po-

TABLE 3.4 Compensation of Top Five Executives at Prime Defense Contractors, 1989–1994 (in thousands)*

Company	1989	1990	1991	1992	1993	1994
General Dynamics	$2,496	$2,607	$12,910	$19,200	$56,425	$6,043
Martin Marietta	$3,167	$3,152	$3,493	$4,029	$4,823	$5,435
Lockheed	$2,557	$3,383	$3,881	$4,480	$5,076	$6,438
McDonnell Douglas	$1,956	$2,238	$3,135	$2,623	$3,958	$7,555
Raytheon	$3,521	$3,910	$3,647	$4,021	$4,662	$5,023
Northrop	$1,966	$3,459	$3,448	$3,228	$2,987	$4,472
Loral	$4,027	$6,406	$6,489	$10,018	$8,302	$9,052

SOURCES: U.S. GAO, *Defense Contractors: Pay, Benefits, and Restructuring During Defense Downsizing*, October 1996; company annual reports.

*Figures exclude exercised stock options.

sition to maintain capacity and pressure the state for additional contracts at higher prices (Oden 1999; Korb 1996; Sapolsky and Gholz 1996).

Profit margins on development and production costs for new systems continue to escalate, but contractors may not be redirecting their profits toward innovation-oriented research. In fact, scholars have found that the largest prime contractors had very low research and development-to-sales ratios during the first half of the 1990s (Oden 1996, 17; Gansler 1995, 59). As long as these contractors can win contracts, maintain profit levels, and satisfy their shareholders through downsizing and financial restructuring, they are unlikely to consider serious actions toward commercial markets or innovation-oriented research.

The Post–Cold War Regulatory Regime

Defense contractors like General Dynamics responded to declining procurement funding by withdrawing capital from the industry, slimming down to vestiges of their former selves, and returning the surplus to their shareholders and senior executives. The few remaining defense conglomerates now have near-monopoly power to raise the prices of weaponry and steer the services toward systems that will provide them with higher profits. Their restructuring devastated the unions and communities that depended on jobs, local purchases, and tax revenues. Their strategies may also jeopardize national security objectives by redirecting funds from research and development and quality improvement to financial manipulations with short-term payoffs. Nonshareholder constituents appear to have borne the brunt of this misallocation of public resources.

Given the legal-institutional structure of corporate governance in the United States, we cannot expect publicly held defense contractors to possess an internal commitment to restraint in the area of profit making. Nor can we expect that contractors will treat all corporate constituents equitably. Corporate governance and financial market rules, as I have explained, constrain corporations, pressuring management to forgo long-term, intangible, and risky investments, such as defense diversification, in favor of quick-fix increases in share prices.

American corporations—whether civilian or defense—are not likely to highly value their ability to respond to other public interests, unless the state or other affected parties (e.g., labor unions) put pressure on them through public policy. Regulation can enter the tenaciously guarded sanctum of managerial authority and force a redistribution of profits. By articulating mandatory standards of corporate behavior, regulation prevents management from falling back on its default mode of investment decisionmaking, namely, shareholder privilege and short-term horizons. Health and safety requirements, pension fund regulation, and labor organizing potentially cut off the possibility of certain kinds of behavior and steer investments toward nonshareholder constituents.

The federal government has a substantial amount of leverage with defense contractors because it acts as a single buyer of their products. Unfortunately, it took a rather passive approach with its contractors in the 1990s, choosing to subsidize private wealth accumulation rather than engage in serious conversion planning. Although the Clinton administration initially articulated a high standard of private adjustment behavior, it ultimately gave in to its prime contractors and even sanctioned their distributional priorities. Rather than ease the adjustment of workers and communities to defense cutbacks, the federal government spent most of its money subsidizing restructuring and foreign arms sales. The following section assesses the fate of the Clinton administration's initial commitment to diversifying the military-industrial base in light of ensuing political realities. I analyze the state's different adjustment policies: (1) dual-use technology development, (2) support for industry mergers and consolidation (3) support for foreign military sales (4) worker retraining and (5) community adjustment. In doing so, I disentangle the various state actors and multiple public interest claims articulated in the defense adjustment policy debates.

Many organizations and policymakers saw the end of the Cold War as an opportunity to rethink military priorities and craft new relations between the state and the network of private arsenals it had nurtured. The Clinton administration originally articulated its desire for a strong government role in influencing the goals and structure of the new defense industrial base—beyond just serving the nation's defense needs. Policy advisors and administrative agencies saw an opportunity to create a publicly funded science and technology policy based on fostering defense conversion and innovation in commercial industries (Borrus 1992; Borrus and Zysman 1992). Unions, grassroots organizations, and state and local governments saw an opportunity to redeploy federal resources toward more basic domestic needs such as infrastructure, education, transportation, and health care (Rose 1993). Ultimately, however, defense contractors enjoyed the freedom to respond to the budget cuts on their own terms. Except for some limitations of antitrust, liability for contract completion, and loss write-offs for tax purposes, defense contractors were free to pursue a wide array and mix of strategies, no matter what their ultimate effect on defense workers, communities, or the public purse. They chose to let the stock market govern their adjustment.

In the years following the breakup of the Soviet Union, the federal government was divided in its approach to aiding the various constituents of the defense industrial base. Long-standing political coalitions supporting defense spending were disrupted, while defense policy debates were opened up to new groups of actors, such as high-technology and local economic development advocates, environmentalists, and state and local governments (Rose 1993). Defense adjustment brought together formerly disparate groups of citizens and bureaucrats whose claims on the future of the defense industrial base conflicted and coalesced in often surprising ways. For example, hawkish Republican Congressmen and -women seeking aid for their districts fought with military planners who sought to streamline the forces, even while they endorsed the Department of Commerce's efforts to dismantle the export control system to allow for less encumbered foreign arms sales. The cacophony of conflicting interests involved in defense procurement, combined with the apparent consensus about the supremacy of "market solutions," contributed to the development of a series of uncoordinated and decentralized adjustment policies. Essentially, the federal government devolved responsibility for adjustment to individual, profit-seeking defense firms and to local actors in areas hard hit by spending cuts (Christopherson and Weber 1994).

Individual presidents have great leeway in framing issues and setting policy agendas, and when Bill Clinton took office in 1992, he pledged to promote defense conversion and state-governed adjustment. His enthusiasm contrasted greatly with that of the previous administration, headed by a chief executive who had tried to avoid this unpopular topic and was reluctant to support any new programs that resembled industrial or employment policies. Clinton assembled a group of economic and technology policy advisors who shared his passion for advanced technology, consortium-based manufacturing, and free trade.[7] His administration shied away from bolder demilitarization strategies that called for dramatic cuts in military spending, choosing instead to revive the idea of "competitiveness" proposed as a basis for science and technology policy during the Reagan and Bush administrations (Slaughter and Rhoades 1996; Stowsky and Laird 1992; Tyson 1992; Cohen and Noll 1991).[8] Clinton and Gore insisted that their competitiveness agenda departed from traditional U.S. technology policy, which, they claimed,

> has been limited to support of basic science and mission-oriented research in the Defense Department, NASA (the National Aeronautics and Space Administration), and other agencies. This strategy was appropriate for a previous generation but not for today's profound challenges. We cannot rely on the serendipitous application of defense technology to the private sector. We must aim directly at these new challenges and focus our efforts on the new opportunities before us, recognizing that government can play a key role helping private firms develop and profit from innovation. (Clinton and Gore 1993, 1)

This statement committed the Clinton administration to a technology policy that would encourage the development of civilian technologies and other advances with "dual uses" in defense and civilian applications. No longer would American technology policy rely on military-civilian technology "spillovers" (Alic et al. 1992; Tyson 1992; Borrus 1992). The new agenda sought to fund defense contractors directly to commercialize science and technology in hopes that they would increase their global market share, reinvest in high-performance manufacturing processes, and ultimately increase the number of high-technology, high-wage jobs in a streamlined defense industry (Misheloff 1994; Alic et al. 1992).[9] For those who could not preserve their jobs or businesses in the face of re-structuring, the government offered to mop up the damage with the pro-vision of funds, albeit scant, for small business start-ups, retraining, and unemployment assistance (Christopherson and Weber 1994).

In March of 1993, President Clinton outlined a four-year, $20 billion program designed to help the United States make the transition to a de-militarized economy. The Defense Authorization Act of 1993 established the logic and architecture that the administration adopted for its longer-term conversion program. The act revolved around three core areas: (1) the transition to manufacturing "dual-use" technologies, technologies that are critical to defense and yet also have sufficient commercial viabil-ity; (2) worker adjustment; and (3) community adjustment to a lower level of defense expenditures (Christopherson and Weber 1994; Lessure 1994; Oden and Bischak 1995). Dual-use and other advanced technology subsidies comprised the bulk of the administration's initiative: Of the al-most $2.6 billion of the Department of Defense spending dedicated to de-fense reinvestment programs in fiscal year 1995, approximately 60 per-cent was devoted to dual-use technology programs, designed to fund research and development on technologies with potential commercial applications. Personnel programs (primarily for enlisted military person-nel) received nearly 30 percent of these funds, and community transition programs received only 9 percent (Lessure 1994).

Although the administration wanted to craft new commercial technol-ogy policies, it was reluctant to reform an entrenched bureaucracy or build new interagency capacity. The executive branch ultimately yielded to the Pentagon's desire to take the lead role in the adjustment agenda and funneled new dual-use technology programs through its existing in-stitutional framework. By taking the helm of the defense diversification strategy, however, the Pentagon walked a fine line between maintaining the productive capabilities of its contractors on a tighter budget and pro-tecting its political power by supporting the President's dual-use agenda.

On the surface, the Department of Defense appeared to embrace the general ideal of global economic competitiveness.[10] But the agency also had strong overarching interests in maintaining its own capabilities and keeping the defense industrial base "warm" in the event of future conflicts (Kaminski 1995). Looking out for these interests implied protecting or keeping in business certain companies as a hedge against military uncertainty. Fearful of being labeled an advocate of industrial policy, Secretary of Defense Perry tactfully claimed that he cared little for saving the defense industry per se, but that he was concerned about the "technical talent, the brains, the know-how" and the future defense capabilities. Accordingly, the Pentagon's Bottom-Up Review of 1993 continued to call for a relatively large force structure and the resupply of major weapons systems. Production rates for remaining capacity were kept high with continued domestic purchases and major arms sales abroad. The federal government saved such "unnecessary" systems as the Seawolf submarine, the V-22 Osprey aircraft, and the ABRAMS tank, and it sanctioned the sale of F-16s to Taiwan, F-15s to Saudi Arabia, and ABRAMS tanks to Kuwait—despite the ramifications for international stability (Korb 1996).

With calls to balance the budget and lower taxes, however, the Pentagon was under pressure to trim fat and cut programs. The problem was keeping contractors in each key weapons and systems area active and profitable, capable of producing current weapons and developing new ones, all at lower costs. The Pentagon justified its support for both dual-use technologies and defense contractor consolidation on the grounds that these programs allowed the military to balance its capability needs with the budget pressures placed on it by Congress. Dual-use products, defense officials argued, could advance national security objectives by stimulating the development of process or product technologies with both military and civilian uses (U.S. Department of Defense 1995, 10).[11] The goal was not to support the commercial technology base for its own good, as the President had originally intended, but to integrate the defense and commercial industrial bases to create a single industrial base flexible enough to meet both sectors' needs. By helping defense firms increase their volume of sales in commercial markets, the Pentagon could also procure technologies at lower per unit costs.

A variety of financing and planning programs, involving the participation of federal, state, and local agencies as well as local lending institutions, federal laboratories, and institutions of higher education, were designated to serve the needs of firms wishing to engage in dual-use technology development (Defense Conversion Committee 1992). The Technology Reinvestment Project (TRP) was the administration's showcase diversification program, with appropriations totaling $1.2 billion between 1992 and 1995 in cost-shared grants administered through eight statutory programs.[12] The executive branch organized a group of representatives from six agencies led by the Advanced Research Projects

Agency (ARPA) at the Department of Defense to oversee the TRP initiative.[13] ARPA funded firm-led consortia to develop dual-use technologies and placed a heavy emphasis on teaming and joint ventures. In 1993, the year in which the TRP was first unveiled, applicants submitted 2,850 grant proposals. The applicants expected big pay-outs, but by the time each contractor paid its multiple partners and proposal costs, they found themselves with rather small allocations. By early 1995, the program was able to fund approximately 251 projects totaling $751 million (U.S. Department of Defense 1993). The most generously funded of the eight programs, the Defense Dual-Use Critical Technology Partnerships, required an industry cost-share for 50 percent of the federal contribution. The program funded projects that developed lithium ion batteries, advanced display technologies, and uncooled infrared sensors (Stowsky 1999).

The Pentagon's other strategy for balancing capabilities and costs involved subsidizing contractors' merger activity by "allowing" and reimbursing the eligible costs contractors incurred on restructuring. The Federal Acquisitions Regulations (FAR) govern the allowability of restructuring costs incident to a merger or acquisition, although they do not define these costs or provide clear guidance about the specific coverage to contractors if they are working under cost-plus contracts. On July 21, 1993, in the middle of the merger movement in the defense industry, then Under Secretary of Defense for Acquisition William Perry issued a memorandum clarifying the Pentagon's policy. Perry indicated that the costs of severance, early retirement and relocation payments, closing plants, moving equipment, continuing health care coverage for laid-off workers, and other merger-related actions incurred by defense contractors would be considered "allowable" if the company could demonstrate two things. First, savings to the government as a result of the restructuring would have to exceed the costs of the' subsidy, and second, the merger would have to preserve a critical defense capability. The directive was formalized after several major defense contractors approached the Department of Defense, arguing that, without such subsidies, they would bear all the costs of merger-related restructuring whereas the Pentagon would reap all the benefits (*Economist* 1997). Congress ultimately passed the legislation endorsing the provision—although it imposed additional auditing, certification, and reporting requirements (U.S. GAO 1995b; 1996).[14]

Allowing such costs, in the words of the General Counsel of the Department of Defense, would "motivate cost effective and timely downsizing, and produce a more efficient defense industry" (Miller 1993).[15] The expected savings were to result from fewer redundancies (e.g., fewer duplicated assembly lines) and reduced overhead (e.g., smaller headquarters staffs). Because more than half of the prime contractors' business was with the Pentagon, officials said much of the savings would be passed through to the state in the form of lower prices on defense contracts. Meanwhile, federal antitrust and procurement statutes were interpreted leniently to allow for the increased merger activity (Kovacic 1991). During the early 1990s, the Pentagon instituted other procurement reforms to reduce costs: rationalizing the defense acquisition system and encouraging the substitution of generic, commercial components for specialized, expensive ones under the Federal Acquisition Streamlining Act of 1994. However, the expected savings through such reforms and the dual-use strategy were dwarfed by those anticipated from the industry's consolidation.

Only a small number of contractors (seventeen requests from eleven contractors between 1993 and 1997) met the eligibility requirements, but the Pentagon was able to assist several large, prime contractors in purchasing the operating units of their competitors. For example, the Pentagon reimbursed Martin Marietta $110 million to help with its $208 million purchase of General Dynamics' San Diego–based rocket plant.[16] Similarly, the Pentagon agreed to pay $132.5 million of Hughes Aircraft's $366.1 million merger costs to purchase General Dynamics' missile operations (U.S. GAO 1996).

The Pentagon's support for mergers and dual-use technology development was challenged by various members of Congress. Congressional representatives, especially those from jurisdictions that had experienced restructuring-related layoffs, opposed the Pentagon's reimbursement of costs related to mergers and consolidations. Trying to protect the interests of the targeted firms, workers, and communities they represented, public officials lashed out at "corporate welfare at its worst" when federal dollars promoted downsizing. The policy's most vocal foe, Representative Chris Smith (R.-NJ), joined other members of Congress to introduce a provision to ban such payments in the future. "This [restructuring] policy," he said, "is the direct cause of some 3,200 layoffs in my district alone, and it uses the tax dollars of these very same people to do it" (Smith 1996). He coined the expression "payoffs for layoffs," and accused the government of ignoring its free market mandate in order to underwrite corporate mergers. A bipartisan coalition of representatives led an effort to halt these reimbursements whose bill, although successful in the House, was later rejected in the Senate in the summer of 1996 (Velocci 1996a, 30).

Meanwhile, other members of Congress challenged the Pentagon's dual-use programs on the grounds that they jeopardized the public interest by diverting resources from traditional defense roles, such as combat readiness and strategic missile defense, to ill-defined civilian missions.[17] Although the concept of dual use was heavily supported by a centrist administration with a passion for advanced technology, it came under attack when the Republicans gained control of Congress in 1994. The Republicans challenged the President's diversification efforts, slandering them as "industrial policies" and "wasteful subsidies to private contractors who should have to compete in the marketplace" (Cassata 1995). They voted to cut $300 million from the TRP in 1995 with the warning that the Pentagon should "refocus its increasingly politicized and commercially oriented dual-use programs back to traditional military purposes" (Green 1995, 13).[18] In the summer of 1995, the Pentagon announced that civilian agencies would no longer have formal involvement in selecting applicants for TRP awards and that their positions would be filled by military officials (*Defense Week* 1995).

Interagency conflict over defense adjustment was rife as different interest groups sought representation and protection through different arms of the administration. As "global economic competitiveness" came to dominate the discourse of post–Cold War industrial production, the Departments of Commerce and Labor (and to a lesser extent the Departments of Transportation and Energy) saw an opportunity to insert themselves as defense policy players. In contrast to its role in previous administrations, the Commerce Department became a key agency in the management of jointly funded technology development and adoption programs with firms (Mowery and Ham 1995; Alic et al. 1992). The newly established Office of Economic Conversion was moved to the Commerce Department from the President's Council of Economic Advisors, and the department's research and development budget more than doubled between 1993 and 1996. Most of this increase was linked to the Advanced Technologies Program (ATP), which provided matching funds for firms and consortia for the development of "pre-commercial" technologies.[19] As the main supporter of the President's dual-use agenda, the Department of Commerce objected to the Pentagon's support for the consolidation of the industry because, it intimated, mergers slowed both the transfer of defense assets to the commercial sector and the product development process crucial for diversification.

The Commerce Department was involved in other ways, working closely with the Pentagon, Congress, and contractors to redraft the Export Administration Act. It sought to allow for the export of dual-use products and complex weapons systems. In keeping with the administration's free-trade stance, the Commerce Department sought to lower the barriers to trade for American companies and increasingly exerted its influence to permit the sale of weapons abroad (U.S. Congress OTA 1991; Pearlstein 1991; Kapstein 1992). The Departments of Defense and Commerce under Bush had approved two large foreign deliveries from General Dynamics—a $600 million tank order to Kuwait and a $2.3 billion

fighter jet order to Taiwan (Sennott 1996). These approvals reversed earlier policies and were announced in the waning days of Bush's 1992 pres-
idential campaign. Clinton's reforms went beyond those of his Republican predecessor in the degree of export-oriented financing available to
defense contractors (Savage 1994). His reforms made the sale of dual-use
items (once they passed muster on national security grounds) eligible for
the same subsidized government financing available to commercial exports through the Export-Import Bank. The Commerce Department also
funneled export subsidies through its Office of Strategic Industries to
manufacturers of defense subsystems and components by waiving re-
coupment fees, providing marketing assistance, and assisting buyers
with financing (Sennott 1996, B1-B2).

The Defense and State Departments were more ambivalent about foreign military sales. On one hand, they viewed these sales as a way to
keep key contractors profitable without having to support weapons programs unpopular with a budget-conscious Congress. They also wanted
to assist American allies and weapons buyers, such as Saudi Arabia and
Turkey, in fending off potential attacks from "rogue states." On the other
hand, arms proliferation increased the potential for international conflict
and active military engagement. Moreover, dual-use technology development may create new channels for proliferation (Reppy 1999).

Like many Congressional representatives from defense-dependent districts, the Department of Labor was directly in conflict with the Pentagon
over the unemployment effects of defense industry consolidation. Although the Labor Department never served as a center for policy innovation regarding defense adjustment, it played the critical role of overseeing the funds for worker retraining and some unemployment benefits.
The agency fought to wrest a portion of the defense adjustment funds
away from the Pentagon (Mueller et al. 1994).[20] Congress allocated
roughly $225 million in employment and training assistance to displaced
defense workers between 1993 and 1995, with an extra $75 million added
to the existing Economic Dislocation and Worker Adjustment Assistance
Act (EDWAA), the primary federal program designed to assist displaced
workers. Funds for workforce development, such as basic and remedial
education, the acquisition of new occupational skills, on-the-job training,
out-of-area job search, relocation, and entrepreneurial training were intended to supplement normal unemployment benefits and ease the pain
of layoffs. These funds were distributed to the states based on an unem-
ployment-based formula and administered by business-dominated, re-
gionally based Private Industry Councils (PICs), a deliberate shift away
from the public sector (King 1995, 193).

Although several communities experimented with innovative responses to defense downsizing (Markusen and Powers 1999), eligibility

requirements and the unique circumstances of defense workers hindered the effectiveness of EDWAA and related retraining programs. Firms could only access these moneys if they faced a loss of 25 percent of their sales or 80 percent of their workforce as a result of defense cuts. Thus, most workers were forced to defray retraining costs themselves, which sharply reduced their interest in such endeavors. EDWAA was designed to provide basic readjustment services to "generic" displaced workers and was often administered by the same organizations that provide job counseling to disadvantaged youth and young adults (Mueller et al. 1994). Laid-off defense workers shared unique characteristics: They tended to be older, enjoyed substantial job tenure, and were in occupations with little growth potential, such as durable manufacturing. Trained in the Department of Defense's arcane contracting and engineering practices, many former defense workers confronted different barriers to reemployment than other more flexible workers. Worker retraining schemes for both defense and civilian workers were also inadequately and unevenly tied to new job creation. The question "retraining for what?" haunted program administrators who themselves were skeptical about the prospects of laid-off defense workers finding comparable work at comparable pay in an increasingly service-oriented economy (Mueller et al. 1993).

State and local governments had their own interests in defense adjustment. After all, they were the political units most immediately affected by restructuring-related layoffs and plant closures. Direct pressures for action and the economic consequences of corporate adjustment strategies fell squarely within the local policy domains. Yet state and local governments were perhaps the weakest units of political authority to address the challenges. They were constrained by smaller budgets and by legal strictures that gave them few powers over the behavior of corporations. State and local governments were primarily interested in creating new jobs, attracting firms, and retaining defense firms and workers, all of which would contribute directly to their revenue bases. Expenditure pressures to aid laid-off workers and ailing suppliers coincided with a shrinking revenue base and impeded the ability of municipalities like San Diego, St. Louis, and Groton, Connecticut, to meet the normal service needs of their constituents.

Because the health of state and city governments depended heavily on the resources of the federal government, local policymakers developed intergovernmental lobbying and grantsmanship skills to secure financial support for defense adjustment. Congress appropriated approximately $245 million to the Office of Economic Adjustment (OEA) at the Department of Defense and the Economic Development Administration (EDA) at the Department of Commerce for local community adjustment between 1993 and 1995 (Oden and Bischak 1995, 54).[21] These two agencies assisted state and local governments in planning and implementing economic diversification programs for communities that suffered from economic downturns due to the loss of a military facility or reductions in defense contracts. The OEA was primarily responsible for guiding communities through the initial planning phase, and other federal agencies, primarily the EDA and Department of Labor, were responsible for implementation and actual job creation.[22] EDA implementation grants funded industrial parks, seed capital funds, incubators, and revolving loan funds for small businesses as well as infrastructure construction projects, such as access roads to industrial plants (National League of Cities 1992).

Both the OEA and EDA programs were a low priority of the administration; their small budgets (the OEA's budget was $39 million in FY 1994) could not adequately address the scale of problems associated with community adjustment, and they could assist only a few communities each year (School for Workers 1993, 45–48). Officials at OEA characterized their programs as "firmly 'outside-the-gate' . . . we have no real control over the terms of individual procurement contracts or the behavior of the firms who are laying off people" (Official at OEA, interview by author, Fall 1996). As with the EDA and state and local governments, OEA officials were essentially bystanders to the adjustment process; they did not intervene into the labor relations of defense firms nor did they meet with Pentagon procurement managers to lobby for the inclusion of economic development provisions in defense contracts.[23] Their role was remedial and reactive, providing emergency funding to soften the blow of decisions made far beyond their reach. Most community adjustment programs turned to the noncontroversial, noninterventionist task of building local, institutional capacity so that community leaders would be better equipped to deal with future layoffs.

Taking their cue from efforts at the federal level, state and local governments also developed their own programs to address the needs of defense-dependent businesses, workers, regions, and municipalities. States and municipalities provided tax incentives, marketing assistance, loan guarantees, venture capital, and product development grants to companies they determined were in growth or emerging-technology sectors. For example, the Connecticut Department of Economic Development and its technology development agency, Connecticut Innovations, Inc., coordinated the state's response to defense cutbacks. After convening meetings with local prime contractors, the state established a $22.5 million Defense Diversification Fund in 1993 and passed legislation that provided Connecticut manufacturers with tax credits for research and development, capital investment and job training activities, sales tax exemptions for aircraft manufacturers, loan guarantees, and bonds for credit relief (Connecticut Department of Economic and Community Development 1996). Subnational governments considered these public-private partnerships necessary to retain existing defense firms and jobs.

Unfortunately, the available evidence suggests that large defense conglomerates did not respond to these federal, state, and local adjustment initiatives in ways that would improve the transition to nondefense manufacturing, the stabilization of communities, or the creation of jobs (U.S. GAO 1996; Oden and Bischak 1995; Markusen and Powers 1999). The large prime contractors, for the most part, ignored the 1993 Defense Authorization Bill, or took advantage of funds for dual-use development, restructuring, and foreign military sales without significantly altering their corporate strategies. Of all the contractors I interviewed, not one said that adjustment policies had any bearing on its investment strategy. This finding correlates with other studies (Lovering and Curran 1996; Markusen 1997a) and public statements by contractor executives (Anders 1991, 1992). Pressures from financial markets, rather than state planning, drove their behavior.

State Support for Shareholder Primacy

The Clinton era adjustment policies did not expedite the shift to nondefense manufacturing nor did they necessarily save or create jobs. Instead, contractors pursued the three adjustment paths I described earlier in this chapter, specialization, rationalization, and foreign market penetration, which left a few very large and very powerful defense firms remaining in the industry. State support for dual-use technologies, retraining, and community adjustment merely eased the move to a more concentrated, specialized, and globally oriented defense industry (Christopherson and Weber 1994). The high degree of defense-dependency among the remaining contractors perpetuated pressures for high degree of defense expenditures, subsidies, and arms exports, resulting, some argue, in further resource misallocation and diminished national security (Markusen 1997a).

After the Cold War, the federal government did not engage in conversion *planning* per se. Under the Clinton policy regime, defense diversification was a voluntary and uncoordinated activity, determined by the desire of individual contractors and their shareholders, not by a more public, system-steering directive. If defense firms chose not to explore or undertake diversification activities, the government did not impose any penalties on them.[24] Without any disincentives, defense contractors were free to restructure in any way they saw fit, regardless of negative externalities or social costs incurred by groups outside the purview of corporate governance. Perhaps government officials viewed capitalism's propensity for "creative destruction" as a natural means by which the economy makes way for new industries, new products, and new forms of work organization. Laid-off workers, they believed, would find work in growing sectors of the economy, and defense-dependent communities would find ways of revitalizing themselves—through, for instance, casinos, tourism, and service development.

That the defense adjustment process was firm-led is not surprising, considering that in the United States, system-steering and coordinative mechanisms that unite firm interests and national interests, like those in the Western European and Japanese economies, are largely absent (Christopherson 1993). Adjustment to changes in product, consumer, and financial markets is made by corporate management based on their calculations of projected returns, rather than within a broader policy or institutional framework that may constrain the actions of *individual* firms but enable *groups* of firms to be competitive (Samuels 1994). In place of conversion planning, Oden and Bischak remark, "each component of the (military-industrial) complex bargains to minimize its individual losses and an entropic, ex-post adjustment process results" (1995, 40).

The state's response to contractors' behavior was not just permissive; the federal government actively subsidized their financial restructuring and foreign sales. The Pentagon never directed specific companies to merge with one another or to sell off specific divisions. However, by providing incentives to defray the costs of restructuring and exhorting industry leaders to consolidate, it made its goals known. Restructuring would allow contractors to remain specialized in defense work and was expected to create more savings than dual-use development. Initiated by an administration with strong ties to the financial sector, the adjustment programs made it easier for financial markets to reshape the military-industrial complex. Then Secretary of Defense Perry, for example, embarked on an aggressive program to dismantle antitrust regulations as they applied to defense contractors (Markusen 1997a). The Pentagon and the Department of Justice quickly approved most mergers and acquisitions among contractors. By underwriting the costs of takeovers, the federal government not only offered its stamp of approval to mergers, but also absorbed many of the costs that otherwise would have accrued to private contractors and their shareholders.

Why did the state support defense contractor restructuring over other adjustment strategies, such as defense diversification? The primary reason for the support was that the Pentagon expected consolidation in the industry to reduce overhead and operating costs and therefore unit prices. A Department of Defense study of three business combinations confirmed this expectation. It revealed that the Pentagon share of projected costs was $256.3 million, while its share of projected savings was estimated at $1.146 billion (Kaminski 1996). But calculating the costs and benefits of the Pentagon's restructuring subsidies was more an art than a science. Speculation in an uncertain market translated into rough initial calculations. Inflation effects were ignored in certain instances, and five-year projections were questioned. A GAO study of the merger between FMC Corporation and Harsco Corporation's tracked-combat-vehicle divisions found that the actual savings to the government were much less than originally projected. Rather than $10 in net savings for each dollar in costs as predicted, there was only $1.49 in net savings (U.S. GAO 1996). This fell below the two-for-one savings-to-costs ratio the Defense Department required to subsidize the merger. Although the company claimed that the reduction in unit price for their combat vehicles was entirely due to lower overhead costs, many other factors may have contributed to the lower price. Economies of scale from purchasing several vehicles, lower inflation rates, and workforce reductions unrelated to mergers could also have contributed to the lower price. Moreover, the government savings figures never factored in the higher costs associated with the ripple effect of layoffs, such as increased services needed to assist workers, or the effects of decreased competition in the industry (Markusen 1997a).

Absent regulations or contracts protecting other stakeholders' claims to defense revenues, management can ignore the interests of workers, communities, and taxpayers. The government, like the nexus of contracts scholars, wrongly assumes that all of the economic actors in the firm are equally equipped to enforce their claims on profits and protect themselves in the face of fundamental corporate restructuring (Macey 1989). But because workers have no right to influence these decisions through the traditional collective bargaining process, they have no guarantee that directors will weigh their concerns when formulating strategic corporate policies (O'Connor 1991; Stone 1988). Similarly, community groups, state and local governments, and taxpayers possess few ways of protecting their interests under the current system of corporate governance.

Rather than rectifying this inequity, the federal government further marginalized nonshareholder groups. The state did not use government authority to make private economic decisionmaking more responsive to workers or communities. The federal government, for example, did not give organized labor or state and local governments an official role in the evaluation, selection, and implementation of its diversification programs. Neither the Department of Labor nor other labor representatives were involved in the TRP review and selection process. Unions were ineligible to apply for TRP moneys despite management's traditional lack of enthusiasm for diversification (Bischak, Oden, and Klock 1995). Although the administration justified the TRP on the grounds that it would help companies retain and retrain existing workers, the criteria for evaluating TRP proposals submitted by consortia did not consider job impacts in determining awards. Adhering to the ideal of voluntariness that permeated the defense adjustment agenda, stakeholder participation was encouraged, but not mandated or enforced.

Meanwhile the administration's adjustment policies favored those large defense contractors with established relations to the Pentagon. Many of the same firms that enjoyed intimate relations with the Pentagon during the Cold War salvaged their privileged positions with restructuring subsidies, TRP grants, technology transfer relationships with federal laboratories, and the few remaining defense contracts. In addition, the Pentagon, as opposed to a commercial agency, administered the defense adjustment agenda, even though the agency and its suppliers were ill-equipped to advance new standards for commercial, even dual-use, innovation. The TRP, for example, reflected the predominance of military objectives, because the "criticalness" of the technology, not commercial marketability or cost-conscious production, was the most important criterion for an award (Bischak, Oden, and Klock 1995). Rather than weaning defense contractors from their dependency on the Pentagon or encouraging them to alter their marketing, cost structure, and product development to civilian markets, the defense adjustment policies of the 1990s allowed firms to continue to focus primarily on defense contracts and shareholder value.

In the years following the end of the Cold War, state actors cobbled together a very weak defense adjustment agenda, capitulating to the contractors' objective of preserving a hollowed-out but financially dynamic defense industrial base. Those policy measures that did attempt to alter contractors' investment behavior did so in a manner that strengthened the decisional autonomy of management, the claims of shareholders, and the interest of their financial intermediaries. The weak adjustment agenda and the degree to which prime contractors were free to restructure in (almost) any way they saw fit points to the collusion between the private interests of key defense suppliers and certain segments of the state.

The "iron triangles" that connected Congress, the Pentagon, and powerful corporate interests, defining Cold War state-market relations, did not disappear; these three entities have in fact became more mutually dependent. Rent-seeking coalitions, reinvigorated by defense spending cuts, used their political power to ensure that adjustment regulations were promotional, rather than disciplinary. The defense industry, for example, launched vigorous efforts to defeat the proposal to repeal the federal subsidies for restructuring and to approve loan guarantees for sales abroad (Velocci 1996a, 30). The lack of competition in the industry increased the dependence and price inelasticity of the Pentagon, which had to ensure that its few remaining systems suppliers remained financially viable.

Because contractors wielded a disproportionate amount of influence over public policy, the agency relationship I have discussed in previous chapters broke down. The agents effectively became the principals. In a system where managers of defense contractors were insulated from market competition, enjoyed privileged access to funds, and pressed for excessive benefits to fulfill their obligations to shareholders, the needs of the contractors became those of the Pentagon. In the 1990s, the administration generally supported contractors' financial viability, distributional priorities, and increasing profitability, turning a blind eye to excessive profits and executive compensation packages. Only through weaker government agencies did it inadequately fund state and local governments to deal with the dislocating restructuring strategies of its suppliers.

An adjustment policy based on subsidies to business tacitly supports the redistribution of publicly created wealth to senior management and shareholders, or regards it as an unfortunate, but private, decision protected by explicit contracts and the implied consent of all the parties involved. Whatever its motives, the state was an ambivalent accomplice— content to go along with corporate adjustment strategies as long as its remaining weapons systems were built. Although restructuring the defense industrial base jeopardized long-term social investments in skills and innovation and the economic security of millions of workers and residents of defense-dependent communities, it was politically easier to keep feeding the military-industrial complex in peacetime than to overhaul it.

Notes

1. These figures do not include direct commercial sales, which are negotiated directly between manufacturers and foreign governments. These sales can account for up to $6 billion a year and are much less regulated (Sennott 1996, B11).

2. Harrison and Bluestone (1988), Lazonick (1990), Appelbaum and Berg (1996), and others have noted how American corporations choose to attack costs associated with labor and location to weather contract cutbacks rather than make long-term investments in new forms of work organization, new product development, or new process technologies.

3. The meaning of the term "conversion" remains elusive. Some define conversion generally as the planned transformation of excess military production to

civilian purposes (Renner 1993). Others delimit specific types of conversion such as company, local economic base, worker, and facility conversion (Sandler and Hartley 1995, 288–289; Hill et al. 1993). I am primarily concerned with company conversion, when contractors reorient their production capabilities, products, and markets to nondefense work.

4. Observers were quick to point out that Hughes had not been a prime contractor on an aircraft platform for several years and that its missile systems—its bread and butter—had not made any efforts to diversify.

5. If contractors are willing to convert some of their operations to commercial production, they are more apt to acquire new, nondefense units. Even among those financially equipped to make the transition internally and commit funds for preliminary research and development, few are willing to take the financial risk to invest in actual production activities. Many of the large primes have developed commercial prototypes but lack the leadership commitment and institutional capacity to see these projects through initial years of low returns.

6. An index of defense stocks rose to a higher level than the Standard and Poor's 500 between 1991 and 1993. The defense stocks increased in value by 140 percent while the Standard and Poor's 500 stocks increased by 38 percent (Borrus 1993).

7. Before joining Clinton's Council of Economic Advisors, for example, Laura Tyson advocated for a more strategic approach to the defense industry as a national technological resource instrumental to confronting increasing foreign competition (Tyson 1992).

8. See, for example, the Federal Technology Transfer Act (1986); National Competitiveness Act (1989); North American Free Trade Agreement (1995).

9. Many of Clinton's initiatives actually originated in the early 1980s in response to changes in the international economic and technological environment that reduced U.S. technological dominance and deepened the interdependence of the U.S. and foreign economies (Mowery and Ham 1995).

10. The Pentagon created a new position, Assistant Secretary of Defense for Economic Security, to help the agency adjust to the changed environment. Joshua Gotbaum, formerly an executive with the investment banking firm of Lazard Freres, was appointed to this position and put in charge of the defense industrial base, dual-use technology, base closure, and community reinvestment initiatives.

11. Although there was resistance in the ranks, defense officials, such as former Assistant Secretary Kenneth Flamm of the Office of Dual-Use Technology Policy and International Programs, claimed that dual-use strategy had gained acceptance among the upper echelons and within the Pentagon (Jacobsen 1995).

12. Defense Dual-Use Critical Technology Partnerships; Commercial-Military Integration Partnerships; Regional Technology Alliances Assistance Program; Defense Advanced Manufacturing Technology Partnerships; Manufacturing Extension Program; Defense Dual-Use Assistance Extension Program.

13. Department of Defense; National Science Foundation; National Institute of Standards and Technology; National Aeronautics and Space Administration; Department of Transportation. ARPA (or, as it was known before 1993 and again after 1995, the *Defense* Advanced Research Projects Agency, or DARPA) is separate

from the military services and has historically funded basic research on dual-use technologies.

14. Subsequently, the Defense Contract Management Command (DCMC) and the Defense Contract Audit Agency (DCAA) issued detailed guidance to contracting officers and auditors to assist them in evaluating a contractor's restructuring plan, and the Department of Defense issued interim regulations to address the allowability of these costs.

15. In an interview, Paul Kaminski noted, "From a competitive standpoint it might be very desirable to keep three competitors in a given area, but if there's no business to give them, we pay a very expensive penalty in overhead" (1995).

16. In this transaction, the government made an entirely new kind of payment to Martin Marietta: a $30 million transfer designed to share with the firm the savings the government would enjoy from less expensive rocket launches. The CEO of Martin Marietta, Norman Augustine, stated that had the Pentagon refused to subsidize this acquisition, his company would not have made the purchase because it would have been a bad business deal (Yeager 1996).

17. In contrast, a National Commission for Economic Conversion and Disarmament report found that 80 percent of TRP development awards from the first competition went to projects that were closely linked to the Department of Defense's own list of new technology priorities (Bischak, Oden, and Klock 1995).

18. Congress appropriated $496 million for the TRP in FY 1994 and $550 million for it in FY 1995.

19. Likewise, the Commerce Department received increases in budgets for industrial technology adoption, such as regional manufacturing extension programs that provide technological and management assistance to firms. Funding for the Manufacturing Extension Partnership program, which is administered by the National Institute for Standards and Technology (NIST) of the Commerce Department, increased markedly under the Clinton administration.

20. This is not surprising given the degree to which agency autonomy and turf is tenaciously defended. Secretary of Labor Robert Reich was reluctant to single out former defense workers for special benefits. He had hoped to consolidate all the available retraining money and spread it out to workers who were displaced not only by defense cuts but by capital flight, imports, and restructuring in general. The Department of Defense, which in turn was reluctant to work with the Department of Labor in the first place, retaliated by delaying additional funds for Labor's retraining and adjustment assistance programs.

21. The Department of Defense transferred $130 million to the EDA to provide grants to state and local governments in areas severely affected by defense cuts and other sudden and severe economic disruptions.

22. Eligibility for both EDA and OEA grants depends upon the number of jobs lost and whether the job loss resulted from the actions of a single employer or within a single industry. The OEA distributes grants worth between $200,000 and $300,000, with a 25 percent matching fund requirement, to help communities respond to base and plant closures. The EDA awards about 20 planning grants (averaging $65,000 each) and 20 implementation grants (averaging $630,000 each) each year.

23. This bystander role is both assumed by choice—i.e., by officials philosophically opposed to market intervention—and because of the existing constraints of legal precedent. As I have discussed, corporate and labor law delimit certain arenas as open for state intervention and others as only market-dependent.

24. The elusive market may penalize nondiversifying contractors in the long run, but management's myopia may not let such worries influence their present investment decisions.

4

General Dynamics:
The Shareholder Success Story of
the 1990s

Even though General Dynamics' situation is replicated by many firms and industries, its response and ultimate achievements are remarkable, serving as the preeminent management and shareholder success story of the 1990s.

Jay Dial and Kevin Murphy, 1995

In 1990, General Dynamics was the second largest defense contractor in the United States (trailing only McDonnell Douglas in sales). With more than 45 production sites worldwide, the company manufactured a variety of defense products, including the M60 and M1 series Abrams battle tanks, F-5 and F-16 aircraft, cruise missiles, and nuclear submarines. But with more than 90 percent of the company's sales dependent on the Department of Defense and most in shrinking product lines, General Dynamics was on the verge of bankruptcy in 1990 and poised for disaster in the decade to come.

Much to everyone's surprise, the conglomerate reversed course and dazzled Wall Street by making a bold, unprecedented play for shareholder value. In two years, it sold its F-16 fighter plant to Lockheed, its missile business to Hughes Aircraft, its space launch business to Martin Marietta, and its nonmilitary aircraft business to Textron. Unlike other contractors that sold off their assets, General Dynamics did not reinvest the proceeds but returned them to the company's shareholders. General Dynamics' strategy was based on the principle that it was both possible and desirable to create wealth in a nongrowth market. The company's president during the early part of this period, William Anders, took every opportunity to preach the gospel of the financial markets, arguing that by merging, divesting, and downsizing, contractors could move underutilized assets to the true residual risk-bearers of the firm: shareholders. Shareholders, not the government, he argued, were best suited to determine the future of the military-industrial complex. This chapter provides an overview of General Dynamics' shareholder-oriented adjustment strategies as well as the justifications for these strategies and their impact on other corporate stakeholders.

Warning Signs

General Dynamics' continuing profitability was threatened in the latter half of the 1980s by declining government orders and changes in procurement practices, including more dual-source supply, fixed-price contracts, and a greater focus on cost competition. The story of the corporation's oldest division, the Electric Boat facility in Groton, Connecticut, illustrates the changing environment in which General Dynamics operated during this time. Electric Boat built nuclear submarines for the Navy. The decline in submarine orders initially did not faze the shipyard, which in 1990 still had a backlog of $23 billion in submarine contracts from the Carter-Reagan build-ups.[1] General Dynamics had remained profitable throughout most of the 1980s, and profit margins on Electric Boat's backlogs were sufficiently high to guarantee large cash flows and financial solvency well into the 1990s. During its peak years of production in the mid-1980s, Electric Boat often had eight submarines under construction at one time, including many of the Los Angeles–class attack and Ohio-class Trident missile submarines. Then Electric Boat won the lead ship contract for a new faster, quieter submarine with more firepower: the Seawolf. The Navy announced it would be purchasing twenty-nine Seawolf submarines, and Electric Boat based its long-term planning on the Navy's projection.

The fall of the Berlin Wall in 1989 and the dissolution of the Soviet Union in 1991 precipitated a reassessment of military strategy and acquisition needs. All of General Dynamics' divisions were threatened, as the Pentagon began to wind down many of the $10.2 billion defense contractor's major programs. Analysts predicted that the contractor would probably lose a third of its sales by 1995. With the demise of the Soviet Navy, it had become increasingly difficult to justify the extraordinarily expensive nuclear submarine program. The Navy decided to move beyond its Cold War strategy of tracking attack submarines on the high seas, responding instead to the new threat posed by shallow water, littoral (coastal) warfare overseas, and smaller regional conflicts (Krepinevich 1996). Advocates of the submarine program insisted that an advanced submarine fleet was still necessary because the Russians were improving their submarine development programs and selling state-of-the-art vessels to "rogue nations" in regions of strategic interest to the United States (Center for Security Policy 1995).

Nonetheless, the Navy decided that it needed to procure cheaper and smaller submarines with more advanced acoustic and signal-processing systems and decrease the overall size of the fleet (Kaufman and Steinbrunner 1991; Krepinevich 1996). The Navy announced that it would be scaling back the Seawolf program from its original projection of twenty-nine ships to, at most, three. Then, in his 1992 State of the Union address, George Bush announced the decision to reduce the Seawolf program to the single submarine under construction at Electric Boat and rescind funding previously approved by Congress for the second and third ships.[2] Electric Boat's backlog of orders was dwindling, and Connecticut's Congressional representatives pleaded that the shipyard risked going out of business if the two ships were not reinstated. Running a tight race against Jerry Brown in the Connecticut primary, Bill Clinton made a campaign pledge to extend the program if elected. In the fall of 1992, Congress overruled Bush's cut and in a compromise bill rescued the second Seawolf. In 1995, Congress approved a third.[3] Even with these three Seawolfs, the Navy ordered no more than five submarines during the 1990s, compared to the thirty-seven contracts Electric Boat won during the 1980s. At these low production rates, management predicted that the yard would be unable to break even during the 1990s (Hamilton 1996j).

The end of the Cold War precipitated not only a reduction in the volume of government orders, but also changes in the general procurement environment. With smaller defense budgets and fewer contractors, competition for the fewer, bigger contracts intensified. Just as Boeing and Lockheed competed tooth and nail to win the Joint Strike Fighter program, Electric Boat and its main rival, the Newport News shipyard in Virginia (owned by Tenneco), stepped up competition for the few remaining submarine contracts. The sole-source, cost-plus contracts of the past had allowed contractors to keep their prices high. Contractors were unfamiliar with the accounting and budgeting methods necessary to oversee and rein in costs. When the Navy began switching to fixed-price contracts in the mid-1980s (primarily because of billing scandals in which General Dynamics was implicated), the two shipyards began competing on the basis of costs for the few remaining fixed-price contracts, each bidding low in an attempt to undercut the other.

There were fewer big programs in the 1990s, and if a contractor lost one contract, it had difficulty reentering the market. Electric Boat and Newport News, for example, competed viciously for the twenty-five New Attack Submarine contracts, valued at $1.5 billion each (Hamilton

1995b). Electric Boat was at a disadvantage because, manufacturing only submarines, it had a smaller backlog of defense orders than Newport News. Newport News built aircraft carriers and other surface ships in addition to submarines. The new competitiveness was evident not only during the pre-award bidding, but also in the legal fights following the award of contracts.[4] After a court battle with Newport News over the Seawolf, Congressional representatives were able to assuage the Virginia-based shipyard by negotiating a work-sharing compromise in which Newport News and Electric Boat would *jointly* construct the New Attack Submarine.

Following a burst of orders during the Gulf War, General Dynamics' other divisions were also prepared for the worst. Its missile division saw orders drop precipitously. In 1985, the Pentagon purchased more than 31,000 new missiles, whereas in 1994 it bought fewer than 2,500. In its facility in Fort Worth, Texas, General Dynamics was building the A-12 Navy attack jet, which was billions of dollars over budget on a fixed-price development contract and almost two years behind schedule. In 1991, the Navy finally canceled the beleaguered project, causing thousands of layoffs at the Fort Worth plant. Rumors circulated that the Air Force was planning to phase out General Dynamics' most profitable program, the F-16 fighter. Moreover, the contractor struggled to find orders from abroad and to keep its two tank-building plants (in Michigan and Ohio) open beyond the middle of the decade.

With intensified competition and the decline in defense contract revenue, General Dynamics appeared to be headed toward serious financial troubles. The company's monthly closing stock price fell from $79 in February 1987 to $25.25 at the end of 1990 (Bloomberg Financial Services 1996). Accounting returns declined between 1987 and 1990 (G. D. Annual Reports 1987, 1990).[5] Its $636 million long-term debt had increased more than twentyfold since 1985. Standard and Poor's and Moody's downgraded the firm's debt ratings, citing its poor financial condition, and the Pentagon's internal audits confirmed that General Dynamics had a "possible chance for bankruptcy" (Jefferson and Pasztor 1990). In 1989, the contractor announced that it would lay off 8,500 of its employees the following year.

Shareholder Values

In 1990, General Dynamics embarked on a radical turnaround. William Anders, a former test pilot for the Air Force and an Apollo 8 astronaut, was recruited to the position of chairman. Anders had held many prestigious appointments in government, serving as the head of the Nuclear Regulatory Commission (1975–1976) and as Ambassador to Norway

(1976–1977). He also had a reputation for being a savvy defense industry insider who had made a name for himself as the general manager of General Electric's nuclear energy products and aircraft equipment divisions, and subsequently as senior executive vice president of the Rhode Island–based defense conglomerate, Textron.

When Anders took office on January 1, 1991, he stated that his goal was to transform General Dynamics into a shareholder-driven enterprise (Dial and Murphy 1995). To accomplish this objective, he first needed to alter the corporate culture so that it would be more responsive to the stock market. In the 1980s, the company's relationship to shareholders was characterized as one of benign neglect, with occasional bouts of head-to-head antagonism. General Dynamics' stock prices were depressed, selling at a price-to-book value of 0.4 in 1990.[6] General Dynamics' majority shareholder for over twenty years, Chicago millionaire Henry Crown (who over the years had owned major stakes in both the Empire State Building and the Chicago Bulls), wielded a substantial amount of control over the board of directors and watched management like a hawk. A boardroom struggle with Crown had left the company cash-strapped and limping along financially for a period in the 1960s, and he was not willing to jeopardize the value of his assets again (Goodwin 1985; Wrubel 1992).[7]

Anders quickly changed the composition of the company's board of directors and top management. He brought in outside managers who, he believed, would have fewer personal attachments to workers, customers, and communities, attachments that could impede the implementation of potentially painful adjustment strategies. Eighteen of the top twenty-five executives Anders brought in were either new to General Dynamics or new to their positions. He, for instance, recruited former Secretary of Defense Frank Carlucci to join the board in 1991. In that year, Anders also moved the company's headquarters from St. Louis to Falls Church, Virginia, to be closer to the company's main customer. He brought in Wall Street analysts and professors from elite business schools to educate his top managers in the virtues of shareholder wealth creation. He wanted them to "think like business people, not like aerospace engineers," in order to transform a long-standing corporate culture focused on sales growth to one more focused on profitability, financial strength, and improving shareholder value (Dial and Murphy 1995, 271–273).

Anders and his new team were vocal about their commitment to shareholders and to improving the financial strength of the company. The chairman frequently gave interviews and speeches in which he sang the praises of shareholder value, galvanizing support from industry leaders for this goal. In a speech Anders gave to *Defense Week's* annual conference, he outlined his strategy for financial strength. He chided executives at other defense firms for neglecting the most important corporate stakeholder—shareholders—without whose support they would be unable to improve the financial performance of their companies and their service to the country.[8]

Anders and his team offered several defenses for the company's fixation on shareholder value. The company recognized that it was under the intense scrutiny of institutional investors, unions, the Department of Defense, financial analysts, and the general public, and took advantage of every opportunity to explain why it would pursue financial performance in a shrinking market. The corporation's lawyers insisted that the company had legally enforceable, fiduciary obligations to its shareholders. Shareholders, they argued, are the only owners of corporations; they invest in the company and bear the risk that the company will underperform. Managers echoed the contractarian scholars of corporate governance, who paint shareholders as the only corporate stakeholders to have legally recognized claims on the corporation's residual profits. One observer noted, "To the extent that General Dynamics is increasing stock price while laying people off, you could argue they are doing a good job of catering to their primary constituency—the shareholders. That is simply the foundation of the economic society we live in" (quoted in Remez and Taylor 1992, A1).

General Dynamics officials believed that by removing underutilized assets at their continuing operations, management was fulfilling its commitment to "constructively redeploy excess assets back to their rightful owners—the company's shareholders" (General Dynamics 1993). At the end of the Cold War, the defense industry was at a crossroads, and General Dynamics' financial performance had suffered. Many in the industry believed that defense stocks were heavily "discounted" because of volatile procurement markets, negative growth, overcapacity, and low profit margins.[9] In other words, if investments in two companies offered the same returns but one company was a defense company, investors would prefer to purchase the nondefense stock. As a result, investors would demand higher returns from defense contractors than commercial businesses in exchange for their continued support. This behavior was not based on an irrational distaste for the defense industry; for General Dynamics and other contractors, the late 1980s was a period characterized by low price/earnings ratios. The market price of General Dynamics' stock was substantially below book value (*Aerospace Daily*, March 14, 1990). With its stock already depressed, Anders argued, the company had no other option than to satisfy the short-term interests of shareholders. Anders claimed that shareholders had stood by the company during these hard times, and that they should be rewarded for their risk-taking and perseverance: "The cash we are accumulating comes from past investments made by [shareholders]. Therefore, as I have said before, it's only right that excess funds be returned to the investors for reinvestment as they see fit" (1991, 17–18).

Although they may have fulfilled their legal obligations to shareholders, management had the opportunity to reject their legal obligations for what they believed was pragmatically necessary to achieve business success. So why did they turn somersaults to satisfy the company's stockholders? Several extra-legal reasons explain why management pursued its shareholder-oriented restructuring strategy. First, senior managers at General Dynamics argued that focusing on shareholders was an institutional necessity, regardless of their legal obligations. If returns to investors were good, they believed, shareholders would invest their money to generate new research and fund plants, equipment, jobs, and growth. If returns were bad, investment would abandon the industry, and debt and other more expensive replacement capital would be a drain on the cash flow. Chairman Anders's comments in a *Fortune* interview reflect this sentiment:

> Now even if we didn't have a fiduciary responsibility, even if we didn't care about shareholders, we'd still have to have them. Because they are the people whose investment provides the capability for us to do the government's business. . . . Sure our program has been shareholder-oriented. That's not to say that we don't give a goddamn about anything else. If you don't have shareholders with you, you eventually lose the employees and the customers and vice versa. (Perry 1993, 56)

One could argue, however, that defense contractors are able to secure working capital through their government contracts and should be less interested in courting shareholders and other forms of external financing.

During this period increasingly powerful shareholders were bullying management to serve their interests. In the 1980s, activist shareholders and institutional investors began to change the rules and practices of corporate governance, pressuring management to forsake long-term plans for short-term gains (Finnegan 1990). Reluctant to sell their shares when they were disappointed with management's decisions because they had such substantial holdings, these groups attempted to exercise their rights to influence policy and improve stock prices, performance, and returns on investment. Anders took office in the midst of a particularly bitter proxy fight at fellow contractor Lockheed, which was about the same size as General Dynamics. In 1989, Texas billionaire Harold Simmons began a proxy fight to unseat several members of the Lockheed board. Simmons was the largest shareholder, owning 19.8 percent of the stock, and had criticized the company's financial performance and diversification plans (Stroud 1991; White 1991; Kovacic 1991). Although Simmons's efforts ultimately failed, this experience reinforced the fears of defense contractor executives; they had to maximize value vigilantly for their shareholders or risk challenges to their authority.

Anders had his own shareholders to occupy him. He was brought to General Dynamics at the behest of the majority stockholders since the 1950s, the Crown family. The Crowns, who had watched their stake in the company plummet from a high of $817 million in 1986 to as low as $184 million in early 1991, took strong measures to protect their interests and keep close tabs on their investment (Wrubel 1992, 26). To reassert control, they had increased their presence on the board of directors and brought Anders in with the explicit mandate to protect their assets. The press predicted that Anders would choose the restructuring strategy that would bring the Crowns the most nontaxable income (Weisman 1992b).

Other institutional investors had begun amassing General Dynamics' stock at bargain basement prices, and these investors were very frustrated by the way defense stocks had performed in the late 1980s (Gilpin 1994). The Crown family holdings, which once totaled 22 percent of the common stock, declined to 14.3 percent. Although their holdings still entitled them to a strong voice in the affairs of the corporation, and Lester Crown, son James, and cousin Charles Goodman still held positions on the board of directors, their power became increasingly diluted by the rise of more aggressive institutional investors. In 1990, Battery-March Financial Management became the largest institutional investor, and in 1992, Warren Buffett paid more than $330 million for a 15 percent stake in the firm, enough stock to equal the holdings of the Crown family. Rather than challenge management (as was his wont), Buffett gave the company his proxy to vote his share conditional upon Anders's tenure as chairman of General Dynamics (G.D. Proxy Statement Summer 1992, 6–7). Buffett was followed by Delaware Management, the FMR Corporation, and Fidelity Investments so that by 1996, institutional investors held approximately 60 percent of the company's stock (Hamilton 1996a).

Second, management pursued its own interests by maximizing shareholder value, as its own compensation was so tightly tied to share prices (Dial and Murphy 1995). In 1991, the company took one of the most aggressive paths to financial performance within (and outside) the defense industry. Anders proposed an executive compensation program in which the twenty-five top executives at the company would receive enormous cash bonuses for graduated improvements in stock price. Typical executive compensation plans, including General Dynamics' existing compensation package in 1990, tied managerial bonuses to some measure of *accounting performance*, such as the return on equity. However, Anders believed that to achieve rapid increases in stock price and to change the company's strategy and ingrained culture, he would have to try something more dramatic than stock options (options to buy shares directly from the company anytime within a specified period at a preset price) or accounting-based bonuses. The company would have to develop a bonus system that linked managerial rewards to *shareholder value creation*, as opposed to firm size, accounting profitability, or survival, as a way of making managerial goals more consonant with the short-term interests of shareholders.[10] Generous bonus packages would also help the company to attract and retain the best managers.

On May 1, 1991, shareholders approved a plan known as the "Gain/ Sharing Program" at their annual meeting. As Anders had proposed, the plan stipulated that the top twenty-five executives at General Dynamics would earn lump sum cash bonuses (not mere stock options) for improvements in stock price. One hundred and fifty upper-level executives would receive accelerated stock options and restricted stock grants, and 1,150 managers were eligible to participate in an "option exchange" program in which previously granted options could be exchanged for new ones at a lower exercise price (G.D. Proxy Statement 1991, 4). The most controversial element was the first, where the company's top twenty-five executives would receive a bonus equal to 100 percent of their base salary if stock prices closed at $10 above the February 1991 price for at least ten consecutive trading days. For each additional $10 jump in stock price, these executives would receive 200 percent of their base salaries. There was no limit to the bonuses as long as stock prices continued to jump.[11] The plan also included provisions to encourage lower-level employees to invest in the company's Savings and Stock Investment Plan, which covered approximately 62,000 employees.

A 1991 proxy statement noted that "(the Gain/Sharing Program) reflected the Board's recognition of the urgency and the importance to have a powerful motivation for a very few key personnel whose decisions, judgments, and actions could most directly produce the intended objective of shareholder value." The plan rewarded value creation and provided management with an incentive structure to accelerate the process of "rightsizing, repositioning and restructuring" Anders believed was necessary to survive and thrive in the changing defense marketplace.[12]

After discussions with the management consultants Booz, Allen, and Hamilton and an analysis of the corporation's procurement markets and competitive strengths, management announced that it would focus on the company's "core competencies" instead of growing or diversifying out of defense production. Anders's plan called for dividing the company into business areas and pushing decisionmaking authority downward to the few remaining unit managers. In the next four years, management

dismantled the once diversified and "General" conglomerate and embarked on a course of divestiture, reorganization, and downsizing. After
every surgery, the market rewarded stockholders by buoying stock price
and providing management with huge payoffs.

During this time, Anders was making speeches encouraging contractors to rid themselves of excess capacity through consolidation and divestiture in order to restore the health of the defense industrial base. He
likened the defense marketplace to a jungle where only the strong would
survive and urged weaker players to manage for cash and leave the jungle. He exhorted them:

> My challenge to you is for our entire industry to close down and write off
> truly excess capacity. . . . Step back, look at the field and start doing some se-
> rious buying, selling, or swapping of businesses to create the kind of Critical
> Mass each business needs to be a strong and reliable supporter of the future
> Defense Industrial Base. (Perry 1993, 56)

At the end of the year, General Dynamics moved aggressively to apply
these criteria to its own operations. The company went on a selling spree
starting in November of 1991, when it sold its Data Systems Unit for $184
million and shortly thereafter sold the company's commercial aircraft
subsidiary, Cessna, to Textron for $600 million. With these divestitures,
General Dynamics was able to "reduce liabilities, add substantially to
our financial strength, and eliminate a management diversion, thus allowing us to more clearly focus on core defense competencies" (G.D. Annual Report 1992, 2). Management determined that the company's core
competence was the design, integration, and production of major
weapons platforms. Anders said that if the company could not be number one or number two in a particular procurement area and if it could
not justify dedicated factories in these areas—what he called the "market
leadership" and "critical mass" criteria, respectively—the company
would sell these units to companies with whom they had a better strategic fit (G.D. Annual Report 1992, 4).

The four core businesses that passed both tests were tactical nuclear
submarines, military aircraft, armored vehicles, and space launch systems. The company announced a formal "plan of contraction" in its 1992
proxy statement and began to sell off divisions that did not meet its core
competence criteria (see Table 4.1). In May of 1992, the company sold its
Missile Systems business to Hughes Aircraft, a subsidiary of General Motors, for $450 million. In the fourth quarter of 1992, the Carlyle Group
purchased General Dynamics' Electronics Division for $52 million.

Speculation about whether or not General Dynamics was liquidating
itself out of existence surfaced in the second half of 1992. Warren Buffett

TABLE 4.1 General Dynamics' Divestitures and Acquisitions, 1991–1997

Disposition Date	Division	Buyer	Sale Proceeds ($million)
1991	Data Systems	Computer Science Corporation	$184
1992	Cessna	Textron	$600
1992	Missiles	Hughes Aircraft	$450
1992	Electronics	Carlyle Group	$52
1993	Military Aircraft	Lockheed	$1,525
1994	Space Launch Vehicles	Martin Marietta	$208
1994	Material Services		$50

Acquisition Date	Company	Seller	Purchase Price ($million)
1995	Bath Iron Works	Bath Iron Works	$292
1996	Teledyne Vehicles	Teledyne	$55
1997	Defense Systems & Armament Systems	Lockheed Martin	$450

SOURCE: General Dynamics Annual Reports, 1991–1997

had purchased 15 percent of the company's stock, displacing the Crown family as the majority shareholder of General Dynamics. Wall Street interpreted Buffett's interest in the company as evidence of an imminent breakup, and not of prospects for growth in the defense industry (Weisman 1992b). Buffett was known as a harbinger of liquidation, interested primarily in the breakup value of ailing corporations. Then, the company announced that it would sell its tactical military aircraft business to Lockheed. This announcement startled the financial community, because, earlier in 1992, the company had asserted that tactical military aircraft was one of its four core competencies. News of the sale incited rumors that the company was on a "liquidation path." Later in 1993, General Dynamics sold off the second of its core competencies, its space systems division, to Martin Marietta for $208 million. "General Dynamics is hardly a corporation anymore," said a former employee. "But a bunch of loosely aligned divisions with a tiny holding company on the top that manages tax issues" (Mintz 1994a, 1).

The company's two remaining core competencies, nuclear submarines and armored vehicles, held uncertain futures within the rapidly shrinking giant. Both were mature, stagnant markets where General Dynamics now held monopoly power. In 1992, the company closed one of its two tank-producing plants outside of Detroit. In 1993, Anders announced at the company's annual meeting that the "nuclear submarine business screams out for consolidation" (Weisman 1993b). The government was paying dearly to support the overheads of two fully outfitted shipyards that were forced into a vicious, cost-cutting competition because of the government's decision to keep both Electric Boat and Newport News afloat. That year General Dynamics began peddling Electric Boat to its rival's owner, Tenneco. The conglomerate spurned General Dynamics' offering price, judging it to be too steep given the rapid depreciation of the company's assets. In the fall of 1995, Tenneco sought federal funding for a proposed buyout of Electric Boat. Shortly thereafter, the Electric Boat division became the Electric Boat Company and went from being a division of General Dynamics to a wholly owned subsidiary. This move gave the shipyard additional autonomy and its own board of directors (Hamilton 1995d). General Dynamics also wanted to make the shipyard easier to sell in the event that it lost a major contract or faced certain bankruptcy. Said one observer, "[This move] essentially creates a perforated line which you can rip off" (Hamilton 1995c).[13]

During this time, Anders swiftly reduced capital expenditures and research and development spending. General Dynamics cut its capital spending faster and deeper than other defense contractors (Dial and Murphy, 1995).[14] In 1991, annual capital expenditures were $82 million compared to $321 million in the previous year. Research and development spending was cut in half from the $390 million allocated in 1990.

General Dynamics also reduced employment at a more rapid rate than other downsizing defense contractors. Through divestitures and layoffs, it cut its workforce by 76 percent between 1989 and 1994, from 102,200 to 24,200 (including cuts from divestitures) (U.S. GAO 1995). Shortly after the generous executive compensation plan was instituted, General Dynamics began laying off its employees faster than the rate at which the defense budget declined (Ellis 1991b). At its corporate headquarters in Virginia employment fell from 650 to 60 in 1994 alone.

The combined and almost immediate effects of the executive compensation plan and the subsequent divestitures and layoffs triggered an unprecedented rise in General Dynamics' stock price (see Figure 4.1). When the projected workforce reductions were announced in 1991, the market responded favorably; just five days later, the company's stock closed for

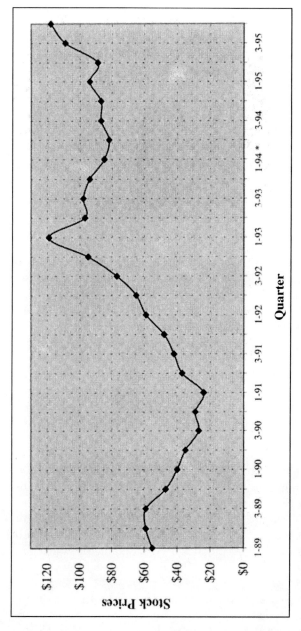

FIGURE 4.1 Quarterly Stock Prices of General Dynamics, 1989–1995

SOURCES: Jay Dial and Kevin Murphy, "Incentives, Downsizing and Value Creation at General Dynamics." *Journal of Financial Economics*, 1995, Appendix B. Bloomberg Financial Services.

*A stock split took place on April 1994, after which stock prices were doubled for consistency's sake.

the tenth consecutive trading day above the designated hurdle, triggering $5.1 million in Gain/Sharing bonuses to nineteen executives. In March of the same year, shortly after Anders introduced the Gain/Sharing plan, its stock jumped over 30 percent (from $22.75 to $30) in a few days based on the strength of "buy" recommendations from three Wall Street investment banks. These analysts commended Anders's "willingness to take dramatic actions," noting the new incentive plan, reductions in spending, and the possibility of stock repurchases to return cash to shareholders (Dial and Murphy 1995; *Investor Daily* 1991). The Gain/Sharing Program was in place from February 15, 1991, to December 3, 1991, during which time shareholders made over $980 million. Even after the Gain/Sharing Program was modified and the company reverted back to the practice of stock options, its stock price continued to rise.

With the funds from its sale of business units totaling almost $3 billion, General Dynamics was flush with cash. Part of the cash was used to retire approximately $600 million of debt, bringing the company's debt burden to a mere $38 million in December 1993. True to the company's promise, it returned much of the remaining cash to the shareholders through dividends, stock repurchases, and special distributions. General Dynamics increased annual dividends from $1 per share to $1.60 per share in 1992 and up to $2.40 per share in 1993. In June of 1992, the company repurchased some of its stock for $960 million (an average of $72.75 per share), and then paid a lump sum $20 per share distribution to shareholders. During 1993, the company returned $50 per share to shareholders through special distributions (Dial and Murphy 1995; Velocci 1994).

The effect of these distributions and the increases in share prices presented a $4.63 billion return to shareholders between 1991 and 1993, a three-year return of 440 percent (Dial and Murphy 1995). No other defense contractor, or commercial enterprise for that matter, approached General Dynamics' record returns. The Crown family alone made $740 million from General Dynamics stock between 1991 and 1993, and Warren Buffett made $280 million during this period. The employee-shareholders made $450 million. Even with these record returns and distributions, the company's remaining cash balance totaled over $600 million and grew to over $1.1 billion by 1995. James Mellor, who subsequently became chairman of General Dynamics in 1995, contentedly noted that the company "had the strongest balance sheet in the defense industry" (Philpott 1995).

Because executive compensation was tightly tied to stock price, the top executives of General Dynamics enjoyed phenomenal bonuses in the early 1990s. During the 1991 Gain/Sharing Program, bonuses for the nineteen participating executives totaled $22.3 million in one year. In addition to his Gain/Sharing bonus of $2.95 million, Anders exercised stock options in December 1992 worth over $21.2 million and his remaining options in 1993 for $14.9 million. He held $15.7 million of additional stock in 1993. By the end of 1993, Anders had received $67.6 million, which included his salaries, bonuses, restricted stock, and payments associated with the termination of his tenure with General Dynamics. Anders's overall incentives (including stock options and stock owned) represented about three times the average incentives for CEOs in the defense industry and twice the average incentives for CEOs in commercial industries (Dial and Murphy 1995; U.S. GAO 1995a). Even after Anders stepped down in 1993, his replacement, James Mellor, was the highest paid executive in the defense industry and had a salary much higher than that of his commercial counterparts (Hamilton 1995e). In addition, General Dynamics instituted a generous golden parachute plan for its executives in 1996. The company announced that it would pay almost $20 million to its top five executives if the contractor were acquired, and that it would pay twenty-two key executives a multiple of their base salary and a large bonus (G.D. Proxy Statement 1996, 3).

As early as 1991, the press renamed the company "Generous" Dynamics and sarcastically noted how the proposed "peace dividend" had ended up in shareholders' and executives' pockets (Ellis 1991b). Rather than reinvest the proceeds from its sales in the company or make acquisitions, General Dynamics distributed them to managers and shareholders. The prospect of these windfall gains provided the necessary incentive to consolidate into two mature, low-growth markets—tanks and submarines. Nonetheless, the increase in executive salaries and incentives during a time of cutbacks and layoffs prompted a Congressional inquiry into the salaries and benefits packages of executives in the defense industry in general (U.S. GAO 1995a).[15]

The company defended the salaries by insisting that all but a fraction had come out of the company's newly created wealth. Company spokespeople justified the huge salaries and executive bonuses on the grounds that shareholders "paid" the overwhelming portion of this compensation and that the company's management team had managed the company very successfully through the downturn in defense spending. More suspicions would have been aroused about the executive compensation packages had not the company's shareholders done so well. A spokeswoman summed up General Dynamics' distributional philosophy:

> At most companies the issue is that compensation increases while shareholders suffer with declining returns. However, at General Dynamics we've returned almost $5 billion in cash back to the shareholders since 1991 when the company was near financial ruin. If the shareholders don't win, then management doesn't either. (Hamilton 1995e)

Senior managers are motivated by a complex set of overlapping interests. While their interests may be consistent with those of shareholders, they are fundamentally related to maintaining and increasing their own compensation. This is the general problem of moral hazard that the corporate governance literature addresses (Easterbrook and Fischel 1991). Managers are vested with fiduciary duties to shareholders in order to guard against self-dealing. However, when both share prices and executive compensation increase and the company is flush with cash, the problem of self-dealing is assumed to go away. The genius of General Dynamics' strategy was that it was able to serve *both* management's interests and those of their shareholders. Managers saw no harm in appropriating a relatively small proportion of total shareholder returns; after all, many insisted, they were responsible for creating these gains in the first place. Corporate law does not judge whether or not the amount of executive compensation (or the number of stock options) is excessive, justified, or fair, as long as there is a concurrent increase in share price.

Nonetheless, the federal government did initially object to the highly publicized salaries of General Dynamics' executives. The Gain/Sharing Program of 1991 upset and embarrassed many of the Pentagon brass, because executives at one of its prime contractors were rewarding themselves with huge bonuses—at a time when the company was charging more for its products and the services were cutting or reducing most of their programs (Ellis 1991a). Under the Federal Acquisition Regulations (FAR), contractors may claim up to $250,000 of the chief executive's compensation as an allowable cost, but the regulations have little to say about stock options and bonuses. In a letter to CEO Anders dated April 18, 1991, the Pentagon warned that it did not want the taxpayers to foot the bill for General Dynamics' generous bonuses. The letter stated, "Should you choose to bill the enhanced compensation to government contracts, the government will take appropriate action to withhold from billings and subsequently disallow any and all excessive compensation" (Ellis 1991a). A top-level meeting of Department of Defense officials was held in 1991 to discuss the bonuses, which spurred a probe of General Dynamics' pay policy. No conclusive evidence, however, was found to charge the company with any wrongdoing.

Third, and least persuasively, Anders and his team focused on shareholders because, they argued, shareholders were the corporate constituency best equipped to decide the future of the defense industrial base. Anders's speeches evoked themes of industrial democracy and reciprocity to justify his shareholder-oriented adjustment strategy. He regarded shareholders, not the government, as the only real arbiter of the public good. Returning cash to shareholders was the most efficient means of "converting" excess defense capacity and redeploying these assets to other growth segments of the economy (General Dynamics 1993). Anders stated, "As an American, I'd like to see money invested in the right places. Who can decide how to reinvest in America? The answer is the American people. Give money back to shareholders and let them decide what the next best thing for America is" (Perry 1993, 57). With these kinds of statements, Anders coyly indicated his suspicions of any state-mandated diversification policy.

Sticking to Its Knitting

General Dynamics' management also spoke out publicly against defense diversification. In September of 1991 Anders made a speech in which he announced for the first time that the company would not buy or create nondefense businesses. Not only did he vow not to lead his company down this path, but he ridiculed the very notion, citing a study conducted for the company by the consulting firm McKinsey and Co. that showed an 80 percent failure rate for nondefense acquisitions by defense contractors. In the same breath, Anders predicted that the company's cash flow would be in excess of the firm's current investment needs and suggested a record return of the excess cash to shareholders. These announcements, dubbed by *The Washington Post* as the "$1.6 million speech," caused the company's stock to rocket up for ten consecutive days and gave those executives participating in the Gain/Sharing Program a $12.6 million bonus (McCartney 1991a).

There were many reasons for the company's adamant refusal to explore commercial production opportunities. Most significant, the company assumed that its stockholders did not favor defense diversification because it would undoubtedly involve a redeployment of investment capital into labor and other assets, investments that were likely to have only long-term and diffuse payoffs. These long-term, intangible returns were likely to be misjudged and misunderstood by the stock market and hence undervalued. The company was organizationally reconfigured to fixate on shareholder value and would not consider any new investment project that could not guarantee high returns. Indeed, General Dynamics' stockholders, at the urging of management, overwhelmingly defeated a resolution in 1993 that would have required the company to report its efforts to prepare General Dynamics workers and plants for the post–Cold War era (G.D. Proxy Statement 1993, 5). Many analysts attributed the company's popularity with shareholders to its strong refusal to diversify out of defense work and its core competencies. Management consultants argued that "focused" firms generate greater shareholder returns (Berger and Ofek 1996; Denis et al. 1997). Dial and Murphy (1995, 280) note that "an indicator of Anders' strategy of creating shareholder value is the fact that early on Anders pledged not to pursue diversification into non-defense industry."[16]

Part of Anders's strategic plan for the company included more stringent standards of risk and return for new investments. General Dynamics told its shareholders that the company would consider selling or merging with competitors to remain in core businesses, but that diversification was too risky a venture to be profitable in the near future (G.D. Annual Report 1993, 2). Developing new products would certainly involve more risk than reducing inventory or increasing control over working capital while staying in the defense market. In order to compete with a single $1.5 to $2.5 billion submarine contract and a guaranteed profit margin, the company would have to produce new products in mass quantities—a challenge management was not ready to take. Moreover, the company's antiquated asset base in both tank and submarine production was not particularly well suited for commercial production. "It's not that we don't want to or wish to diversify. It's just not very practical," said James Turner, general manager of Electric Boat (Nagy 1994).

Anders noted that "conversion is a formula for disaster. . . . If you feel you are on a sinking ship, diversification may seem attractive despite the risks. But I think we should all pay close attention to the history on this issue" (1991, 11). The irony is that General Dynamics' history with diversification had produced quite a few successes. The company had manufactured commercial ships, tugboats, and ferries until after the Vietnam War. After World War II, Electric Boat even built bowling pin resetters and transferred its steel processing skills to a number of large, local infrastructure projects, including bridges on the Merritt Parkway.

At the end of the Cold War, the company received thousands of inquiries and conversion project ideas from engineers and subcontractors around the country (former employee of Electric Boat, interview by author, Summer 1996). Electric Boat opened an Office of Business Development in March of 1992 to explore some of these possibilities. During its brief history (the office was closed in March of 1995), a staff of twenty-four engineers and marketing specialists examined diversification possibilities and worked to establish three new product lines. The shipyard received a contract from the city of Boston in 1991 to manufacture egg-shaped sludge tanks that were intended to float in Boston Harbor. One and a half years into the project, it became apparent that the tanks were not going to be profitable. "We've spent over $3 million of our own money (on diversification) . . . and we managed to lose $4 million" complained Donald Norman, Electric Boat's vice president for human resources (*Norwich Bulletin*, March 13, 1994, 1). The company probably lost money on the sewerage digester tanks because its initial cost and schedule estimates were too low, and the company was unfamiliar with nondefense accounting practices (former employee of Electric Boat, interview by author, Fall 1996).

The company briefly pursued other projects. General Dynamics began looking for investors to underwrite a partnership with Westinghouse Electric to build barge-mounted power stations for roving service in the islands of the Caribbean Sea and other developing regions with volatile energy demands (interview by author, Summer 1996). Electric Boat designed and fabricated racks for storing spent fuel rods from the Maine Yankee nuclear power plant in Wiscasset, Maine, and briefly considered a joint venture with a Finnish company, Wartsila Diesel International, to build large marine diesel engines for sealift ships. The company also built liquefied natural gas tanks at its facility in Charleston, South Carolina, and barged them up to Groton to save on labor costs.

The Massachusetts sewerage tank experiment, however, was the flagship diversification project for the company. When it failed, General Dynamics' support for future diversification projects dried up. One former employee of the Office of Business Development noted after the fact, "You just can't expect to manage a start-up and downsize at the same time" (interview by author, Fall 1997). The unions, selected management at Electric Boat, and local community organizations continued to urge Electric Boat to use its cash flow to diversify. They suggested that the company retrain its workforce to produce nondefense products or acquire nondefense businesses. In 1992, Connecticut economic development officials suggested that proffered state money, combined with Electric Boat's own investments, could create or preserve 1,500 to 2,000 jobs over the following five years. In 1993 the states of Connecticut and Rhode Island each awarded Electric Boat $1 million in matching grants to perform marketing and engineering studies to explore nondefense market opportunities in the fields of marine power, marine transportation systems, and industrial fabrication. Less than a year after receiving the awards, however, the submarine builder suspended its efforts to diversify and agreed to return the $2 million in state matching funds (Weisman 1993a). Corporate officials also pledged that the company would not take advantage of any federal adjustment programs.

Although Electric Boat may have earnestly tried to find new markets, its corporate parent never disguised its contempt for what it considered wasteful adventures outside of defense work. The company chose instead to pursue the few remaining submarine and tank contracts and reorganize excess capacity in order to weather the cutbacks. Also, with almost 100 percent of the facility's resources dedicated to the submarine program, Electric Boat lacked the Navy's support for diversification (employee of Office of Supervisor of Shipbuilding, interview by author, 1996). The Navy wanted to keep its contractors on a short leash—a holdover from the Admiral era, in which Hyman Rickover controlled every facet of the nuclear submarine progam—and was concerned that if the company did anything other than build submarines, it would not be completely devoted to its main customer.

As if to confirm the company's commitment to defense markets, General Dynamics strayed from its divestiture strategy to acquire the Bath Iron Works in Maine in the summer of 1995. The Bath shipyard is one of the two yards that build the Arleigh Burke–class destroyers (DDG-51), the Navy's newest generation of surface ships. The company was owned by Prudential Securities, which had financed the yard's $580 million buyout in 1986. With a $1 billion cash reserve, General Dynamics easily met the asking price of $300 million without any outside financing (Hamilton 1995g). The acquisition added more than $2 billion to General Dynamics' backlog. At the time of its purchase, Bath employed 8,000 people, but the yard had been facing cutbacks from a declining backlog of work. General Dynamics vowed to honor all preexisting labor agreements, including an agreement that placed a two-year moratorium on layoffs (which expired in 1996).

Why did General Dynamics choose to purchase another shipyard, let alone an old facility that analysts considered the weakest of the six remaining shipyards?[17] Although Bath's physical assets were valued at zero, General Dynamics was able to purchase an $800 million income stream for a very small amount of money (interview by author, Fall 1996). Bath had been unable to achieve satisfactory profit levels after the Cold War, primarily because of its unwieldy debt burden. With an injection of $300 million in cash, much of that debt load was erased, and General Dynamics believed that, with proper restructuring and new destroyer contracts, the shipyard could regain its profitability.[18] Some observers speculated that purchasing the yard would strengthen Electric Boat's position on Capitol Hill because key lawmakers, such as former Maine senator and current Secretary of Defense William Cohen, would be inclined to protect the company's contracts (former employee, local office of Sam Gejdenson [D.-CT], interview by author, Fall 1996).

Directors and analysts touted the potential operating efficiencies that Electric Boat would enjoy with the purchase of the shipyard. Perhaps, some speculated, the company would make bulk purchases of steel or use one machine shop to do tooling on both ships and submarines (Hamilton 1995g). At the 1995 annual meeting, General Dynamics chairman James Mellor noted that government agencies were encouraging consolidation with the quick approval of mergers because the Pentagon saw financial restructuring as the key to keeping weapons systems affordable (G.D. Annual Report 1995). The companies soon discovered that most of the components for Electric Boat's nuclear-powered submarines were considerably different from those used in Bath's gas turbine-powered ships. To date, cost efficiencies have not clearly been achieved because of the incompatibility of their manufacturing processes, and no new work has been created at Electric Boat facility because of the purchase. Nonetheless, the market responded favorably to the news of the purchase, and General Dynamics moved into the position of fourth (from sixth the previous year) largest defense contractor in the country in 1995 (Kaplan 1995a; Hamilton 1995f). The company went on to purchase Teledyne Vehicles and Lockheed Martin's tank business in 1996 and 1997, respectively.

Reorganizing Production at Electric Boat

In addition to changing the corporate form through divestitures and acquisitions, General Dynamics initiated a strategy of in situ restructuring to streamline operations at its divisions. The Electric Boat plant was the most likely target; its propensity for cost overruns, poor labor relations, and scheduling delays was exacerbated by the rapidly shrinking backlog of submarine orders. The company set about reducing the overall capacity of the shipyard so that it would be better calibrated with the falling demand for submarines. Electric Boat also engaged in heightened price competition with its rival, Newport News, forcing down overhead and labor costs through downsizing, productivity measures, outsourcing, and union concessions. Although all divisions of General Dynamics experienced mass layoffs, the situation at Electric Boat most captured popular attention. Photos of blue-collar workers streaming out of the shipyard gate with hard hats and lunch boxes appeared in the pages of local and national newspapers as proof that the costs of ending the Cold War would be great for some. Articles and publicly commissioned studies offered bleak pictures of the region's future (Arthur D. Little 1993; Midwest Center for Labor Research 1996; Connecticut Center for Economic Analysis 1993).

General Dynamics hired consultants Booz, Allen, and Hamilton to help it turn the Electric Boat shipyard into a leaner and more efficient company. Several departments were eliminated, along with layers of management and thousands of hourly workers. In 1989 Electric Boat employed close to 22,000 people, but following some of the steepest cuts in 1996 and 1997, only one-third remained. In 1998, the Groton yard employed under 6,000 workers, and employment at its Quonset hull fabrication yard (in nearby Rhode Island) dropped from 3,000 in 1996 to close to 1,000 in 1998. "Although actions like these are unfortunate," said general manager James Turner, "they're a continuation of what the division must do in the face of declining workloads. We don't have any other option" (quoted in Carbone 1993). The layoffs, management insisted, were purely "workload-driven," although it admitted that deciding how many workers were needed to maintain a full service shipyard capable of building and maintaining submarines was "not an exact science" (employee of Electric Boat, interview by author, Summer 1996). The company proudly announced that it was making smaller, but more frequent, cuts than in the past and giving advance notice to the workers and community (Nagy 1994).

Management made other organizational changes at the shipyard to enhance the productivity of workers and their ability to compete with Newport News. The company announced that it wanted to make Electric Boat into a "flatter organization with less oversight and more individual responsibility" (Nagy 1994). As many middle management layers were eliminated, most of their former responsibilities devolved to first-line supervisors.[19] General manager Turner said, "The new structure will empower our employees, providing them with the responsibility and the authority they need to perform more effectively" (Nagy 1994).

Whether this form of job enlargement empowered workers or simply overextended them, the company actively sought to work with less to achieve more. Management reconfigured labor-management relations at the shipyard when the main bargaining unit, the Metal Trades Council, was weakened by declining membership and the threat of no new work. In 1988 the Metal Trades Council had gone on strike for 103 days to press their demands for higher pay, but in the early 1990s the unions were unable to employ such powerful leverage. Management regained the upper hand with threats of layoffs, the dreaded "exit scenario," and plant closure (member of Metal Trades Council, interview by author, Summer 1996).[20] The unions settled for more modest goals; in the 1980s they fought for pay increases and better terms of employment, but in the 1990s, they were primarily concerned with the protection of existing seniority structures, retirement, and benefits packages (Kaplan 1995b).

The Metal Trades Council fought an uphill battle simply to secure these baseline demands. Management cut benefits by 59 percent between 1993 and 1998 in order to meet new cost projections set by General Dynamics. As one of Electric Boat's highest and fastest-growing overhead costs, the topic of benefits had always been at the top of the shipyard's reform agenda. Management insisted that workers receive lump sum "awards" instead of graduated raises in wages. This change was implemented so that the company could hold down the cost of benefits, which were tied to the base-wage rates (Hamilton 1995i). In 1995 the union agreed to the change, although a similar demand in 1988 had prompted a bitter strike and protests where yard workers shouted angrily, "Dump the lump!" (member of Metal Trades Council, interview by author, Summer 1996). In lieu of pay raises between 1995 and 1998, union members received a $1,000 bonus payable in 1995 and a $500 bonus payable in July of 1996. Starting in 1991, the company reduced its contributions to health and dental benefits, shifting these costs to the employees and imposing higher deductibles. In addition, the company's tuition reimbursement program, which had allowed workers to take classes to enhance their job-related skills, was abolished in July of 1995.

Other productivity-enhancing policies were introduced into the yard in the early 1990s. The 1991 collective bargaining agreement gave the company the right to reassign workers within their trades, loosening the grip of restrictive contract language governing job tasks and increasing task flexibility. Electric Boat instituted a major change in February of 1992 whereby workers were no longer compensated for the first five hours of overtime no matter how many hours they worked a week.[21] Workers were afraid to complain about the change because, in the words of one employee, "It's very clear if you don't do it, you can expect to be on top of the next round of layoffs" (Hayden 1994b). As of January 1995, the amount of maximum accrued vacation time was reduced from two years to one, and paid personal time was eliminated (Hayden 1994a). The company also eliminated paid leave for certain holidays and began offering "prizes" to white-collar workers who did not use their sick days (Hamilton 1996b).[22]

Management threatened to initiate additional layoffs if the yard was not cost-competitive with Newport News. When workers at the Newport News shipyard ratified a contract that cut vacation days by 10 percent and offered bonuses in lieu of raises, management increased the pressure on Electric Boat workers to ratify a similarly "realistic" contract (Hamilton 1995h). Management was also concerned about how the Navy perceived labor relations at the yard. Before the third Seawolf contract was awarded to Electric Boat, management warned workers that any cost increases or delays for the ships already under construction could jeopardize any future funding. Signing collective bargaining agreements with little labor struggle, said one official, would "send a good message to the Navy and to Congress that we have a stable, energetic workforce" (Hamilton 1995h).

After 1991, Electric Boat began shifting production interregionally to adapt to the declining submarine market. The company transferred more work to its nonunion yard in Quonset, Rhode Island. Quonset was outfitted with more modern process technologies than Electric Boat, and the company claimed that it needed to increase the return on that capital investment. Electric Boat also wanted to avoid the union work rules and higher wages by performing more work at Quonset (former employee of Electric Boat, interview by author, Summer 1996).[23] Although the company decided to continue operating the Quonset facility, it shut down other operations, such as its engineering office in Tampa, Florida (closed in 1992), and its Charleston, South Carolina, steel fabrication plant (closed in 1994). It also shut down a prototype nuclear reactor plant in West Milton, New York, which employed 600 in 1994. Management's goal was to cut facilities by 55 percent between 1993 and 1998.

The regional economy in which laid-off Electric Boat workers found themselves had changed dramatically since the late 1980s. The first notable transformation was the growth of the service industry and the concurrent decline of manufacturing in New London County, the region in which the Groton shipyard was located. Goods-producing employment in the county declined by 22 percent between 1989 and 1995, while service-producing employment increased by 12.5 percent. Second, fewer defense jobs were available after the layoffs at all Connecticut prime contractors, the demise of local subcontractors, and the realignment of the Naval Laboratory and Submarine Base. In 1988, defense-related industries provided 116,000 jobs in Connecticut. By 1995, this number had fallen by over 20 percent to 74,000—the second highest defense-related job loss in the country, behind only Virginia (Robinson 1996). The defense drawdown threw Connecticut into a bitter recession from 1989 to 1992. The city of New London, home to many Electric Boat workers, was especially hard-hit; its unemployment rate in 1992 was 9.5 percent compared to the state's average at 7.3 percent.

The region's long-term dependence on Electric Boat and the relatively high costs for energy and worker's compensation had been disincentives for local business development. Compared to the Hartford aerospace complex, where vertically disintegrated tool and die and machine shops clustered close to prime contractors like Pratt & Whitney, the nuclear submarine complex never developed the same healthy agglomeration of small subcontractors. New London County was more dependent on a single company and less diversified than the other defense-dependent areas in Fairfield and Hartford counties. Electric Boat did develop important backward linkages to approximately thirty-five local subcontractors who supplied the shipyard with components and services. With the decline in procurement funding and a vanishing backlog of submarine orders, however, Electric Boat and the Navy severed ties to these few subcontractors in their efforts to find the cheapest products. For example, the Navy took a subcontract for nuclear reactor cores away from United Nuclear in Montville, Connecticut, and gave it to Babcock and Wilcox in Lynchburg, Virginia. United Nuclear promptly went out of business in 1992. Noted one observer,

> As the volume [of submarines] goes down and budgets get cut, Electric Boat has less and less commitment to local suppliers. When they were flush, they

could support all of them. But when they're under cost pressures to find the cheapest guy and he happens to be in Arizona, they'll go with him. Electric Boat's vendor base stretches across forty-four states; it hasn't widened since 1989, but the local ones who survived because of Electric Boat's business are now falling out of the race. (manager of subcontractor to Electric Boat, interview by author, Summer 1996)

Electric Boat's local vendors and other small businesses in the area experienced the pinch as the shipyard made fewer purchases. Workers at those small firms that supplied janitorial supplies, office equipment, parts, and other services for Electric Boat were laid off, as well as "downstream" workers employed by businesses that sold goods and services to former Electric Boat workers. Laid-off workers tend to postpone purchasing "big ticket" items, like homes and automobiles, and forgo services outside the home. A study by the Midwest Center for Labor Research estimated that in addition to the 4,000 workers laid off from Electric Boat between 1994 and 1996, 1,635 other jobs disappeared in the region because of the "ripple" or multiplier effects of the loss of these shipyard jobs (MCLR 1996).

Average manufacturing wages in the county showed some subdued growth between 1989 and 1993, which may have resulted from the total loss of manufacturing employees or from an increased workweek (from 40 hours in 1990 to 41.7 in 1992). However, the 1.8 percent increase in factory production wages between 1989 and 1992 was well below the Department of Labor's Urban Consumer Price Index of 3.1, suggesting that wages rose more slowly than inflation during this period (Connecticut Department of Labor 1993). Most manufacturing workers experienced a decline in the standard of living, as competition for new jobs drove wages down. Between 1988 and 1994, New London County's per capita personal income was consistently lower than that of Connecticut as a whole.

In 1992, the region experienced a dramatic change of course that no one had predicted. New London County became a tourism hub after the opening of Connecticut's first high stakes bingo and casino complex by the Mashantucket Pequot Indians in Ledyard in February of 1992. Called the Foxwoods Resort Casino, the complex included two hotels, sixteen restaurants, a theater, and a gambling space of over 193,753 square feet. It is currently the largest casino (in terms of area) in the western hemisphere. Reflecting the "dawning" of southeastern Connecticut's service-based economy, the Foxwoods complex and the new Mohegan Sun casino (opened in October of 1996) created over 15,000 jobs in four years.[24] In 1989, 11,480 county jobs were directly and indirectly attributable to the tourism industry, whereas by 1995 this number had more than doubled.

Hiring at the new casinos helped to cushion the defense job cuts at Electric Boat to some extent. Although regional employment indicators show that, in the aggregate, more new jobs were created than old jobs lost, few of the laid-off welders and pipefitters from Electric Boat found work as blackjack dealers and car attendants at the casinos. The local transition center estimated that less than 10 percent of laid-off workers found employment at the casinos (employee of Private Industry Council, interview by author, Summer 1996). Another study found that only 300 of the 10,000 employees at Foxwoods had ever worked at Electric Boat (Peppard 1995). Those who did find employment at the casinos experienced a decline in wages. Casino workers earned 25 to 40 percent less than the $14.74 or so hourly wages that the shipyard paid in 1993.[25] Many workers returned to their home states or left Connecticut in search of other manufacturing work. On a brighter side, the Pequots began manufacturing high-speed ferries in New London to shuttle visitors from Long Island and New York City to the casino complex. The Pequot River Shipworks employed 100 shipbuilders in 1996—most of whom were former Electric Boat employees.

The financial machinations that occurred in the intermediate space between the halls of the Pentagon and the military-industrial complex determined the fate of many other corporate stakeholders, not just shareholders. Wall Street watched with great interest as General Dynamics' defense markets dried up. It applauded when the company sold off its divisions and when layoffs were announced, rewarding "shrewd" managerial decisions with higher stock prices, which meant record bonuses. The corporation's adjustment strategy was decidedly shareholder-oriented, but because shareholders are not spatially concentrated or embedded, the local landscape did not reflect the outcome of its ingenious strategy: the stunning balance sheets of the early 1990s. Instead the local outcome was one of dislocation and hardship.

Within the Purview of the Law

There is nothing unusual about publicly held corporations focusing on increasing shareholder value. Given the power and influence of a growing cadre of activist, value-oriented shareholders and the increase in proxy fights and hostile takeovers, managers must do everything in their power to assure investors that they are responsive to shareholders' concerns. The challenge for a corporation is convincing investors of this commitment. With a proven track record and good accountants, managers can emphasize the company's good performance. Managers can demonstrate how they have increased earnings and cut costs and overhead. They can also meet personally with shareholder groups and solicit their advice. They can hint about stock repurchases to return cash to shareholders, or make specific announcements about the possibility of such actions. The practice of rewarding management with stock options also demonstrates a company's commitment to shareholders by further riveting management's attention to short-term returns.

General Dynamics not only took advantage of each of these signaling mechanisms; it pushed them to the limit of acceptable legal behavior. By partially liquidating, this most defense-dependent contractor was able to generate an exorbitant amount of cash, which it subsequently allocated to shareholders and top management. General Dynamics did not adjust to changed market conditions in a vacuum, but developed its strategy within an inherited framework of corporate governance rules and financial institutions. Restructuring, after all, involves judgments about the relative value of different stakeholders' claims, the proper boundaries of corporate membership, and the relationship between economic imperatives and social obligations (Clark 1993). This framework guided senior management at General Dynamics and allowed it to privilege the interests of shareholders above those of all other corporate constituencies without ever actually breaking the law. What looked like avarice and opportunism—shareholders and senior management making record returns in a declining government market—fell squarely within the bounds of the laws governing corporate obligations, because the laws themselves privilege profit making and financial imperatives over loosely defined social obligations.

The layoffs at General Dynamics' many plants did not generally violate the unions' collective bargaining contracts, nor did they violate the National Labor Relations Act (NLRA), the Worker Adjustment and Retraining Notification Act (WARN), or the Employee Retirement Income Security Act (ERISA) governing pension funds.[26] In the 1990s, General Dynamics generally honored its obligations and liabilities under existing contracts with the government, existing collective bargaining agreements with its workers, and contracts with vendors. General Dynamics complied with the federal regulations governing executive compensation, and, at least during the early 1990s, the acquisition regulations governing which costs could and could not be passed on to the government. If specific terms were not in the actual contract or regulated by the statutory limitations, however, management had the authority to act in its own interests and the interests of its shareholders. Under the dominant system of corporate governance in the United States, General Dynamics had no legal obligation to share any of its record returns with the state, taxpayers, local communities, or workers.

In general, however, legal rules are signposts for corporate behavior. They do not necessarily represent what is most equitable or fair, but rather mark out, in very broad terms, what is legitimate conduct. Often that conduct, even when it is encouraged in an economy based on the ideology of free enterprise, is inequitable or morally questionable (Kadish 1964, 436; Selznick 1992). The case of General Dynamics demonstrates just how large a role the law plays in validating the inequitable distribution of risks and returns of corporate adjustment.

Notes

1. A backlog reflects current orders for future deliveries, and it allows defense firms to maintain their levels of production with only small declines in employment and investment for years even after actual orders decline.

2. The law requires full funding of ship programs. Once Congress authorizes and appropriates funds, they tend to be relatively secure—unless, of course, the executive branch intervenes.

3. There was some suspicion that Clinton's approval of the third Seawolf reflected his gratitude to Connecticut senators Joseph Lieberman and Christopher Dodd for their Congressional support.

4. In 1991, Newport News set a new precedent by challenging the award of the second Seawolf contract to Electric Boat in court (*Defense Daily*, May 31, 1991). Electric Boat was able to underbid Newport News by about $80 million because it had already won the first Seawolf contract and therefore had the cost and learning curve advantage in the program. Newport News argued that the Navy had not considered industrial base concerns in awarding the contract but took only cost and technical information into account. A federal judge issued an injunction, required the Navy to rebid the contract, and temporarily blocked construction on the ship (Weisman and Fitzgerald 1991).

5. Most of the decline was due to a $578 million net loss in 1990 (on $10.2 billion in sales) from its troubled A-12 aircraft program.

6. "Price-to-book value" is a measure that compares the stock price to the net value of a company's assets. It is used as a guide in determining underpriced or overpriced stocks and is an indication of the ultimate value of securities in the case of a liquidation.

7. After a merger agreement gave Crown preferred stock in the company, General Dynamics was obliged to pay Crown about $1.8 million annually on his initial holdings. When Crown refused to convert his preferred stock to common stock, General Dynamics pressured Crown into selling out his preferred stock for cash. The corporation was forced into $40 million of debt in order to repurchase the stock and had to dig into its working capital to pay the millionaire (Goodwin 1985).

8. A copy of this speech, entitled "Rationalizing America's Defense Industry: Renewing Investor Support for the Defense Industrial Base and Safeguarding National Security," was included in the company's 1991 annual report to shareholders.

9. In 1990, defense stocks were trading at price-earnings multiples of no more than eight times earnings—a fifty percent discount to the average Standard and

Poor's 500 multiple (*Aerospace Daily*, March 14, 1990). It seems reasonable to argue that defense stocks may actually be less risky for investors because there is an assured market, a guaranteed cash flow, and prompt payments from the government.

10. The 1991 proxy statement noted that the plan makes "employees' interests more aligned to those of shareholders, and [rewards] them accordingly for increases in the price of the corporation's stock, that is, improved shareholder value." Anders told shareholders he wanted to make the management team "your partners" through shared interests and shared rewards.

11. The program was modified and then expired on December 1991.

12. Management scholars believe that "pay-for-performance" incentives are particularly important in declining industries, with little potential for future growth. Otherwise managers will hold on to their old ways and old loyalties (see Jensen and Murphy 1990).

13. Becoming a wholly owned subsidiary can insulate each unit of a conglomerate from the potential financial liabilities of the other. If one unit goes bankrupt, it might not affect the assets of the other. This way General Dynamics could reduce its total financial liabilities in a sector where there was a considerable amount of risk.

14. The ratio of capital expenditures to depreciation expresses the rate at which a company invests in its capital stock. Ratios exceeding 100 percent indicate that a firm is investing more than it needs to replace depreciating assets, whereas ratios of less than 100 percent indicate that the firm is not fully replacing depreciating assets. The average ratio among eight prime defense contractors fell from 108 percent in 1989 to 79 percent in 1992, but General Dynamics cut its capital spending faster and deeper than other contractors, plummeting to just over 16 percent in 1992 (Dial and Murphy 1995, 296).

15. The GAO (1995a) found that average pay for defense contractor executives increased 34 percent between 1989 and 1994. The value of stock options increased from $918,000 in 1989 to $26 million in 1994.

16. Management may also have noted that Lockheed's governance troubles and proxy fights began when investor Harold Simmons opposed the company's efforts to diversify.

17. It is unusual for shipyards to purchase other shipyards; this phenomenon is more prevalent in the aerospace sector.

18. Bath had engaged in some diversification efforts, but these efforts were stymied by General Dynamics' purchase of the yard. The company had been seeking a $100 million cash infusion to move into commercial shipbuilding, having studied shipbuilding in Japan and Finland (manager at Bath Iron Works, interview by author, Summer 1994).

19. By tripling the ratio of first-line supervisors to middle managers, the company hoped to "increase efficiency and reduce costs by pushing down decision-making to the level of first-line supervision" (Hamilton 1995k).

20. Hostility ran so deep during the 1980s that workers booed and heckled James Turner at a rally in 1989 when he announced that Electric Boat had won the first Seawolf contract (interview by author, Summer 1996).

21. The U.S. Department of Labor began conducting an investigation to confirm that Electric Boat was complying with the Fair Labor Standards Act, the fed-

eral statute covering wages and hours. Under the law there is no limit of hours that employees are required to work, but hourly employees must be paid time and a half for any time worked over forty hours per week. Some of the yard employees had quasi-managerial positions and may have been exempt from the overtime requirement.

22. Blue-collar workers were not eligible for these prizes because of union rules.

23. Electric Boat originally manufactured only the submarine hulls at the Quonset facility and then barged them to Groton, where the components were added. Since 1990 the company has begun loading the hull with components at Quonset so that most of the floors, equipment, and wiring are installed before the submarine reaches Groton.

24. In 1995, 10,136 people were employed at Foxwoods, and 5,000 at the Mohegan Sun Resort in 1996.

25. The casinos have no union, although there is an employee group council to voice workers' concerns.

26. The layoffs at General Dynamics' aircraft manufacturing plants in Tulsa and Fort Worth following the A-12 cancellation in 1991 *did* lead to a suit under WARN. WARN requires a business that employs more than 100 workers to provide at least sixty days' written notice before a "plant closing" or a "mass layoff" (29 U.S.C. @ 2101-02).

5

Redistributing Risks and Rents
at General Dynamics

Executives of defense companies, like senior managers at any corporation, have discretionary power to allocate surplus revenues. They have certain contractual commitments that they must honor, perhaps remunerating a supplier for the delivery of a component or paying wages to their employees, but beyond these explicit obligations, upper-level managers have scope for independent action regarding the use of residual profits (Clark 1993). They may choose to reinvest their profits in the corporation, expecting that a facility expansion or the purchase of new machinery will help achieve economies of scale or improve productivity and boost earnings. In the case of defense production, such a strategy might deploy assets, technology, and labor into new nondefense product lines. Reinvesting profits may lower the price of their products, ingratiating the company with the federal government and taxpayers. Such a strategy might help to chip away at the federal deficit defense spending created in the first place. Alternatively, profits can be used to retire debt so that interest payments will not be a drag on earnings. Management may also return the excess cash to their shareholders in the form of dividends or stock repurchases. Despite the fact that each of these choices has a different effect on different constituencies of the corporation (i.e., employees, shareholders, the state), the American system of corporate regulation makes minimal attempts to control management's distributional priorities, apart from protecting existing contracts and stressing fiduciary obligations. Such decisions are close to the core of entrepreneurial control, and both corporate and labor law confine them to the domain of management alone.

When General Dynamics distributed its record profits to shareholders, Wall Street swooned. Analysts argued that the returns reflected overall "efficiency gains" to society from diverting capital and labor to more highly valued uses (Dial and Murphy 1995; *Investor Daily* 1991). Likewise, the company made few rhetorical distinctions between what was best for itself and what was best for the public interest. Throughout the twentieth century, defense contractors have tried to convince Congress and the voting public that their success or failure in meeting their own financial goals has a strong correlation to the government's success in meeting its own objectives and, by association, societal ends.

But it could also be argued that the record returns and shareholder gains came at the expense of other stakeholders who, since the beginning of the century, had been making investments in the contractor. Indeed organized labor, local governments, and certain federal agencies interpreted the stock price increases and the phenomenal give-backs to shareholders not as the improved utilization of resources, but as a wealth transfer from other parties that had economic relationships with the corporation (giving the shareholders "redistributional gains"). In other words, the highly profitable General Dynamics may have reaped phenomenal returns not because it was innovative and efficient, but because it appropriated rents from other stakeholders. The company was able to both raise prices and cut costs by shedding labor and fixed capital. Some even went so far as to accuse the contractor of cutting quality. Moreover, shareholders did not entirely deserve such gains. They were buffered from risks because of General Dynamics' oligopolistic relations with the government and the various concessions they received from other stakeholders.

Thus, restructuring did not result in a Pareto optimal situation, where everyone was better off, because it involved a redistribution of wealth from one group to another. The gains to General Dynamics' shareholders and managers accrued primarily at the expense of the state, taxpayers, and the company's labor force. These nonshareholder constituencies possessed contingent claims on the company's residual profits and even held implicit contracts for job security, high-quality products, and the preservation of the defense skill base. Although contractors appeared to have taken their fiduciary obligations to shareholders very seriously, their concern for the state and their employees did not extend much beyond the letter of the law. The state held implicit contracts for the maintenance of the defense technological base that were undermined by the hollowing out of the industry for financial gain. Because workers held only implicit and legally unenforceable contracts for job security, management incurred few costs in reneging on them. With few opportunities for sales growth, pressure increased for the company to breach these implicit contracts in its pursuit of shareholder and executive wealth.

Corporate law's inner justification for privileging shareholder claims on the corporation's residual returns above all other stakeholders' claims rests on the perceived relationship between risk-bearing and reciprocal obligation. Underlying corporate doctrine is the belief that shareholders risk and invest the most, and thus, managers have reciprocal obligations to act in their interests. Even if legal justifications are simply smoke screens under which managers can strategically pursue their own interests, the contention that General Dynamics' shareholders should be the primary beneficiaries of the company's adjustment strategy needs to be examined critically in light of their purported role as the sole, residual risk-bearers of the firm. I challenge this logic, because other corporate stakeholders—most notably, the state and taxpayers—have played equivalent roles. Thus, the shareholder-oriented adjustment strategies of prime defense contractors force us to name the beneficiaries of contractor activities, reexamine the claims of different corporate constituencies on contractors' profits, and define the "public interests" in whose name military spending is ostensibly predicated. The following sections explore the contributions that different stakeholders made to General Dynamics and, in turn, the extent of corporate obligation to them.

The State and Taxpayers as Risk-Bearers

In their efforts to maximize profits, corporations frequently seek to insulate their operating units from financial liabilities by shifting the risks of loss to other parties. Defense contractors are no exception; in fact, their capacity to protect themselves is enhanced by the fact that they may have only one customer and that customer typically has few suppliers. Its strong position in several product markets gave General Dynamics enormous bargaining power with the military services, the Department of Defense hierarchy, and Congress. In a more indirect manner, contractors also shift the risks of production to taxpayers. Given that taxpayers finance government expenditures, the public investment in defense contractors can be considered investments in which each individual taxpayer holds a very small share.[1] Throughout its history, General Dynamics took advantage of the contract negotiation process and its lobbying capabilities to aggressively shift the costs, risks, and liabilities of production away from its shareholders to the state and taxpayers. It did so primarily through five mechanisms: contractual changes, bailouts, government-furnished property, investment subsidies, and accounting tricks.

Contractual changes

Procurement contracts are the primary mechanisms for the allocation of risk and liability in defense production. Traditional commercial contracts respond to future conflict—such as schedule delays or design defects—without shifting the risks of resulting losses away from the seller. In contrast, weapons contracts are continually negotiated and create elaborate administrative mechanisms to allocate the costs of changes *between* the government and the seller (MacNeil 1978, 861; Goodman 1988, 397). Armed with a corps of lawyers, contractors improve their ability to deliver current backlogs profitably and shelter their shareholders from potential losses through contractual means. That contract negotiations are habitually extended and perennially contentious indicates the importance of this process to the contractor's risk and profit levels. Defense-dependent contractors like General Dynamics have few opportunities to increase their profits by increasing their market share; aside from the United States and a few other foreign nations, the market for nuclear submarines, for example, is rather limited. Thus, General Dynamics has always bargained hard and even at one time engaged in occasional illegal dealings with the Pentagon to maintain and increase profits levels. In the 1980s, the company's name became synonymous with cost overruns, fraud, and bill padding, although it has managed to avoid any new criminal allegations since the end of the Cold War.

The process of avoiding risks and costs begins even before the bidding for the contract begins. A contractor can reduce its level of risk and communicate its future profitability to shareholders if it can guarantee that it alone will receive a lucrative procurement contract. Although the tactic is unpopular with Congress, the Department of Defense frequently grants specific contractors a monopoly through "sole-source" awards, because they are often less expensive and the bidding process less cumbersome.[2] General Dynamics has been the sole source for many of America's submarines since the 1960s, when the federal government decided to withdraw from its own active naval production and close its shipyards. Electric Boat's market position was not necessarily the outcome of its own increased competitiveness or productivity; it was due, in part, to the increased concentration in American shipbuilding caused by the demise of the public yards (Goodwin 1985, 100–101; Sapolsky and Gholz 1996). Newport News Shipyard in Virginia and Electric Boat emerged as the only manufacturers of nuclear submarines in the nation, and both shipyards have struggled to secure sole-source contracts for many of the last submarine classes.[3]

In addition to lobbying for sole-source awards, General Dynamics has always bargained hard for cost-plus contracts. The company has claimed that the magnitude of uncertainties involved in the design and production of submarines (e.g., the design of a submarine can take over eight years) should preclude the use of fixed-price contracts. Contractors generally prefer that the government bear the risk of any additional cost increases resulting from design changes or schedule delays. Operating under these types of contracts, the contractor's own financial risk is minimized, as all allowable costs are reimbursed by the government.[4] The prevalence of cost-plus contracts has varied over time with shifts in government priorities. In the late 1970s and early 1980s, the services had a preference for cost-plus contracts because of the intense Cold War pressure for rapid technological innovation, but after the billing scandals of the 1980s, fixed-price contracts became more politically palatable (McNaugher 1989). Nonetheless, General Dynamics has contrived to win large cost-plus-fixed-fee design contracts. Even in the early 1990s, most of the contracts for engineering technical support services for the design, manufacture, and test phases of the lead ships have been cost-plus-fixed-fee contracts (Hamilton 1996h).

During cost-plus contract negotiations, contractors inevitably bargain for higher fixed profit rates. These rates are supposed to be based on the Federal Acquisition Regulation's (FAR)"weighted guidelines," which detail the process of calculating a "fair and reasonable return." The weighted guidelines provide a broad range within which the fee may fall, but actual rates are more likely to be negotiated based on the rates of similar contracts let to competitors or on projections of what contractors require to boost next quarter's earnings.[5] These negotiations involve a great deal of compromise as well as a fair amount of puffery. Contractors exaggerate the potential financial loss they will have to declare if the government's choice of profit rate is below their target rate. The government has a difficult time verifying these projections of future loss.

The government also, however grudgingly, has an interest in the company's financial solvency. An official in the Navy's Supervisor of Shipbuilding's office at Electric Boat noted:

> The general manager of Electric Boat wants 17 percent profit, and we're offering 11 percent. Now, he has got to go back to his corporate board and come away with the feeling that they have trust in him. And he's not going to them with an 11 percent profit because his corporate board will just say "Forget it." We have to be sensitive to the company's financial needs without letting them take advantage of us. (employee of Office of Supervisor of Shipbuilding, interview by author, Summer 1996)

Even if it refuses to capitulate to contractors' demands for higher profit rates, the Pentagon may offer other perks in order to strike a bargain. On the third Seawolf contract, for example, the Navy held to its lower profit rate but agreed to an "accelerated payments clause," which provided Electric Boat with more cash up front.

If contractors are unable to negotiate higher profit rates on their cost-plus contracts, they may resort to illegal means to maximize the profits (DeSouza 1985). Some contractors knowingly break the law, whereas others blame the laws themselves for not being adequately explicit about what kinds of behavior are forbidden. The numerous infractions associated with cost-plus billing in the 1980s demonstrate how the benefits of breaking the law, discounted by the probability of getting caught, were high enough to encourage many contractors to take advantage of the government's largesse. General Dynamics was at the epicenter of the controversy; Congressmen and the press routinely attacked the contractor's "catch-me-if-you-can" billing as an example of the defense industry's wasteful spending of the taxpayer's money (Vartabedian 1990). Between 1983 and 1990, three of General Dynamics' executive vice presidents were indicted on criminal charges by grand juries in different areas of the country.

Under cost-plus contracts in the 1980s, for example, Electric Boat charged a variety of unallowable expenses to the Navy. These charges included country club dues, executive travel, liquor at promotional parties, and even boarding fees for an executive's dog (Goodwin 1985, 273). The company admitted that a few dubious expenses had been submitted improperly but generally maintained that its overhead charges conformed to government acquisition regulations. In addition to charging unallowable costs to the government, General Dynamics engaged in a practice common amongst contractors: covering losses on fixed-price contracts by presenting bills to the Pentagon for work under separate cost-plus contracts where reimbursement is permitted. A federal grand jury in Los Angeles charged General Dynamics with using this practice to fraudulently obtain $3.2 million from the government for expenses stemming from the development of a prototype for an Army divisional antiaircraft weapon, the DIVAD (Vartabedian 1990). No other contractor's behavior more incensed the public or created more doubts about the integrity of the defense acquisition system—especially the use of cost-plus contracts.

Although contractors prefer cost-plus contracts, they have many opportunities to reduce the financial risks inherent in fixed-price contracts through the practice of change orders and contract claims. In a fixed-price incentive contract, the contractor is reimbursed for allowables up to a limit called a "ceiling price," and this price, as well as the target cost, is negotiated at the outset of the award. Contractors dislike fixed-price contracts because they are forced to share the risks of contract performance; the contractor must accept certain cost overruns as losses on their balance sheets if they are responsible for incurring them. Fixed-price contracts, in the words of one government employee, "force shipbuilders to cut their own throats" (interview by author, Summer 1996). Fixed-price contracts foster the illusion that all possible costs for weaponry can be predicted at the outset. In reality, however, they encourage the submission of wildly optimistic cost and productivity projections to show that the deliverables will be on budget. The government expects a "buy-in," the submission of an unrealistically low bid from the contractor. As costs increase, the contractor will subsequently attempt to "get well" and recoup its costs through changes, claims, and follow-on contracts (McNaugher 1989).

One particular episode in General Dynamics' history sheds light on the manner in which contractors transform fixed-price contracts into cost-plus-like contracts through change negotiations. In 1974, the Navy awarded Electric Boat fixed-price incentive contracts to build eighteen Los Angeles–class submarines, because the service realized that fixed-price contracts were more likely to be approved by Congress.[6] In a few years, the company had submitted a staggering number of contract changes (U.S. GAO 1988). Some of the changes were "directed" changes, in which Electric Boat was ordered by a Navy contracting officer to change some technical deficiency, eliminate a recently discovered safety hazard, or satisfy the performance demands of a particular officer (Fox 1974, 227). For these changes, the government agreed to pay an "equitable adjustment" to cover the costs the contractor incurred in making these changes.[7]

Other changes were so-called "constructive changes," which resulted from some government action or inaction that indirectly affected the contractor's costs. Electric Boat claimed that the Navy's directive to change thousands of welds and its changes made to Newport News' drawings caused long delays in construction work on the Los Angeles–class submarines. Meanwhile the Navy insisted that the contractor's poor management had caused the delay (Goodman 1988). General Dynamics submitted a series of constructive changes and asked for reimbursement for the ensuing cost overruns. When the government denied its request, the company reasserted its claim through the mechanism of a "contract claim" to the Navy Claims Settlement Board.

Inevitably some changes had to be made, given the long construction cycle and the uncertainties surrounding the production of a new vessel, but no one expected Electric Boat to claim $544 million as a result of these changes.[8] The changes had increased the cost of each of the eighteen submarines by $23 million (U.S. GAO 1980, 3). To underscore its insistence that the Navy pay these claims, Electric Boat laid off 8,000 of its 14,000 workers and threatened to stop work on the Los Angeles program until the government acceded to its demands.[9] Though the Secretary of the Navy threatened to pull the unfinished submarines out of Electric Boat and place them in other yards, the only other shipyard capable of building nuclear submarines, Newport News, was also locked in a contract dispute with the Navy. Essentially, the Navy was held hostage to Electric Boat's demands because, in the interest of national defense, it could not delay or cancel a program considered necessary for countering Soviet naval capabilities.

During these claim negotiations, the nation's security interests were less important to the company than the interests of the contractor's shareholders. "This will destroy investor confidence in General Dynamics," CEO David Lewis complained in a telephone call to the Navy Secretary (Tyler 1986, 133). To avoid declaring a massive fixed loss, General Dynamics insisted that the Navy effectively absorb the company's losses by making multimillion-dollar concessions in the negotiating process.[10]

For the sake of a quick settlement, Congress used its authority to go beyond mere contractual remedies and the Navy Claims Settlement Board to settle the Los Angeles claims. In an unusual turn, Congress passed Public Law 85-804, which allowed the Executive to grant "extraordinary contractual relief whenever such action would facilitate the national defense."[11] In June 1978, after four years of heated wrangling, the Navy and General Dynamics signed an $843 million agreement in order to settle the $544 million contract claim. The final cost figure had increased by nearly $300 million to account for the additional cost growth and inflation that had occurred after the claim was filed. The bailout provided General Dynamics with a quick infusion of money, including a $300 million "advance payment" check. Not only did the company's shareholders avoid swallowing a huge deficit, but General Dynamics' stock increased 50 percent in value over the next few months (Tyler 1986). When President Carter signed the defense bill officially authorizing the settlement, a copy was flown to the Chicago office of Henry Crown, the corporation's controlling stockholder, where it was framed and hung on his wall.[12]

Even while its claims were being negotiated, Electric Boat continued to work on the submarine contracts and receive progress payments from the government. "Progress payments" are regular payments made by a military service to its contractors that reimburse contractors' allowable costs. Unlike the practice in civilian contracting, the government will make these payments regardless of whether a change dispute or claim is under way. The rationale behind progress payments is that the contractor should not have to finance a large portion of the allowable costs of performing under a contract that may extend five or more years (McNaugher 1989). Contractors prefer that the government cover their upfront costs in order to minimize their own debt service payments.[13] By securing the cash flow, progress payments are another means by which the government reduces the contractor's need to borrow money and shields shareholders from potential financial losses.

Also during this period, the Justice Department opened an investigation on charges that Electric Boat illegally inflated the prices of some submarines it was building to cover losses incurred on the Trident contracts

(U.S. GAO 1985). Although the investigative team did not find sufficient evidence to indict any individual at the yard, Electric Boat once again came under fire in 1983 when its general manager, Takis Veliotis, was indicted for accepting $1.3 million in illegal kickbacks from a subcontractor (Goodwin 1985; Tyler 1986). Veliotis had already fled to Greece where, as a fugitive from the law, he provided the Justice Department with evidence that General Dynamics had indeed submitted fraudulent claims to the Navy during the 1970s. The investigation was closed a little over three years later, however, when the department announced it had insufficient evidence of criminal wrongdoing.

The company was also accused of intentionally withholding pessimistic information about the Trident submarines from the government and shareholders (Goodwin 1985). According to the accusation, Electric Boat had realized that there would be massive cost overruns and delayed delivery dates for the Tridents. But in an effort to bolster the price of its stock and clear its name with the government, the company told stockholders and the Navy that the Trident program was profitable and that the first ship was on schedule.[14] The Securities and Exchange Commission (SEC) investigated charges that the company had misled its stockholders about the claims and progress of the submarines at Groton, although it never made an indictment. These issues would resurface when the Navy terminated the A-12 carrier-launched attack plane program in 1990. The Navy accused General Dynamics of intentionally withholding evidence that the plane was over the weight allowed by the contract. Because the Navy was unable to prove this contention, the company was later awarded almost $1 billion and its stock was boosted to a new high (Hamilton 1995a).

General Dynamics' actions, although consistent with its strategy of profit maximization and risk-shifting, pushed the parameters of legal behavior. These actions also demonstrate how the company so often held the trump card in contract negotiations. Once design changes had been made, the contractor gained the dominant bargaining position, and the government was pressured into shielding shareholders from financial risks.[15] General Dynamics was able to make money on the modifications of fixed-price contracts because there was no competition once the award had been won. The federal government was also under pressure to deliver the products on time. One official noted, "Electric Boat has always put in a lot of constructive changes. Change orders are the only way they can make more money off of the government on a fixed-price contract. In the end, it doesn't matter who asked for the change. If it's an emergency, no one will stop to figure out who owes whom, or how much extra it'll cost" (employee of Office of Supervisor of Shipbuilding, interview by author, Summer 1996).

"Simply put," notes author Roger Franklin, "the company was just too big to whip" (1986, 74). Contrary to the belief in institutional economics that concerns about reputation deter bad behavior, General Dynamics' past performance was rarely scrutinized because of its near-monopoly position and the perceived necessity of building specific weaponry. Although it was barred on a few occasions from bidding on new contracts and endured the public's wrath against corporate welfare and government fraud in the 1980s, the company continued to build the nation's arsenal.[16] The government subsequently granted the company immunity from suspension for related fraud cases. Immediately after the contract claim imbroglio, the Navy announced that General Dynamics would receive another $1.1 billion in Navy business in 1985 (Biddle 1985b). Given the dozen or so investigations (three grand jury and ten to fifteen others) under way at the time, it was a surprising development.

Senator William Proxmire (D.-WI), a long-time critic of the company, said the new contract awards were the most demoralizing actions since the Nixon pardon. "I haven't seen any of these contractors getting knocked off their jackasses," said Congressman John Dingell (D.-MI). "Nobody lost contracts because of misbehavior. Nobody paid" (quoted in Vartabedian 1990, A1). The Department of Defense inspector general even recommended that General Dynamics chairman David Lewis and two other top company officers be suspended from doing business with the Navy because "adequate evidence exists to demonstrate [they] lack the business integrity and honesty required of high level officials in corporations that do business with the government" (Biddle 1985b). Then Secretary of the Navy Lehman said he decided against singling out the three executives because of a more "pervasive corporate attitude" intent on "maximizing profits and maximizing the interests of stockholders without regard for the public trust" (Goodwin 1985, 315–317).

Bailouts

General Dynamics emerged from the scandals of the 1980s financially solvent and ethically renewed. The company instituted a new accounting system to track unallowable costs, underwent a series of independent audits, and developed a new code of ethics. During the early 1990s, Congress and the Pentagon again shielded General Dynamics from financial losses by coming to its rescue when its financial viability was threatened. Despite evidence that certain technologies were no longer needed in order to fulfill military missions, the Pentagon found creative ways to avoid severing its relationship with General Dynamics.

One of the most glaring bailouts of the post–Cold War era was introduced in Chapter 4: the reinstatement of the contract for the final two

Seawolf submarines.[17] President Bush announced that he was cutting the program from twenty-nine submarines to one because military need for these $2.5 billion behemoths did not exist. The existing force of Los Angeles–class submarines was equipped to operate in regional conflicts until the smaller New Attack Submarine would be available at the turn of the century, making the Seawolf obsolete. The Seawolf program had become less important, given that its original mission was to combat Soviet attack submarines in deep waters. Independent estimates from the comptroller of the Department of Defense and the Navy indicated that the net savings of canceling the two submarines, after subtracting all direct termination costs, would be at least $2.8 billion and could be as great as $3.3 billion (U.S. GAO 1993).

Electric Boat threatened that it would go out of business without the Seawolf contracts. In testimony before the House Armed Services defense industrial base panel, CEO of Electric Boat James Turner said that unless changes in government spending plans were made quickly, his facility would lose the ability to build nuclear-powered submarines (U.S. House 1995). The division would be unable to prevent its suppliers and its corps of skilled welders, nuclear engineers, naval architects, and other specialists from moving into civilian work. They would then be unavailable to build the New Attack Submarine slated for 1998. The yard's advocates insisted that Electric Boat should build the two final Seawolfs in order to keep the two nuclear shipyards "warm" and preserve the submarine industrial base. Studies by RAND and the General Accounting Office (U.S. GAO) confirmed the industrial base argument (Birkler et al. 1994; U.S. GAO 1994b).

In the end, President Clinton capitulated and ordered a second and then a third Seawolf in late 1995. The procurement was intended to keep the yard in business until 1998, when it began production of the New Attack Submarine. Many in Congress viewed the order as a bailout for a contractor that, contrary to the image it projected to the Navy and to Congress, was in fine financial form. Senator John McCain (R.-AZ) criticized saving the Seawolf as "an extremely expensive subsidy to a limited number of firms at the expense of others" (1995, A16). Letters to the editor denouncing the bailout appeared in national newspapers, but were conspicuously absent in southeastern Connecticut. "This is not a bailout," responded Defense Secretary Perry, the policy's intellectual architect. "I explicitly reject the idea of sustaining a defense company just to keep it in business. We're not doing it to save jobs or help shareholders. We expect defense companies to go out of business, and we will stand by and let that happen" (Mintz 1993). Acknowledging that the state actually *invests* in contractors, expanding their productive capacity just as shareholders do, Electric Boat's spokesman, Neil Runzel, responded to criticisms: "Finally, your question whether Congress is willing to subsidize Electric Boat to the tune of $1 billion per year is off the mark. The $1 billion would be allocated throughout the entire submarine industrial base, and is *not a subsidy as much as it is an investment* in the nation's continuing capability to design and build nuclear submarines" [emphasis added] (Runzel 1994, 3).

Had Congress decided to cancel its contracts for the Seawolf submarines, the company's shareholders would not have suffered as much as one might have expected. The Navy is required to pay penalty fees for contract cancellations, and between the available cash on the books, the value of the physical plant, and the money it would get from the termination of contracts, those shareholders that held on to their stock would have faced only minimal risks of financial loss. If the Navy had canceled the third Seawolf, it was estimated that the company would have received a $500 million penalty fee in cash (Hamilton 1995j). Financial analysts assured stockholders that the company shares would retain their value: "Basically the possible Electric Boat shutdown should not cost the company a penny. At this moment in time it's a cash-positive event for the company. The moment it [contract cancellation] happens you get millions of dollars to settle" (quoted in Hamilton 1995j). Even if the shipyard had closed, the Navy would have paid for the clean-up of the company's property and would have reimbursed Electric Boat for its inventory at current value. Shipyard workers and the region's residents would have been less fortunate.

General Dynamics' radical restructuring of the early 1990s raised concerns about the public impact of the Seawolf bailouts. Electric Boat reduced its investments in capital and research and development (R&D), investments critical to the production of high-tech defense products. Electric Boat had last invested in its facilities during the 1970s, and most of its production equipment had not been modernized since that time. By vastly reducing spending on plant, equipment, and R&D, management "starv[ed] the company's future" (Wrubel 1992, 26). General Dynamics' disinvestment in physical and human capital resulted not in pure efficiency gains for the federal government, but, many contended, in a decline in quality, faulty construction, and a disorganized and demoralized workforce. An article in *Aviation Week and Space Technology* entitled "Profit Wave Uncovers Nagging Paradox" suggested that the financial vibrancy of contractors like General Dynamics was hiding a "hollow" industry with few prospects for maintaining its high-tech capabilities over the long term (Velocci 1995, 36).

Shortly after the contractor's executive compensation plan was made public, concerns about the quality of the workmanship on the lead Seawolf surfaced. In the summer of 1991, small cracks were found in the hull of the ship, which the yard had been constructing for two years. This revelation led the yard to tear down and rework sections that were already welded and to start from scratch on certain segments using new steel. Ultimately the Navy paid $58.8 million for the welds to be redone (Weisman 1991b). Other major design flaws were found in subsequent years; for example, torpedo hatches on the second Seawolf were unable to open correctly (U.S. GAO 1993). Quality problems cost the state and the taxpayers an exorbitant amount of money; at one point, it was estimated that shoddy workmanship alone added 10 to 30 percent to the cost of weapons (U.S. GAO 1980; Gerth 1985b).

Electric Boat had quality problems dating from its entry into the submarine market in the early 1900s, so these construction flaws could not be blamed solely on the company's pressures to service the short-term interests of shareholders. Nonetheless, many in the government believed that submarine quality was being compromised for these very reasons. After the weld cracks on the Seawolf were discovered, Navy Rear Admiral Gene LaRoque from the Center for Defense Information fumed, "Management is under pressure to make a profit, which shouldn't be a consideration when you're building weapons to defend people. It's all profit-driven, and it's leading these companies to cut corners" (Weisman 1991b). The Navy's supervisor of shipbuilding at Electric Boat admitted that he was under short-term pressure to invest his increasingly limited resources in programs other than the Seawolf, such as the Trident program (interview with author, summer 1996). The Trident had a higher profit margin and its delivery would increase Electric Boat's immediate cash flow (U.S. GAO 1994b).

Government-Furnished Property

The federal government and taxpayers also paid for many of the specialized components, machinery, land, and facilities used in defense production (all falling into the category known as "government-furnished property," or GFP). Many of General Dynamics' plants and facilities were once government-owned yards made available to the contractor under special arrangements. Following the attack on Pearl Harbor in 1941, the government purchased the Groton Iron Works plant just south of Electric Boat, where it constructed ten additional shipping ways. The government invested $9.5 million in building the new yard, which was "a huge undertaking, with much of the yard being blasted out of solid rock" (Rodengen 1994, 81). The new yard, known as the Victory Yard, opened in July of 1942. The Navy leased and then sold the yard to Electric Boat in the mid-1960s for a price well below market value. The Navy also sold its shipyard in Quonset Point, Rhode Island, to Electric Boat for a below-market price.

To accommodate the increased workload in the early 1970s, General Dynamics undertook a huge modernization and facilities investment program at Electric Boat (Rodengen 1994). It received interest subsidies through a government program that cost $3–5 billion a year.[18] The company installed a $120 million automated frame-and-cylinder-manufacturing facility there. The submarine's hull, cylinder shells, and frames were fabricated in Rhode Island and then barged down to Groton for component installation. Financed by the Navy, Electric Boat also invested in a $150 million, eight-acre submarine construction facility at the Groton yard. The new facility allowed for a modular assembly process in which hull cylinders could be moved on an elaborate grid system of rail tracks and transfer cars.

In addition, the federal government paid for the high acquisition costs of specialized process technologies and equipment, even though General Dynamics was able to retain rights to the GFP after contract completion. Admiral Rickover once noted,

> What usually happens is that initially the government probably has a real need to put government-owned machine tools in a particular supplier's plant. Often, after a few years this need passes. Government contracting officials authorize him to use the government-owned tools on the new work on the basis that the government should get its money's worth out of the tools. . . . Once a company gets the government to provide him with machine tools, he almost certainly can keep them forever. (U.S. House 1966)

Electric Boat also relied on expensive government-furnished equipment (GFE) specialized for incorporation into a particular contract's end product. Since the mid-1950s, the Navy had purchased nuclear reactors and turbines directly from General Electric and Westinghouse and then provided them to Electric Boat as part of their procurement contracts. Nuclear reactors and turbines are economies of scale purchases; the government can more cost effectively purchase eighteen of these items rather than require Electric Boat to negotiate the sale of each reactor one at a time. As a submarine class matures and the learning curve declines, government negotiators try to "migrate" (move responsibility for) the provision of property back to the contractor.

The government provided many complex electronic components as GFE. The asset value depended on the vessel; for example, the supervisor of shipbuilding at Electric Boat estimated that 30 percent of the total value of the first few Tridents was GFE, or $330 million per submarine (interview by author, summer 1996). The Seawolf-class submarines contained an unusually large amount of new computer electronic equipment, and the estimated government-furnished portion was about 50 percent of the submarine's total value (U.S. GAO 1994).

Tax Avoidance

Corporations serving commercial markets must factor in a sizable tax burden when calculating their cash flows and return on investments. They deduct allowable expenses from their revenues and pay taxes on the adjusted remainder. Defense contractors have operated under a completely different set of rules because they receive progress payments rather than lump-sum payments at the completion of their sales. Federal tax laws once allowed prime contractors like General Dynamics to escape federal income taxes entirely. Between 1972 and 1984, for instance, General Dynamics paid federal income taxes for only one year. The company took advantage of Internal Revenue Service (IRS) provisions that allowed it to defer income taxes until it completed its long-term weapons contracts (Wheeler and Outslay 1986; Gerth 1985e).

Contractors embraced an arcane accounting technique called the "completed-contract method," originally developed for building contractors around the turn of the century, and turned it into a lucrative tax loophole.[19] When defense contractors computed their income taxes, they ignored the progress payments received for incurred expenses and recorded their expenses as a loss, even though they were eventually reimbursed (U.S. GAO 1986b). These hypothetical losses were carried forward indefinitely, as long as their contract was still considered "open" and incomplete. The provision allowed companies to avoid declaring profits for tax purposes until their contracts had been "completed," which for some weapons systems could be as long as ten or fifteen years.[20] The losses were then used to defer, offset, or eliminate taxes on other income.

Between 1973 and 1984, General Dynamics reported over $2.7 billion in cumulative before-tax earnings, according to one study of the company's taxes (Wheeler and Outslay 1986). Yet even though they were reporting record operating profits to shareholders, the company did not pay any federal income taxes during this period. The contractor was able to defer indefinitely paying just over $1 billion in income taxes through the use of these net operating "losses." The company's paper tax losses of over $3.1 billion were "the largest reported net operating losses to carry forward in corporate history" (Wheeler and Outslay 1986, 761). Because the company was able to carry back its losses, it applied them to earlier returns and qualified for a $68.4 million refund for federal income taxes paid in the mid-1970s.

This discrepancy—simultaneously reporting record profits to shareholders and massive losses to the IRS for the same transaction—was considered legal, although, once it was publicized, Congress accused General Dynamics of using "smoke and mirrors accounting" to turn a substantial profit at the taxpayers' expense (O'Shea 1985, C1). The company insisted that it had not deceived taxpayers, and General Dynamics was never found guilty of violating the tax laws. When interrogated by Senator Proxmire (D.-WI) about the nonpayment of federal income taxes, the executive vice president of General Dynamics, Gordon MacDonald, simply replied, "When Congress passes a tax law, a company [that] ignores it wouldn't last very long with the stockholders. You do what the law says, and that's what we feel we have done" (O'Shea 1985, C1).

Moreover, the completed-contract technique provided General Dynamics stockholders with more than $200 million in tax-free dividends between 1979 and 1984 (Wheeler and Outslay 1986). This figure includes $35 to $40 million worth of dividends to the Crown family, which owned about 20 percent of General Dynamics stock during this period. With over $3 billion in net operating losses, corporate distributions were not taxable before 1984. In a letter to shareholders in 1979, General Dynamics identified the completed-contract accounting method as the source of the company's tax-exempt dividends for that year (cited in Alaghband 1983, 1023). They were the first dividends the company had paid since 1970. A report on the company by Duff & Phelps Inc. noted that the completed-contract method of accounting was primarily responsible for the company's strong cash position, which allowed it to buy Chrysler's tank division in 1982 for $366 million and implement a massive stock repurchase ($190 million in 1983 and $560 million in 1984) without increasing its debt levels (O'Shea 1985, C3).

When the loophole was exposed and challenged, General Dynamics and the lobbying organizations to which it belonged—the Aerospace Industries Association and the American League for Exports and Security Assistance—fought hard to preserve it. Despite their efforts, the 1984 Tax Reform Act forced defense contractors to use a different accounting method—percentage of completion—to determine the taxability of their operating and dividend income. This change increased the taxes paid by military contractors, although it did not require them to pay back taxes for the years in which they had no tax bill (Gerth 1985c).

The actual application of the completed-contract method is complex, but the technique—getting tax-free money through progress payments—is often compared to getting an interest-free loan from the government. The taxpaying public, in effect, financed General Dynamics' inventory and works in progress, reducing the need to borrow money from banks or shareholders. Under these tax laws, one study found that ten defense contractors were able to defer more than $1.1 billion in taxes in 1984 alone (MacIntyre and Folen 1984). They were able to retain the deferred tax liability in addition to their after-tax profits, which increased their returns on equity. When profits were recalculated on the basis of taxes actually paid instead of simply provided for, the contractors' average return on equity increased from 25 percent to 35 percent (U.S. GAO 1986a). Observers noted that the prospect of getting tax-free money through progress payments actually gave contractors the incentive to bend the rules. To increase the size of the "loan," contractors overstated the progress on the construction of a ship or other long-term project, for they knew federal auditors rarely challenged contractors' reports.

When a contractor sells a product to the federal government, it provides explicit guarantees that the product will perform to certain agreed-upon standards of workmanship. The Federal Acquisition Regulations (FAR) specify that contractors must adhere to the acquisition regulations and charge the government a "fair price." In the past, General Dynamics took a cavalier attitude toward the legality of its behavior. In the more recent era of budget austerity, the company has realized that legal sanctions have monetary penalties that must be recorded as losses, and they have become increasingly cautious about bending the rules. Nonetheless, the company continued to pursue every legal form of risk- and cost-shifting, starting with the procurement contracts it signed. As a result, the federal government and taxpayers shouldered much of the technical and financial risk that otherwise would fall on the contractors' shareholders. The shareholder-oriented adjustment policies of the early 1990s are clearly unfair, considering that taxpayers and the state have borne so many of the risks of production. They are also a waste of taxpayer money and do not result in a defense industrial base well organized to provide affordable equipment that performs to expectations.

Employees and Local Governments as Risk-Bearers

The huge gains of shareholders and upper-level management at General Dynamics in the 1990s also reflected a wealth transfer from employees. General Dynamics' workforce declined by 79 percent between 1989 and 1994, due in part to divestitures and mass layoffs (U.S. GAO 1995c). Because employees' wages were cut and their jobs eliminated, value was created for shareholders and managers. Employees' overtime, task enlargement, and investments in training had increased the productivity and the income-generating capabilities of the organization. These investments were reflected in the increased value of equity in the corporation, yet were completely ignored when it came time to distribute the surplus. Instead, the labor costs that the company saved by trimming the workforce dropped straight to the bottom line, increasing earnings and buoying stock prices.

At Electric Boat, employment fell from 22,000 in 1989 to 7,000 in 1996. More than half of those dismissed from Electric Boat were not eligible for retirement benefits; they were laid off with sixty days' notice and three to six months' salary, pursuant to labor agreements.[21] The company also gave these workers forty paid hours to use the company's employment transition center. There, a private consulting group provided outplacement assistance, such as counseling and resume editing. Apart from limited computer tutoring at some locations, Electric Boat offered no formal retraining programs.

With the elimination of so many positions, the occupational profile of the shipyard changed dramatically. Several upper-level executive positions at the shipyard were eliminated. In 1988, for example, twenty-three employees reported to the general manager, but only seven did so in 1993. Many middle managers and administrators in the finance, materials, and human resource departments—especially those not directly related to submarine construction or design—lost their jobs in the early 1990s (Hamilton 1995k). The bulk of the layoffs, however, affected workers in the skilled construction trades: mechanics, precision metal workers, hand workers, assemblers, fabricators, and machine setters. Many of the laid-off workers in the skilled trades had over twenty years of seniority, yet were not eligible for early retirement benefits. One observer, concerned about the effect of the layoffs on intergenerational learning, noted:

> Right now, you only have the most experienced workers over there doing the job. At the end of 1996, you won't have anyone in the yards who's under 45 years old. You won't have anyone under 50 by the time you're building the New Attack Submarine. If there are no more young people at the yard, there's no one to learn the practice to fill in as old guys retire. The average age is creeping up because they're not hiring and they're laying off all of the "junior" people. Twenty years tenure is junior now. (former employee of Electric Boat, interview by author, Summer 1996)

The skilled manufacturing trades were organized into ten union locals, all of which were represented by a collective bargaining unit, the Metal Trades Council. In the 1980s, the Metal Trades Council represented 10,000 members at the Groton yard. By 1996, membership had dropped to 4,000.

Few blue-collar workers from Electric Boat were able to find employment at similar wages in the region. Other studies of displaced defense workers found that after a year, almost half had not found comparable jobs (Schoeni and Dardia 1996; Congressional Budget Office 1993; Mueller et al. 1994; Markusen and Powers 1999).[22] Of those seeking jobs in New London County, a large percentage were high school graduates over forty years old and possessed manufacturing or managerial experience. The region continued to pride itself on its educated and skilled workforce, but with the combination of recession and defense cutbacks, many local workers pursued employment opportunities outside the region and outside the state. Sadly, the few local manufacturers that were hiring during this period did not want to hire former Electric Boat employees. A survey of small and medium-sized businesses in southeastern Connecticut found that local employers preferred not to hire former Electric Boat workers because they found them "inflexible" and "single-task oriented" (Moran 1996). The investments that pipefitters and welders had made in their defense-specific skills over the years turned out to be of little value in the service-dominated economy.

These dislocated workers, like most in the country, did not possess the collective bargaining agreements that would have guaranteed them rights to future job security. Instead, they had bargained for present wages, because they were restricted by contemporary labor law from bargaining for long-term job protection.[23] The workers had, nonetheless, relied on the oral assurances of managers, promotion policies outlined in employment manuals, and a corporate culture of seniority to assure them of the security of their employment (Stone 1993). They had made long-term investments in their own technical skills and had contributed to the organizational capital of the company. In legal jargon, they held "implicit contracts" for job security. With the layoffs, General Dynamics reneged on these implicit promises of job tenure and expropriated workers' claims on the future proceeds of the firm. Their hard work and firm-specific investments had created the wealth that shareholders subsequently appropriated.

The company denied that it made distributional choices in laying off its workforce and insisted that executive and shareholders gains did not come at the expense of workers. Said General Dynamics Chairman William (Bill) Anders: "We hate to lay off people, but we also hate to subsidize them if we don't have the work" (Goodman 1991). In contrast to the company's spokespeople, Wall Street analysts openly admitted the connection between the layoffs and General Dynamics' stock price. As one of them put it to a journalist, "All of these bonuses and gains came while General Dynamics was downsizing. . . . It's a scenario that hits you in the gut. This is not a case where somebody's making a lot of money because the company's doing great. This is a case of a guy getting a lot of money, and he's an island of prosperity in a sea of misery" (Crystal 1992, 15).

The unions were appalled by what they saw as unadulterated greed and avarice on the part of General Dynamics' executives. Few employees benefited from the fact that the company had the "strongest balance sheet in the industry" (General Dynamics 1993). They never saw the improved utilization of resources that had supposedly led to shareholder gains and executive bonuses. What they did see were pink slips, longer hours, and eroding medical benefits. This incongruity riled them. The debate over executive salaries was not new, but it grew louder during the recession of the early 1990s when the company was operating under such low rates of production. Dean Giradot, General Dynamics' coordinator for the International Association of Machinists, fumed, "Why is there a Gain/Sharing program just for the top 25 executives—most of them relative newcomers—while people who have worked in the trenches for many years are losing their jobs?" (McCartney 1991b). The employees that demonstrated at General Dynamics' San Diego aircraft plant before it was sold carried placards reading "No Bogus Bonus for Bill." Electric Boat employees joined workers at aerospace giant United Technologies in Hartford to protest executive pay and bonuses in the face of employee sacrifices (French 1994). They wore rubber pig snouts to drive home the union message that defense contractor executives had "pigged out" at the expense of rank-and-file workers.

The massive gulf between shareholder returns and the pay and conditions for employees especially troubled the workers. As part of the restructuring of ownership, General Dynamics tried to encourage lower-level employees to hold the company's stock. The board of directors made changes in the company's Savings and Stock Investment Plan, which covered approximately 62,000 employees. Prior to 1991, the company paid 75 cents for each dollar invested. Under the new plan in 1991, General Dynamics matched dollar-for-dollar in the common stock fund (G.D. Annual Report 1991). Subsequently, the number of employees holding stock jumped to 48,300 (54 percent of employees), and by June of 1992, 15 percent of shares outstanding were held by employees, including the holdings of senior managers. However, few employees were the beneficiaries of the massive shareholder wealth increases because their holdings were so small. Approximately 40 percent of union members at Electric Boat owned stock in the company, but their stock holdings totaled less than the combined assets of the ten top executives. In the words of one union member, "Most folks are just living week to week and simply can't afford [stocks]" (member of Metal Trades Council, interview by author, Summer 1996).

Still, management insisted that employees make sacrifices for the purpose of increasing shareholder value because, they said, employees would ultimately benefit from these concessions. This purported alignment of shareholder and employee interests confused workers; they saw their interests as opposing. The Metal Trades Council president at Electric Boat commented:

All we hear about is shareholder value—even on the shop floor! The company says, "We've got to get our product out on schedule for the shareholders"! I can't really explain it, but the general consensus of almost all of the union leaders and defense workers is that as you downsize, you increase shareholder value. But if we demand more, management says, "Our costs will increase and then you won't have any jobs because we'll go out of business. If we don't do well, you won't do well." Or "If we diversify, shareholders suffer because it will look like a loss and it could take us years before we make 12 percent on the product. If they [the shareholders] don't do well, you won't do well." (interview by author, Summer 1996)

The unions at Electric Boat habitually urged the company to honor workers' claims to the residual profits and use its excess cash to diversify and retrain workers.[24] Management ignored their claims, deeming them illegitimate and legally unjustified. Fulfilling these claims, they insisted, would interfere with the company's fiduciary obligations to shareholders and could potentially be detrimental to the continued viability of the corporation. Observed another union representative, "I've been following the stock market, and quite frankly, they could afford to be a little more generous here [exploring diversification options]" (interview by author, Summer 1996).

Local governments were similarly disgruntled. Electric Boat had served as the economic linchpin of southeastern Connecticut since the turn of the century. The region was one of the most defense-dependent regions in the nation in terms of both employment and output by the end of the Cold War. In 1989, New London County received defense contracts valued at over $2.5 billion, or $10,877 per capita, which was the largest dollar amount of defense contracts in the state (U.S. Department of Defense 1989). In constant dollars, New London County received $13,233 prime contracts per capita in 1989, compared to the $2,316 per capita the state of Connecticut received (see Figure 5.1). The ratio of defense contracts to total personal income earned in the county—another standard measure of regional defense dependency—indicates that New London County was by far the most defense-dependent county in the state and one of the most defense-dependent in the nation. The company's imprimatur could be found on all aspects of the economy, political life, and culture of the region.

State and local governments had long reaped the benefits of defense spending in the form of tax revenues and jobs, but they had also contributed resources to the company through several kinds of direct and indirect subsidies. General Dynamics and Electric Boat took advantage of state and local relocation and retention incentives. For example, when CEO Anders announced the move of the company's corporate headquarters to the Washington area from St. Louis, it set off a bidding war between Virginia and Maryland officials to lure the company (Pearlstein 1993). Electric Boat also received generous tax exemptions from Connecticut and the city of Groton; between 1989 and 1991, the company

156

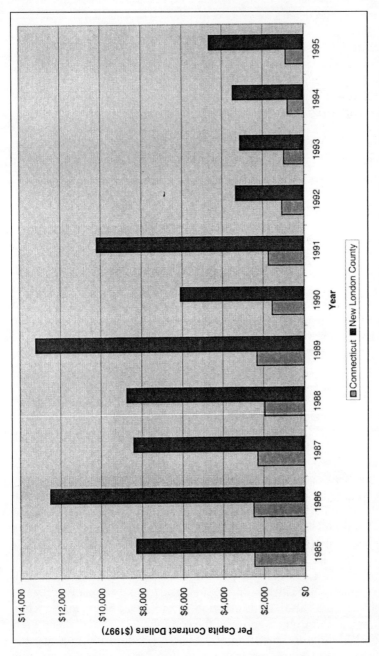

FIGURE 5.1 Per Capita Contract Dollars to Connecticut and New London County ($1997), 1985–1995
SOURCES: DOD Directorate for Information, Operations and Reports, "Prime Contract Awards by Region and State," 1988–1995; U.S. Bureau of Census, U.S.A. Counties, 1985–1995.

paid very modest amounts of state and local income taxes. Moreover in 1992 the Connecticut legislature passed a $4 million tax break aimed at enticing the Computer Sciences Corporation, a former subsidiary of General Dynamics, to remain in the city of Norwich (Pazniokas 1992). The company's computer work for Electric Boat became taxable in 1991 because General Dynamics sold the company at the onset of its spin-off frenzy. The legislation exempted Computer Sciences from the 6 percent sales tax on the data processing it did in connection with the construction of submarines at Electric Boat.

When the contractor's operations contaminated the surrounding environment, the public sector, rather than the contractor, was often liable for the damages (Siegel et al. 1991; Nilsson 1994). The Navy, for example, paid to clean up some of the damages caused by Electric Boat and, in some instances, successfully shifted the costs of environmental clean-up to a third party: the state of Connecticut. In 1994, the Navy realized that it would need to dredge about one million cubic yards of material from the Thames River so that a Seawolf submarine under construction at Electric Boat could maneuver up the river to its home port at the Naval Submarine Base in Groton (Keating and Remez 1995). The riverbed needed dredging because, over the years, it had become clogged with sediments and other waste products from Electric Boat that made it too shallow to accommodate the larger submarines. The Navy convinced the state to pay $14 million for the project, because it demonstrated that homeporting the Seawolfs at the base in Groton (as opposed to the submarine base in Norfolk, Virginia) would bring $20 million to the region from payroll taxes, supplies, and other purchases. No public hearings were held on this issue, and in 1995, a state contractor began dumping the dredge spoils in the Long Island Sound, at the mouth of the Thames River. This elevated the level of contaminants with heavy metals, petroleum, and other toxins, posing a threat to fish in the area. A coalition of environmental and governmental agencies challenged the dredging, but the U.S. District Court judge found that the dumping did not violate the federal Ocean Dumping Act (Tuhus 1995).

General Dynamics workers and local governments were demoralized by the company's adjustment strategies. They had paid for the shareholder windfalls with their loyalty, personal investments, and tax revenues. They had taken the hit of the defense drawdown so that the company's shareholders did not have to. They believed they were pawns in a game that was played over their heads, primarily between General Dynamics, high-ranking Pentagon officers, and Wall Street. It was as if the space between shareholders and local workers contracted suddenly. The company's remaining divisions were put on shorter leashes and forced to become more responsive to the interests of General Dynamics' shareholders.

Shareholders as Risk-Shifters

Management privileged the claims of General Dynamics' shareholders to the residual profits, although, in many ways, they were already very privileged. The state, taxpayers, employees, and local governments anesthetized many of General Dynamics' potential losses through government contracting practices and by absorbing the blow of declining procurement budgets. Taxpayers subsidized the company's tax bill, asset base, environmental liabilities, and daily operating expenses, in effect sheltering the company's shareholders from the competitive risks that shareholders in nondefense firms face. Through progress payments, taxpayers financed General Dynamics' inventory and work in progress, reducing the contractor's need to borrow money. Through cost-plus fixed-fee contracts and government-furnished property, the state accepted the risk of delays, defects, and cost overruns.

The government's practice of bearing shareholders' risks was attacked as corporate welfare that unnecessarily increased the bargaining power of defense contractors and rewarded them for their waste and mismanagement. Generous public subsidies and bailouts encouraged underbidding and cost-inefficiency on the part of contractors, who knew that they would be able to "get well" and recoup their costs through change orders. Many questioned whether contractors even needed financial assistance and risk-absorbing mechanisms in the first place. Large, diversified conglomerates like General Dynamics possessed the financial strength, managerial savvy, and political clout to survive an uncertain future without the cushion provided by these extra subsidies. Indeed, the nation's largest military contractors enjoyed a rate of profit that was much greater than the average for industrial corporations from the mid-1980s through the early 1990s (Dial and Murphy 1995).

Did taxpayers receive benefits commensurate with their investments over the years? It is difficult to say, given that taxpayers are the most diffuse and unorganized corporate stakeholders. They include everyone from contractor management, citizens concerned about their growing income tax burden, parents concerned about the quality of public schools, and others who might consider the government's continued support for an obsolete defense facility a waste of scarce tax dollars. Taxpayers have multiple identities with conflicting stakes in the defense adjustment process and thus perceive the costs of adjustment through different prisms. One interviewee remarked, "As a taxpayer, I don't want the government wasting the hard-earned money I give them each year by keeping a bunch of guys employed at the shipyard—especially if we really don't even need those new ships. On the other hand, I used to be one of those guys, and I know what it feels like to depend on that job" (former employee of Electric Boat, interview by author, Summer 1996).

Taxpayers did save money from the shuttered plants and the procurement budget cuts paying down the deficit. But part of the taxpayers' peace dividend was redirected to generous shareholder dividends, stock repurchases, and executive bonuses. Moreover, it is unclear if cash-conscious contractors like General Dynamics will have the technological capacity to compete for important contracts in the future. The quality of the company's tanks and submarines might suffer for lack of investment in R&D and training, even as General Dynamics uses its near monopoly power to extract higher prices for weaponry.

Compared to taxpayers, the effects on workers and communities were more obvious. These stakeholders bore the brunt of the post–Cold War adjustment. Their investments over the years should have entitled them to more say about how General Dynamics distributed its returns, but their claims to the proceeds were ignored or invalidated. The state tried on occasion to protect the interests of labor and communities; in the end, however, it allowed General Dynamics to redistribute risks and rents in a manner that served management's and shareholders' interests. Contractors' monopoly power, the geopolitics of defense spending, and Beltway favoritism ensured that the corporation was relatively impervious to attack.

Notes

1. Benefit perceptions differ dramatically, and collective action problems prevent taxpayers from organizing and acting as a single "interest group," yet the unitary "interests of the taxpayers" is invoked whenever a politician or interest group seeks to legitimate their demands. All public spending decisions for collectively consumed goods and services contain some notion of serving the taxpayers' interests. However, the phrase's overextension, combined with poor voter turnout rates, has led to profound skepticism about the possibility of state policies producing the greatest good for the greatest number of people at the least cost, the classical utilitarian objective.

2. Multisourcing can diminish the productivity gains associated with mastering the learning curve over time. For example, many attribute the high profit margins on the Trident program to the fact that Electric Boat alone designed and built this class of submarine. The number of labor hours on the last ship in this class, the *Wyoming*, was less than half of the labor hours needed for the lead ship, the *Ohio* (employee of Office of Supervisor of Shipbuilding, interview by author, Summer 1996).

3. The Navy originally planned to give the development and production contract for the New Attack Submarine (worth up to $60 billion) to Electric Boat without any competitive bidding, given the uncertainty of the new submarine's

design. Newport News and the Virginia congressional delegation challenged this designation and ensured that the contract would be bid competitively.

4. When using cost-plus contracts, the government must carry a huge administrative burden—for example, establishing a reliable accounting system to certify pricing data.

5. The profit rate is weighted, and these weightings have changed over time. In the 1980s, the profit rate was based partially (70 percent) on the contractor's incurred costs and partially (30 percent) on the contractor's investment in plant and equipment devoted to military output. Several studies by Congress, the Pentagon, and defense watchdogs in the 1980s found that defense contractor profits exceeded the "fair and reasonable" standard, and that contractors' returns often exceeded those of the Standard and Poor's 500 and other indices (Gerth 1985b; 1985d; U.S. GAO 1986; Field 1993).

6. Admiral Rickover had even convinced the CEO of General Dynamics to submit a bid for these fixed-price contracts by assuring him that they would adjust the contract price down the road through change orders and modifications (Goodwin 1985, 116–119).

7. 48 CFR. 52.243-1(a).

8. A RAND report estimated that contract changes typically increase contract costs by at least 40 percent (1970).

9. In the words of *Washington Post* journalist Patrick Tyler, "[then chairman David] Lewis knew he had to play the wildest game of chicken to find out how deep the Navy would go into its pockets to bail him out" (1986, 143).

10. In each of the fiscal years from 1973 to 1977, the company reported neither a loss nor a profit on the 688-class program, expecting to receive payments from the government to cover its excess costs. Using footnotes and other narratives in its annual reports, the company alluded subtly to serious problems with the program and the necessity of winning sizable claims to turn a profit (Goodwin 1985, 136–137).

11. 50 U.S.C. Sec. 1421-35 (1982). Although relief under PL 85-804 has been used sparingly, large awards were made in 1978, when the Navy provided $1 billion in relief to its three main shipyards, including Electric Boat (Goodman 1988, 415).

12. The claims did not stop there. A year later, the company submitted dubious insurance claims for $100 million to the Navy, withdrawing the claims only after Navy officials promised a higher than usual profit margin on the new contract for three Los Angeles–class submarines (Goodman 1988, 416–421).

13. With the different waves of procurement reform, however, regulations have been introduced to reduce the maximum level of payment. Since the 1970s, the government has paid anywhere from 60 to 90 percent of a contractor's monthly billings. To retain some leverage over the company until work is satisfactorily completed, the services prefer to withhold part of the payments. Exceptions can always be negotiated if "financial need" is demonstrated (Gerth 1985a; Goodman 1988).

14. Relying on tapes that he made public after being convicted on fraud charges, Takis Veliotis accused then CEO of General Dynamics, David Lewis, of hiding this bad news from shareholders. In the tapes, another General Dynamics executive tells Veliotis that Lewis has said he "understands that delivery date [for

the Trident] isn't real. But he wanted to go ahead anyway only to stop our stock from sliding." Lewis was confident that the Navy would carry the financial burden while the Los Angeles–class contract claims were being negotiated (Goodwin 1985, 136; Biddle 1985a).

15. Parties typically negotiate payment for changes about six months after the contractor submits a change proposal. Work has already begun and may even be complete before the negotiations begin. Thus, the government has difficulty proving that costs already incurred should have been lower and typically ends up capitulating to the contractor's demands.

16. The company's first suspension cost it two contracts totaling only $22.8 million.

17. Secretary of Defense Perry also announced that the Pentagon would be committed to saving General Dynamics' tank division, the nation's only tank manufacturer, which saw its workforce drop 44 percent (to 5,800) in six years. The firm delivered its last tank to the United States Army in 1996, and currently depends on work from Egypt and Saudi Arabia (Mintz 1993).

18. In 1976, the Department of Defense began a practice of paying an interest subsidy as an incentive to defense contractors to expand their productive capacities (Mohr 1985). The payment compensated the contractor for part of the cost of the capital equipment devoted to fulfilling weapons contracts.

19. The availability of the completed-contract method for reporting taxable earnings was extended to defense contractors in 1976 through the issuance of Treasury regulations.

20. "There are aircraft that have been retired of old age, but the contract is still open so the company hasn't had to recognize a taxable gain," noted a House subcommittee staff person who investigated defense contractors' use of this tax loophole (Knight-Ridder 1985).

21. One hundred workers claimed that the company had illegally withheld information on a more generous early retirement program with increased pension benefits offered in July 1995. These workers had been with Electric Boat for over twenty years and had retired less than three weeks before the early retirement program was announced. The employees were told no such program was under consideration (Hamilton 1996c).

22. A study of workers laid off from McDonnell Douglas showed that up to a year after losing their jobs, 44 percent of workers studies had not found any work (Oden et al. 1993). A study by RAND of Southern California found that a year after being laid off, most defense workers had not found other work, and if they had, it was at lower pay (Schoeni and Dardia 1996).

23. Contractarian theorists assume that if workers are laid off in response to corporate change, they experience this consequence of their contracts knowingly and have willingly agreed to such terms. They blame workers for relying on implicit contracts and wagering their futures. They urge them to bargain for employment insurance, to demand explicit contracts specifying employment guarantees, severance payments, and retraining (Macey 1989; Easterbrook and Fischel 1991; Dial and Murphy 1995).

24. After five years of increased shareholder returns and no diversification efforts, popular opinion began to side with the unions. An editorial in *The New Lon-*

don Day on December 12, 1995, urged management to use some of the settlement it received on the canceled A-12 aircraft project to further some public interest. The editorial noted that "given the harm the government apparently did to so many through their mishandling of the matter, justice would best be served if corporate stockholders were not the only beneficiaries of the settlement and if some greater good came out of this case."

6

Accommodating Public Interests in Corporate Change

What would an alternative adjustment strategy look like? How could the state take advantage of its corporate stakeholder role to make contractors accountable not only to their own shareholders, but to other public interests as well? How could the federal government more robustly govern its contractors and, in the process, redirect defense resources to foster innovation, decrease the tax burden of military spending, and help to retain and create high-wage jobs in a *civilian* industrial economy? I contend that it can be done, that defense adjustment to lower procurement spending did not and does not have to entail such a bifurcated redistribution of risk and reward.

Many defense conversion advocates believed that more federal and state investment in private firms was needed to encourage contractors to enter commercial markets. They lauded the federal and state policies that provided direct financial assistance to defense firms experiencing contract reductions, hailing these policies as a "revolution" and a "sea change" from the laissez-faire policies of previous administrations (Oden 1996; Pages 1995).[1] The high-technology focus of the Technology Reinvestment Project (TRP), combined with its interagency administration, even invited comparisons to the Japanese system of overt government involvement in the technology development of national "champions." Others suggested that the Pentagon should cut military spending more drastically and use the savings—an enlarged peace dividend—to pay for worker retraining and community adjustment.

Both alternatives have problems. Financial incentives for new technology development provide no guarantee that defense contractors will use their cost savings for training or reinvestment. Like state and local tax breaks, incentives create new opportunities for fraud and misuse. On the other hand, abandoning defense contractors ignores the valuable sunk costs—namely, the physical assets and skills—that have been made in defense contractors over the years.

Rather than suggest that the government simply eliminate all military spending or give away more adjustment funds to defense contractors, my prescriptions place the onus on both the state and its contractors to accept a heavier burden of accountability to other public interests. Accountability suggests a heightened responsiveness to those upon whom the contractor depends and to the community whose well-being it affects (Selznick 1992, 338). In order for contractors to become accountable to public interests in ways that will really address the problems I have described, the public interests themselves must reflect the needs of critically affected defense workers and communities. I suggest ways to democratize the defense adjustment agenda to allow for influence from traditionally neglected stakeholders.

Ensuring that the remaining weapons systems procured with federal funding are both affordable and necessary is one of the most important criteria of public accountability. If defense spending is going to be an effective industrial policy, then the Pentagon should purchase goods the country needs and not just "big-ticket Cold War relics" (Ann Markusen, quoted in Denny 1992). General Dynamics' successful effort to keep a few billion in the defense budget so that Electric Boat could build two Seawolf submarines exemplifies the kind of behavior the Pentagon must leave behind. Regional economist Ann Markusen also noted, "When the Seawolfs are built, we will have two white elephants on our hands, we will be $3 billion deeper in debt and the same 10,000 people will be left with no job prospects" (quoted in Denny 1992). Wasteful make-work pork exemplifies the worst of corporate welfare.

Altered priorities alone, however, will not bring about the intended reforms. In this chapter, I suggest three sets of guiding principles and specific measures that can encourage an amplified public voice in the private investment decisions of contractors. Nonshareholder constituents must be part of the continuing adjustment process. The principles of conditionality, proportionality, oversight, and enforcement must be written into procurement contracts and legislation in order to tie the receipt of federal moneys to specific benchmarks of workplace reform and community reinvestment. I also suggest concurrent changes in the internal corporate governance of defense contractors and their ownership structure to minimize both the economic dislocation and the windfall profits created by defense contractor restructuring. My suggestions ultimately depend on the ability of our political leaders to sustain long-term visions as they do the work needed to transform the legal environment in which contractors operate. In the absence of these transformations, contractors will not behave like the public's fiduciaries but will instead continue to redirect public resources toward narrowly private, profit-seeking ends.

Accountability through Popular Participation

If the government was not acting as the arbiter of broader public interests during the defense adjustment process of the 1990s, who was? The intimate relations between the Pentagon and contractors excluded other state and nonstate actors who, as risk-bearers and corporate contributors, also had legitimate stakes in defense adjustment. Residents of defense-dependent communities, organized labor, and other stakeholders directly affected by the defense drawdown were not recognized through traditional channels of policymaking, or perhaps chose not to articulate their interests through these channels, knowing that their prospects for influence were so limited (Brecher and Costello 1990). These stakeholders had few rights for legal protection or inclusion in private economic and closed-door political decisionmaking. In response, many became activists, articulating broader public interests that directly contradicted the public interest claims offered by defense companies and the Pentagon.

Grassroots organizations, sometimes assisted by national groups such as the National Center for Economic Conversion and Disarmament, Catholic Workers, or SANE Freeze, took on a monitoring and campaigning function with regard not only to defense adjustment, as it was narrowly defined, but to conversion as it related to issues affecting the environment, working conditions, and infrastructure improvements (Rose 1993). They viewed conversion as more than a technological fix to commercialize defense products; for them, conversion was both a means and an ends to fundamentally transforming relations between labor, capital, and the state into a "new social compact" (Call to Action 1994, 12; Bischak and Yudken 1993; Wainwright and Elliott 1982). They sought to end regional reliance on defense manufacturing, but to do so without causing massive dislocation. In St. Louis, Phoenix, Maine, Long Island, southeastern Connecticut, and other cities and regions across the country, these organizations demanded democratic conversion planning initiated by workers and communities.[2]

These coalitions' visions of conversion planning involved participatory processes to produce socially useful, nonmilitary ends, in contrast to the federal subsidies for technology that might only *indirectly* provide jobs, community reinvestment, and technological "solutions" for social problems. For example, the conversion coalition in southeastern Connecticut, A Call to Action, promoted an alternative economic conversion agenda that stressed:

- worker involvement in corporate decisionmaking;
- additional community adjustment funding from federal and state governments;
- new federal market creation by redirecting the peace dividend to government purchases for civilian products;
- increased defense market regulation to encourage high environmental standards and "Buy American" provisions;
- retraining that is linked to economic development;
- additional income support and preferential rehire rights on government contracts for former defense workers. (Summarized from Call to Action 1994, 14–15)

A Call to Action and another private, nonprofit organization called Technology for Connecticut (TECHCONN) attempted to identify and nurture a new industrial base in southeastern Connecticut, one engaged in manufacturing energy- and transportation-related products as well as environmental technologies (TECHCONN 1993). Like A Call to Action, other community-led conversion movements sought to improve the living standards of a wide swath of citizens by organizing and educating communities, staging protests and rallies, and allying themselves with organized labor and progressive state and federal legislators. These labor-government-community coalitions opposed the restructuring strategies of contractors and took a more confrontational approach to management than entrenched federal agencies. In St. Louis, a coalition of peace, religious, and economic justice groups mounted a campaign to pressure McDonnell Douglas to pursue conversion efforts. Led by a Catholic nun, the coalition participated in the annual shareholders meetings and raised the concerns of other stakeholders in these forums.

A Call to Action served as a watchdog organization for the defense adjustment process in southeastern Connecticut, representing groups and community members neglected and yet affected by corporate strategies and the policies that supported them. The organization included other state and federal budget watchdogs, labor leaders, teacher and church groups, peace activists, and professional organizers. A Call to Action published handbooks advising defense workers about organizing "alternative use" strategies to use their facilities and skills to develop new products or modify existing products for new markets (Call to Action 1995). Stressing popular economic literacy, it assisted unions in putting pressure on management to bargain over an alternative use plan and jointly produce such a plan.

After encountering little success negotiating with Electric Boat, A Call to Action turned its attention to assisting those workers laid off by the company. It helped a union-affiliated human resources provider, the

Work and Technology Institute, win a Department of Labor–funded demonstration grant to administer dislocated worker services at Electric Boat, edging out a consulting firm with strong ties to management. With the assistance of local community colleges and the unions, the nonprofit provider conducted a skill survey of workers *before* they were laid off, helping workers develop personal educational, career, and financial plans. They identified sectors that were growing and in which Electric Boat workers were likely to find jobs—namely, the building trades and fiber optics installation. They also tracked dislocated workers after they left the company. A Call to Action funded a study measuring the regional employment and fiscal impacts of layoffs at Electric Boat (Midwest Center for Labor Research 1996) and organized a press conference to publicize the results of the study.

Community coalition building was often difficult, as many of the local groups had conflicting agendas and different definitions of conversion. Although disarmament advocates and community groups generally embraced progressive ideals, for example, their ties to labor were tenuous and almost indifferent before the drawdown of the 1990s (Rose 1993). During the early years of the decade, however, many peace groups realized that their calls to end all defense production would cause massive dislocation and turned their attention away from arms reduction treaties to more local, workplace concerns, such as high-performance manufacturing (Wilson 1993). Similarly, unions realized there would be no imminent upturn in defense spending and looked to conversion as the only means of job security and/or reemployment. Labor law made it difficult for unions to negotiate for conversion measures through the collective bargaining process so they sought out external community support for their initiatives (AFL-CIO Industrial Union Department 1990; Hanley 1993).

Despite the successes of these decentralized efforts, other groups representing local interests, especially business associations, were less sympathetic to the conversion agenda. In southeastern Connecticut, for example, the local Chamber of Commerce and the statewide Connecticut Business and Industry Association (CBIA) acted as boosters for tourism and casino development. They used the defense conversion agenda as an opportunity to push measures for a "favorable business climate," such as lowering state taxes. These organizations supported Electric Boat's disinvestment decisions and consistently praised the company for its timely notification of layoffs. Downplaying the severity of layoffs, they advertised the area's pool of cheap labor as one of its main strengths for future business growth.

At the same time that grassroots struggles were an important part of progressive reform and greater citizen involvement in decisionmaking

at the local level, these organizations also opted for other forms of interest articulation to effect policy changes at the state and national levels.
Whether certain policies were enacted depended not only on interests of
the relevant groups or bureaucrats, or the strength of the idea of "economic conversion," but on the power of each of these stakeholders and
the coalitions they built. Local and regional organizations aligned themselves with Congressional representatives—such as the late Ted Weiss
(D.-NY), Sam Gejdenson (D.-CT), Senator Barbara Boxer (D.-CA)—to
sponsor measures mandating diversification and making the distribution of adjustment outcomes more equitable. No coalition, however,
proved strong enough to dismantle the alliances between the Pentagon
and its prime contractors and their monopoly on the defense policy
agenda.

A more equitable adjustment agenda would be more responsive to
those public actors least able to protect themselves from the effects of
fundamental corporate changes. Workers and communities possessed
few protections from opportunistic conduct by defense firms, and yet
had much to lose. Unlike shareholders, they were not diversified but singularly dependent on defense contractors, entities whose actions they
had no hope of influencing. These coalitions attempted to secure places
for themselves in policymaking circles and pressure legislators so that
the goals of defense adjustment policies would take their welfare into account. When Clinton took office, his administration articulated policy
goals that would have served the interests of these unprotected groups:
commercial technology development, massive cost savings on procured
weapons, and the creation and retention of advanced manufacturing jobs
(Clinton and Gore 1993). In the following years, however, the Clinton administration developed few policy measures to achieve these objectives.

Accountability through Contracts and Regulation

The American corporation is structured to serve the interests of its shareholders. Shareholders have legally recognized rights to residual corporate profits, and managers have legally recognized obligations to distribute that surplus to them. Thanks to corporate law, shareholders—as the
designated corporate "principals"—have at their disposal a repertoire of
incentive and enforcement mechanisms to promote and enforce managers' responsibility to them. Management's fiduciary obligations to
shareholders are codified in and protected by corporate charters and bylaws. Shareholders can vote to replace the board of directors, pursue derivative suits against management for breaching their fiduciary duties,
disapprove of executive compensation plans, and if all else fails, exit easily if they do not believe managers are upholding their obligations. Al-

though structural problems limit the use of these accountability mechanisms, their existence serves the important function of governing shareholders' delegation of power to management.

In contrast, taxpayers, workers, and communities have few enforcement mechanisms to shape the parameters of managerial decisionmaking and protect their firm-specific investments in defense contractors. Accordingly, community groups, labor, and other public actors were unable to compete with stockholder demands in influencing defense contractors' behavior after the Cold War. Despite the recognition that the public sector does not always represent these different public interests, we should not reject the state as a viable medium for furthering corporate accountability to objectives broader than shareholder wealth maximization. Unlike private firms, the state has the opportunity to insert opportunities for public governance in the contracts it writes and the regulations it drafts. Without these changes, individual contractors that attempt to use their profits to serve wider public interests may be penalized for their generosity by financial markets and laws that continue to give priority to shareholder interests. The state, much more so than private companies, *can* respond to democratic pressures; whether it does so depends on its openness to change and the strength of policy networks fighting for reform.

The government has the power to include accountability mechanisms in the procurement contracts that define a contractor's market. Contracts—whether for nuclear submarines or for dual-use technologies—provide some contractor benefit (i.e., profit) in exchange for the fulfillment of a part of the state's interest (i.e., the development of high-quality weapons systems or other technology). I have demonstrated in previous chapters that procurement contracts are incomplete because parties are unable to specify all of the contingencies of their long-term relationships. Nonetheless, contractors insist that they cannot exceed the literal specifications of contracts. Under the existing framework for regulation, management has no legal duty to negotiate with the state about economic restructuring, technological innovation, and job security *unless these measures are included in their procurement contracts or are required by statute.*

It makes sense that a strategy aimed at increasing defense contractor accountability to the public would seek to transform the very documents contractors sign. At the state and local levels, public officials, unions, and community coalitions have organized movements to work their interests into economic development programs since the late 1980s. The movement for corporate accountability, typified by the work of national organizations like the Corporation for Enterprise Development and Good Jobs First and other local groups, such as the Minnesota Alliance for Progressive Action and the Los Angeles Alliance for a New Economy, has attempted to bind those businesses that receive public subsidies to behavior that benefits the communities, workers, and citizens that subsidize them (LeRoy et al. 1994; Moss 1995). Proactive and preemptive strategies involve clearly specifying the terms of the exchange *ex ante*, before public funds change hands.

But to which public interests should contractors be held responsible? The problem of accountability is considerably more difficult when the principal is a complex, heterogeneous constellation of different public interests. It is easier to speculate about labor's interests, as most of the legal and economic scholars who argue for expanded managerial accountability do. Better wages and benefits, job security, and involvement in decisionmaking—these are what labor wants. In contrast, accountability to the state or to "the public" is hard to delimit because of the representative nature of the state, the cacophony of public interest claims, and the dispersed and disorganized nature of taxpayers. In keeping with utilitarian principles of justice, it could be argued that the returns generated by the government's investments should be maximized and distributed so that the least well-off are made as well off as possible. When I refer to corporate obligations to the public, then, I am interested in those obligations that could serve the widest, most diffuse interests of the public as opposed to the concentrated interests of management and shareholders (Banfield 1964). These public interests might include the affordability of weapons systems, the reuse of facilities (instead of mothballing these public investments), technological innovation and competitiveness, rebuilding American manufacturing, high-wage, high-skill job creation, and community reinvestment. A more minimalist variant would simply seek to end the wasting of tax dollars.

Given the differentiated character of adjustment strategies among contractors and the multiplicity of public objectives, the kinds of contractual provisions that would best facilitate the transition to a demilitarized economy are difficult to draft. In this section, I suggest some guiding principles, as well as ways in which the quality of the mechanisms the government uses to delegate public tasks to contractors could be strengthened. If the government finances contractors to pursue public objectives, it must first take measures to prevent the exploitation of public funds and ensure that managers of profit-seeking contractors take some formulation of public interests into account in their investment decisionmaking (Donahue 1989, 39). The following policy principles, if woven into the fabric of future contracts and regulation, can increase the accountability of defense contractors to broader public interests than those of shareholders.

Conditionality

The idea that the public should get something back for providing a private benefit, linking the receipt of public funds to some broader public objectives, is a common policy theme. City planners employ "linkage provisions" in their agreements with developers so that developers will provide a public benefit (e.g., more green space) in exchange for the city's concessions on zoning requirements. At the federal level, provisions in the Omnibus Trade and Competitiveness Act (OTCA) condition access to American consumer markets on our trading partners' respect for internationally recognized worker rights. The Defense Department finances the private development of a particular technology on the condition that it receive a patent or "walk-in" right to that technology. When the state acts as a market participant, precedent supports the state's rights to impose conditions on the market in which it acts.

"Conditionality," then, refers to a quid pro quo policy. The public should receive some specified benefit in exchange for its largesse with defense contractors, instead of silently standing by as shareholders extract its previous investments. The expected public benefits from defense contracts and subsidies can be made more binding by writing provisions into contracts and legislation. As with local linkage policies, the conditions must be related to the original intention or express purpose of the public funding. In other words, conditioning a TRP grant on a contractor's promise to build a community playground would be incongruous and unfounded. But conditioning TRP funds on a contractor's promise to allow for worker participation in defense diversification activities or other benchmarks of workplace reform seems more reasonable. Conditions, therefore, must not be ancillary to the manufacture and delivery of weapons systems.

Contractors could be required to develop labor-management councils to investigate diversification possibilities, inform and consult employee representatives about fundamental corporate changes, set minimum standards in the event of a collective dismissal, and establish an official role for workers in the decisionmaking process. After all, workers are directly affected by a firm's decision to diversify, and their tacit knowledge of products and processes is often a determinant of the success or failure of such a project. If the public sector fails to make this linkage overt or if its goals are not legitimately tied to their original purpose, the courts will have little meaningful guidance in interpreting contracts (Moss 1995). The bargain and the conditioned in-kind benefits must be made as explicit as possible; leaving its expectations vague and unspecified weakens the state's ability to enforce its defense adjustment goals.

Proportionality

Not all contractors receive the same amount of public investment, and not all residual claimants make equal contributions to contractors. Some prime contractors, for example, are almost entirely defense dependent whereas others have more commercial sales. Although 93 percent of General Dynamics' sales were to the Department of Defense (in 1994), most of the aerospace industry is "dual use" and diversified, with large commercial markets in telecommunications (e.g., satellites) and aircraft.

   Thus, the public sector must develop standards for measuring the size of different groups' contributions to each contractor and calibrating the contractor's reciprocal responsibilities and benefits to such standards. This procedure is complicated by the fact that the amount of state support as well as the contractor's responsibilities must be divisible (i.e., have monetary value). Good contracts should aspire to measure outcomes and quantify anticipated public benefits for the sake of defining breach and damages. The benefits to the public are often intangible and ambiguous: for example, *more* participation, *better* jobs, commercial technology development, or, perhaps most difficult, national security. If subsidies are to be effective, they must include more concise measures or proxies of the intended benefits, as well as a time period in which these benefits must accrue. Defense adjustment incentives could include provisions specifying threshold job creation requirements or a target amount of commercial sales.

Oversight

Like shareholders, the public has a strong need to monitor its contractors because of its residual claims on the net proceeds of the firm. The primary purpose of oversight and reporting provisions is to control the discretion of both contractor management and public procurement agencies, since both their interests can be poorly aligned with the interests of the public (McCubbins et al. 1989). Monitoring allows groups to ensure that the contractor is complying with the terms of the contract and assists agencies in gathering data to help evaluate the effectiveness of their programs after the program is completed. Although defense contractors are already enmeshed in a bureaucratic morass of oversight and reporting requirements, this traditionally centralized oversight relies on auditors who may collude with the contractors and who are susceptible to the hazards of political affiliation (Marshall, Meurer, and Richard 1991). I suggest that a more decentralized, local monitoring agency, akin to the supervisor of shipbuilding at Navy shipyards or a board comprised of third-party, nonstate actors, supplement or take over this function.

Enforceability

Having legally recognized obligations to the state through contracts solves only part of the problem; ensuring public accountability requires laying out explicit penalties for noncompliance (Hawkins and Thomas 1984). Contracts can specify the appropriate damages, which might include getting back the amount of public funds originally granted to contractors as inducements (i.e., "clawback" measures), excluding the contractor from future awards (i.e., debarment based on past performance), or even requiring the contractor to perform some kind of community service.

However, the federal government may be reluctant to debar or penalize a corporation that breaches a contract because, as I have noted in previous chapters, it is dependent on a few capable suppliers and may fear alienating them with such harsh penalties. In such cases, contracts should provide for third-party enforcement (Moss 1995). Community groups have begun to sue contractors who breach their government contracts, because these contracts are frequently made with the *intention* of benefiting these groups as taxpayers or interested parties. Unfortunately few of these third-party cases have been successful;[3] scholars and activists, nonetheless, believe that their very existence can serve to deter potential breach and that with federal and state legislation in place, their chances of winning such suits are greater.

Accountability in Practice

These guiding principles are not just an untenable wish list of qualities for better governance; they are being tested in the laboratories of state and local policy-making. Unions and grassroots organizations have lobbied successfully to force public funding agencies to write better, more accountable contracts. They have done so primarily by helping to pass legislation that provides the guidelines for drafting such contracts. In 1994, for example, the Call to Action coalition helped to pass *An Act Concerning Defense Diversification*. This important legislation requires Connecticut-based defense contractors who receive assistance from the state and over $1 million per year in defense contracts to establish an Alternative Use Committee (AUC).[4] An AUC is a group comprised of labor and management representatives organized to identify new commercial products and determine retraining needs. Related legislation, *An Act Concerning Economic Development Program Accountability*, requires members of state granting agencies to report to various committees on the

performance of each business to which they have given financial assistance.[5] This report must include the number of jobs the contractor had
when it applied for state funds, the number it anticipated retaining or
creating (including projected wage rates), and the criteria the state
agency used to determine the economic benefits of providing assistance.

The Connecticut legislation attaches enforceable accountability mechanisms to defense diversification subsidies, incentives, and tax abate-
ments. However, these mechanisms affect only those companies that voluntarily apply for and win state financial incentives. This system allows
many of the largest contractors to fall through the cracks, especially those
who do not seek public financing because of the strength of their own
balance sheets and those who, like General Dynamics, have been
adamantly opposed to the very notion of defense diversification. Only
those contractors already convinced of the necessity of diversification
and those who seek out state assistance, usually small and medium-sized
contractors, shoulder the added public obligations. In order to widen
their reach, I suggest that the accountability mechanisms be applied to
any prime contractor that receives over 75 percent of its sales from public
dollars, regardless of their intended use.

In this vein, several federal legislative attempts have sought to make
the recipients of large federal procurement contracts more publicly accountable. In 1990 Congressman Claiborne Pell (R.-RI) sponsored a bill
that would have required all defense contractors to set aside one-tenth of
one percent of their gross defense revenues—up to a ceiling of $500,000—
to create a diversification planning office within each company.[6] The office would have considered such factors as alternate commercial uses of
the facility and the prospects for retaining and retraining the labor force.
This requirement would not have applied to companies with less than
$15 million in annual defense revenues.[7]

Another important attempt to mandate defense diversification was an
early initiative that originated in the office of the late Congressman Ted
Weiss (D.-NY).[8] Financed by a 1.25 to 2 percent tax on defense procurement contracts, the Weiss bill required contractors to provide full benefits
and 80 to 90 percent of their original salaries to dislocated defense workers during their retraining period. His bill also required that site-specific
conversion plans be drafted by mandatory alternative use committees.
Contractors refusing to participate would be ineligible to obtain defense
contracts for three years. Weiss said his program was necessary because
large contractors could not be trusted to protect workers. "Until you have
the full system in place, where companies are really required . . . to enter
into planning with the representatives of their workforce, they're not going to do it," Weiss correctly noted (Benenson 1990, 89). The Weiss bill
faced opposition on all fronts, and few of his proposals actually made it

into the skeletal Defense Authorization Bill of 1990, a bill that merely allocated additional funding to the existing Department of Labor and Department of Commerce programs.

Even if defense contractors were required to redirect some of their profits to forming AUCs and exploring commercial opportunities, they might not have been able to shepherd workers, technologies, and facilities into lucrative new activities. Conversion would not have been possible in some instances. The skills and assets necessary to build commercial ships, for example, might have been available elsewhere in the United States in better configurations or cheaper abroad in countries like Korea. In some cases, shuttering the plant, helping workers move to other sectors and other locations, and assisting communities to diversify their industrial bases would have been the best alternative for all stakeholders. Nonetheless, public involvement in these decisions would have ensured that more options and interests were considered.

A massive federal investment in outright conversion would be fraught with the risks of economic failure and political embarrassment. But placing the onus on private defense contractors, as the above-mentioned legislation does, forces contractors to salvage some of the investments the public sector has made in them through the years. AUCs would provide excellent incubators for spinning off viable subunits and would give stakeholders a structure in which to cope with downsizing. Such measures would also make undesirable corporate behavior (e.g., ignoring diversification opportunities or seeking excessive profits) more expensive. These progressive policies faced tremendous opposition in Congress because they intervened in the sacrosanct realm of managerial prerogative. In an era with a conservative political climate and simultaneously vibrant stock market, one would not expect support for such interventionist proposals as the Weiss or Pell bills. However, part of the recent backlash against "corporate welfare" has fostered bipartisan coalitions to reform the unwieldy and ineffective tentacles of public financing (Regan 1988). The future is unwritten; there is room for legislative and judicial experimentation with these accountability mechanisms to improve the conduct of recipient firms.

Accountability through Corporate Governance Reform

Regulatory and contractual enforcement of defense contractor accountability is critical, but these vehicles alone cannot stem contractor opportunism. As witnessed by the scores of unchecked violations of the acquisition regulations and individual procurement contracts, profit-seeking agents find ways to get the most out of their government contracts. The measures I have suggested involve tampering with the contours of the principal-agent relationship by imposing external constraints on contractors. Internally, however, the corporation is still singularly focused on shareholder primacy. External constraints have already created a cumbersome maze of requirements for contractors, and they encourage an overly legalistic enforcement ethos by requiring constant oversight and negotiation between the state and its suppliers. Highly contractualized, regulatory constraints provide a "blunt form of relief that cannot remedy opportunistic behavior effectively" (O'Connor 1991, 1258). Defense contractors are not structured to act responsibly toward anyone other than their shareholders, and they will challenge every legislative or contractual measure that cuts into their autonomy. Thus, I suggest that, at an even more fundamental level, corporate governance rules be reoriented so that contractors have an internal commitment and legally recognized fiduciary duties to the state and, by extension, the public.

Several economists and legal scholars have proposed new models of corporate governance that would broaden directorial fiduciary duties to encompass a wider range of stakeholders, primarily workers (O'Connor 1991; Blair 1995; Millon 1991; Mitchell 1995). In Chapter 1, I discussed some of the advantages and shortcomings of their "multifiduciary" models. Unlike some of these authors, I do not believe that fiduciary norms are *the* most important avenue for corporate reform, nor do I overestimate the influence that corporate governance rules alone have on managerial decisionmaking (for an excellent critique, see Simon 1993). However, I do view corporate governance as a fundamental arena in which the distributional priorities of management are reinforced and justified by legal doctrine. Corporate governance rules, therefore, deserve attention and revision, and can be used in conjunction with contracts and regulation to strengthen other means of controlling the behavior of large, subsidized corporate enterprises.

The federal government—along with taxpayers, workers, and communities—makes unrecoverable investments in its prime contractors, investments that are vulnerable to managerial opportunism and abuse. Fiduciary duties should arise in recognition of these public investments, so that decisions about their future at the end of wartime production are not management's alone to make. The law should ensure that managers take stock of the impact of their decisions on the federal government, employees, and taxpayers, measure and weigh alternative investment scenarios, and be prepared to justify their actions to an oversight body other than their own boards of directors. In evaluating different investments, contractors can still aim to enhance shareholder wealth, but if their financial restructuring strategies are found to severely undermine public interests, management should be required to choose less injurious alternatives.

Contractarian scholars object to the idea of managers' fiduciary duties to nonshareholder constituencies, maintaining that these obligations force managers into the role of public servants (Macey 1989). My belief is that such a description is fitting in the case of defense contractors, who as the government's agents should be held to the higher standards of accountability that accompany grants of public authority. I am suggesting that the legal "core" of government contractors be oriented toward public ends, so that their corporate strategies come under the scrutiny of nonshareholder groups.

Fiduciary law responds to the risk of abuse of power inherent in any relationship of delegation, especially those relationships that are long-term. Fiduciary duties are intended to restrict these abuses of power when neither contracts nor statutory mechanisms adequately guard against agent opportunism (Williamson 1975). With their moral undertones and flexibility, fiduciary obligations embody the kind of responsibilities that directors should owe the state and the groups the state is entrusted to protect. Transforming the very core of entrepreneurial control is necessary to subject the distributional decisions of management to additional public oversight and control.

In terms of actual legal reforms, I suggest that prime defense contractors with over 75 percent of sales to the government be federally—as opposed to state—chartered, reviving the doctrine of "concession theory" prevalent in the United States before 1850.[9] Concession theory treated incorporation as a "gift of the state" conferred for public purposes (Horwitz 1992, 72–74). It justified the public regulation of property on the grounds that the state needed to be able to protect the solvency of local communities and workers. The contemporary application of concession doctrine can be found in such "federal instrumentalities" as the Federal National Mortgage Association (Fannie Mae) and Amtrak. These enterprises are chartered by Congress, yet are privately owned. They are chartered to fulfill a government purpose, which is outlined in broad statutes, similar to a private company's articles of incorporation but passed by Congress.

Federal charters could outline the principles governing defense contractors' definition of mission, personnel policy, and fiduciary responsibilities to the state. They would then provide the state with legal mechanisms for *ex ante* and *ex post* enforcement of its interests. Charters could require that defense contractors engage in regular and sustained consultation with a public body (perhaps the General Accounting Office). This body could be apprised not only about the company's profitability but also about the distribution of profits and impact of the contractor's decisions on the government's investments (i.e., infrastructure, workforce, diversification projects). After reviewing this information, the government would be able to negotiate with management *ex ante* over corporate strategies. In a sense, my suggestions aspire to create something akin to the "codetermination" process found in more corporatist systems of government, whereby national unions and trade associations engage in ongoing dialogue with management about industry-wide and individual business strategy (Schmitter and Lembruch 1979). Under German law, for example, workers' supervisory boards have important control and monitoring functions over corporate policy: supervising management, examining the company's documents and assets, questioning management about policy decisions, and approving certain transactions.

Federal charters could also establish the general principles to which the courts would hold defense contractors accountable. If the government suspected a contractor of breaching its codified duties, the government would have the legal grounds to challenge contractors in court. In other words, the charter would allow the executive branch to initiate an *ex post* judicial review to evaluate the fairness of managers' investment decisions.[10] The courts are generally reluctant to second-guess management decisions (Clark 1993). With a statutory change such as federal chartering, however, the courts would possess the institutional precedent and the evidence to consider state challenges to management's authority. They could scrutinize the explicit promise (as outlined in the charter) between the state and contractor management instead of adjudicating on the basis of implicit and vague assumptions about the public interests inherent in defense contracting.

Contractarian scholars would argue that this kind of state intervention is not needed to redistribute control within a firm and that allowing an external body such a large degree of oversight and control increases shareholder uncertainty and deters investment. In contrast, I believe that, with certain institutional reforms, shareholders of defense contractors could enjoy more certainty and more stable returns. If alternative forms of corporate governance were to prevail, financial market rules would encourage more patient, committed, and "relational" forms of investment in defense contractors. Defense contractors, like utilities, could comprise an index separate from other publicly held corporations in the NASDAQ, NYSE, and ASE. Stocks in this index would provide investors with lower returns in exchange for the lower levels of risk inherent in state-supported contractors. The government should decide what level of profitability is reasonable and compatible with a spectrum of contractor responsibilities, a spectrum that includes appropriate concern for employment, technological innovation, and industrial base impacts. If the government assured shareholders of the few remaining contractors that they would maintain a set level of profitability (adjusted by the inflation rate), shareholders would face less uncertainty and contractors could plan longer-term strategies.

There are other reasons why different corporate stakeholders would prefer such arrangements. Federal charters would allow shareholders of defense contractors a "public interest defense" against hostile takeovers, based on the loss of valued technical knowledge and skills, impact on communities, and potential for increased costs to the public purse. Management could also rely on them to fend off shareholder derivative suits. Defense contractors could enjoy the other advantages available to federal government corporations, such as exemptions from certain securities regulations and sovereign immunity (Froomkin 1995). If the legal expectations and obligations between the state, management, and shareholders could be made more explicit and binding in charters, the principal-agent relationships between these parties would be less contested. Under our current form of investment, dispersed institutional investors have become like absentee landlords, exerting power without responsibility and making exacting demands on managers for higher dividends at the expense of other stakeholders. Corporate management has responded by raising hurdles for acceptable rates of return, becoming more secretive, and curtailing investments in assets (such as retraining and research and development) that do not show up on income statements. The kind of cooperation, certainty, and stability encouraged by federal charters and low-risk, low-return indices may ultimately be less costly to the state, contractors, and shareholders than their current relationships of antagonism (Bowles, Gordon, and Weisskopf 1990, 194–195; Crotty and Goldstein 1993).

Strategies aimed at the reform of corporate governance strictures attempt to alter the basic, profit-seeking motivation of the corporation by requiring consideration of other stakeholders' interests. Another more radical means of correcting the agency problems inherent in government contracting involves realigning contractors' profit motive through some form of public ownership. Regulation through modified public ownership is the main mode of economic regulation in most countries outside of the United States. Public ownership gives the state additional powers to impose planning on industries of particular national concern. Even the United States government has considered renationalizing the defense industry, well aware of the profound problem that privatizing public tasks has created in terms of increased authority and freedom from public control. The economist John Kenneth Galbraith, for example, argued that arms companies and others that provide vital services under a virtual monopoly should be treated as public utilities (1969). During the contract claim struggles of the late 1970s and cost-plus embarrassments of the 1980s, even Admiral Hyman Rickover suggested that the Navy take over

Electric Boat and operate the shipyard as a government facility under contract to General Dynamics.

But the courts would probably find such seizures unconstitutional, unless they took place under emergency circumstances, and they would certainly be politically unpopular. Moreover outright nationalization has failed in many countries, not just with respect to economic regulation and control but with respect to sociopolitical objectives of consumer protection and public accountability. Managers of public enterprises frequently create their own empires far from the oversight of citizen-consumers (Baev 1993). Rather than suggest the full-scale nationalization of prime defense contractors, a suggestion that would be met with ridicule or hostility, I recommend that the state employ an alternative legal mechanism for control over the formerly public defense industry: partial share ownership.[11]

The government would like to exercise voice in the decisions of its private contractors, rather than try to write overly inclusive procurement contracts *ex ante* or weakly threaten errant suppliers with sanctions *ex post*. If the state possessed significant property holdings in enterprises of strategic importance, it would be guaranteed a role in setting important business strategy (Baev 1995; Boardman and Vining 1991). The public sector would be able to appoint representatives to the contractors' boards of directors, allowing it access to more information about the contractor and the ability to approve investment programs. Firms would have autonomy to operate their business, with the attendant benefit of "market" efficiency, and at the same time the government would be better able to coordinate defense production needs.

In most countries, "golden shares" and other forms of mixed ownership, where some percentage of shares are held by private shareholders and some by national governments, are used to operationalize the state's investment in companies of national interest (Boardman and Vining 1991, 224).[12] Golden shares originated during the privatization of state-held British firms such as Britoil and Jaguar in the 1980s. When Prime Minister Margaret Thatcher sold these two firms, the British government retained a golden share in each organization. This device allowed the government to outvote all other shareholders and retain veto power over key decisions, even if the government did not otherwise own a controlling number of equity shares (Baev 1995, 20; Pezard 1995).

Golden shares traditionally confer no rights to receive actual dividends or monetary returns, although in some countries, mixed-ownership enterprises provide an important source of state revenue. They do, however, grant their holders an amount of control disproportionate to the amount of equity held. Holders can require a company to undertake new product lines, maintain contractual relations with particular business partners, or refrain from financial restructuring or foreign takeovers, leading some commentators to wonder whether or not golden shares are simply a covert form of industrial policy (Graham and Prosser 1988, 413). Because of these powers, golden shares are held solely by governments and are not transferable to nongovernmental entities.

Aside from a dwindling number of publicly owned arsenals and depots, the United States has rejected outright nationalization of the defense industry, reflecting the generally held belief that the defense market functions well under normal circumstances. Nonetheless, I believe that after the current shakeout, the industry will be poised for a new ownership structure. Defense officials admit that after the restructuring of the industry and lulls in production, America will revert back to its old arsenal system; only this time, defense facilities will be privately owned (Kaminski 1995; Sapolsky and Gholz 1996; Pages 1995). In the restructured defense industry, a handful of contractors will be designated as sole-source providers of technologies not readily available in the civilian sector. Through exclusive government purchasing agreements and subsidies, the Pentagon will continue to sustain these few contractors in a sheltered state, keeping their defense capabilities warm for future conflict (Markusen 1997a). We saw the genesis of this system in the Pentagon's decision to fund the continued production of the soon-to-be-obsolete Seawolf.

At the same time, the increasing monopoly power of these contractors, the barriers of "asymmetrical information," and the high cost of monitoring contractors' behavior provide incentives for these firms to engage in opportunistic behavior. As the defense industrial base dwindles and the stakes increase (i.e., fewer, larger contracts), existing principal-agent problems are likely to be exacerbated. For example, surviving contractors will more frequently challenge awards by the Pentagon through the courts, and, in general, they will use their political clout to further misallocate scarce resources.

Partial ownership rights in the remaining oligopoly would allow a state agency—or, better yet, a more decentralized board comprised of diverse agency, labor, and community representatives—to govern more closely and influence the behavior of the private arsenal system. This board would resolve many of the principal-agent problems that plague both defense procurement spending and adjustment policies. The high transaction costs of government contracting for "idiosyncratic" products would diminish if these transactions took place closer within the hierarchical governance structure of the state, because hierarchies tend to better monitor such exchanges and minimize uncertainty (Williamson 1975). Most importantly, the state would be positioned to engage in synoptic and strategic planning for the nation's future, which would better coordinate the needs, outputs, time horizons, and labor force requirements of the defense industrial base (Lindblom 1977, 314).

Partial ownership rights would have given the Pentagon more say over General Dynamics' record profits and bonuses. They would have accorded state agencies more control over the allocation of resources in the company. The state could have chosen to preserve or redeploy its investments in defense-specific skills and capital, rather than watch as its assets were dismantled, appropriated, and made rapidly obsolete. Funds could have been invested in the interests of national security and cheaper submarines and tanks. They could have been more effectively spent retraining shipyard employees and putting them to work rebuilding New England's tattered infrastructure. A study conducted for the United States Conference of Mayors estimated the impact of a shift from military spending to urban programs and demonstrated how a realignment of federal budget priorities could provide the resources needed to meet cities' urgent needs for infrastructure and social services (1988).

Even partial public ownership, however, is not immune to rent-seeking behavior. Members of the public sector agency entrusted to hold golden shares may become prejudicial, corrupt, or indolent (Lowi 1969). Thus, there is a coincident need for safeguards to ensure public oversight and voice when ownership rights are granted to a state agency. A well-crafted architecture of accountability might include Congressional oversight or citizens' councils to evaluate the government's relationship with its contractors. As owners, the government agency would also carry the same legal obligations as ordinary shareholders, including fiduciary duties to minority shareholders, disclosure requirements, and prohibitions on insider trading (Baev 1995). Like shareholders, the state should have an exit option if, for example, it became clear that a contractor would operate better on its own or at least with less state oversight control. The government could relinquish its shares if the council made such a determination, or it could agree to enter into a golden share arrangement for a limited period of time.

"A Proper Symmetry of Obligation"

If we want to retain our system of contracting out the production of weapons to private, for-profit contractors, we must reshape the way the system operates. Capitalism is compatible with myriad regulatory regimes and institutional forms and can accommodate many types of nonmarket property, such as land trusts and collectives (Simon 1994). Thus, the great challenge facing the defense industry, those who regulate it, and those who finance it, in the words of British journalist Will Hutton, is to create a "new financial architecture in which private decisions produce a less degenerate capitalism" (1995, 298). We must broaden the arena of public stakeholding to create a bias toward long-term, socially useful ends.

The same applies to firms in other heavily subsidized sectors, such as agriculture, utilities, and nuclear power, for in these sectors, the state also acts as the residual stakeholder. Each corporation and sector, however, receives different amounts of federal financing and regulatory assistance. The nature of obligations that should inhere to each enterprise therefore involves a judgment based on the degree or amount of the public contribution. The public sector can develop criteria for measuring the size of its contribution to each enterprise, culminating in a spectrum of reciprocal responsibilities owed by each subsidized company. The few remaining prime defense contractors, as very extreme and expensive examples of state involvement, would be required to submit to a higher standard of state oversight and control, whereas less subsidized corporations would shoulder a lighter burden. However, the amount of public funds that corporations receive is not the sole determinant of the kind and degree of obligation they should owe the public. The nature of the public tasks that each corporation performs is also at issue. Defense contractors are not just heavily subsidized; they are uniquely entrusted with the public good of national security, and expectations about their behavior reflect the deterrent and destructive power of the products they manufacture.

Because of the degree of public contribution and the kind of sensitive tasks they perform, the financial freedom of prime defense contractors must be viewed as a privilege that has to be earned and carries with it a high burden of obligation and responsiveness to the public. This freedom should not be taken for granted or expanded, as many advocates of procurement reform contend; it must be tempered with accumulation and distribution restraints. I have suggested that the state ensure that the contracts it writes and the legislation it passes specify attendant responsibilities to formalize its reciprocal relationship with contractors. The state can use its intimate ties and its largesse to alter the corporate governance rules of contractors to allow for more public oversight and control over investment. Defense contractors will undoubtedly complain about this infringement of their freedom, sacrosanct as it is in our liberal market economy. But since the state acts as the structural equivalent of shareholders and must bear the burden of contractors' destructive strategies, such an arrangement, I believe, would create a "proper symmetry of obligation" (Hutton 1995, 302).

The federal government will also be reluctant to embrace its stakeholder role in defense adjustment because of its fragmented nature, capture by private contractors, and long-standing tradition of pork-barrel politics. Partial ownership rights in defense contractors could encourage the state to view its interests as stakes in long-term relations with particular firms (Simon 1994, 287). Golden shares could provide the state with control rights over a privatized enterprise, so that contractors would be less likely to abuse their property-based prerogatives to weaken communities, organized labor, and the public's trust. Dispersed, disorganized, and increasingly disenfranchised taxpayers also need governance structures to regulate the principal-agent problems between citizens and the state (i.e., the problem of political representation). Citizen oversight, regulatory reforms, and partial state ownership rights may be used to temper the impetus of contractors' restructuring strategies: maximizing shareholder value.

The firm-led adjustment strategy of the last half-decade was very costly. Much of the burden of funding firm transition activities was borne by federal and state governments, labor, and defense-dependent communities. At the same time, money was squeezed from education, health, transportation, and other necessary social and physical infrastructure development to finance what was, in essence, the private accumulation of wealth. Defense contractors and their shareholders siphoned away the excess profits that rightly belonged to the government and others. Both defense industry leaders and persistent critics of defense policy agreed that the political agenda was a woefully inadequate attempt to steer the investment decisions of private firms. Accordingly, in the future the state must take advantage of its stakeholder role—through external constraints and internal fiduciary development—to more robustly govern the military-industrial complex.

Notes

1. "The TRP represents a revolution in U.S. defense industrial base policy. For the first time, Washington has supported efforts by defense firms to diversify into new markets" (Pages 1993, 3).

2. Groups include, among others, the Maine Economic Conversion Project; Center for Economic Conversion (Mountain View, CA); Machine Action Project (MA); and Long Island Defense Diversification Task Force (NY).

3. In *Common Cause v. State*, for example, taxpayers sued the state of Maine, the city of Portland, and Bath Iron Works after the state entered into a tax subsidy agreement that required the state and city to create a dry-dock facility operated by the shipyard. Although state and city officials argued that the agreement would improve the harbor, attract marine commerce, and develop the economic potential of the waterfront, the plaintiffs pointed out that the dry dock would not be available for use by most members of the public nor would its operation directly benefit the public. Although the court eventually refused to reinterpret the intention of the abatement and held in favor of the defendants, other groups have initiated similar actions. *Common Cause*, 455 A.2d 1 (Me. 1983).

4. PA 93-382.

5. PA 92-236.

6. *The Defense Diversification and Adjustment Act*, S. 2097.

7. The bill also proposed that the government and the defense contractors contribute to a second, national fund, called the Defense Adjustment Trust Fund, which would have been capitalized with a treasury deposit of 10 percent of the projected peace dividend savings resulting from the cancellation or termination of defense contracts or closure of bases in each fiscal year as well as a deposit of 1 percent of each defense contractor's gross revenues from new contracts. The latter cost would be waived for contractors who "demonstrated a successful record of having diversified under prior contract terminations." The national fund would assist workers caught in the defense budget squeeze, paying workers' health insurance for two years, as well as relocation and retraining costs.

8. *The Defense Economic Adjustment Act*: H.R. 101.

9. The federal government's authority to charter corporations derives from the "necessary and proper" clause of the Constitution, as expanded by Chief Justice Marshall in *McCulloch v. Maryland*, 7 U.S. (4 Wheat.) 316 (1819).

10. The court system is accustomed to these kinds of decisions, as it frequently evaluates discrepancies between majority and minority shareholders (Romano 1984).

11. Nationalization and privatization are opposite ends of a spectrum of state's property rights in a corporation, but there are a host of middle-range options—only one of which I discuss here.

12. Many governments retain equity shares in electricity, gas, coal, nuclear energy, and oil companies as well as defense. For example, those segments of Russia's defense industry that are being privatized will remain under state control for a designated time period through such mechanisms (Cooper 1994; Kuznetsov 1996). Italian law stipulates that companies who operate in the fields of "defense, transport, telecommunications, energy or other public services contain golden share clauses granting special powers to the Ministry of Treasury" (Baev 1995, 21).

References

Adams, Gordon. 1981. *The Iron Triangle: The Politics of Defense Contracting*. New York: Council on Economic Priorities.

Aerospace Industries Association. 1970. *Risk Elements in Government Contracting*. Washington, DC: AIA.

AFL-CIO Industrial Union Department. 1990. "Resolution on Economic Conversion." January 4. Unpublished document.

Alaghband, Hassan. 1983. "Abolition of the Completed Contract Method: A Study in Legislative Compromise." *American University Law Review* 32: 1009–1037.

Alchian, Armen, and Harold Demsetz. 1972. "Production, Information Costs and Economic Organization." *American Economic Review* 62: 777–795.

Alexander, Gregory. 1993. "Pensions and Passivity." *Law and Contemporary Problems* 56: 111–139.

Alic, John, et al. 1992. *Beyond Spinoff: Military and Commercial Technologies in a Changing World*. Boston: Harvard Business School Press.

Allen, William. 1992. "Our Schizophrenic Conception of the Business Corporation." *Cardoza Law Review* 14 (2): 261–281.

Anders, William. 1992. "Revisiting the Rationalization of America's Defense Industrial Base." Presentation before Aerospace Industries Association, October 27.

_____. 1991. "Rationalizing America's Defense Industry." Keynote Address at *Defense Week* Conference, October 30.

Aoki, Masahiko, et al. 1990. *The Firm as a Nexus of Treaties*. London: Sage Publishing.

Appelbaum, Eileen, and Peter Berg. 1996. "Financial Market Constraints and Business Strategy in the U.S.A." In Jonathan Michie and John Grieve Smith, eds., *Creating Industrial Capacity*. London: Oxford University Press.

Arrow, Kenneth. 1974. *The Limits of Organization*. New York: Norton.

_____. 1969. "The Organization of Economic Activity: Issues Pertinent to the Choice of Market Versus Non-Market Allocation." In *The Analysis and Evaluation of Public Expenditure*, Vol. 1. U.S. Joint Economic Committee, 91st Congress, 1st Session. Washington, DC: GPO.

Arrow, Kenneth, and Robert Lind. 1970. "Uncertainty and the Evaluation of Public Investment Decisions." *American Economic Review* 60(3): 364–378.

Arthur D. Little, Inc. 1992. "Strategic Plan for Economic Development in Southeastern Connecticut." Cambridge, MA: A. D. Little.

Baev, Andrei. 1995. "Is There a Niche for the State in Corporate Governance? Securitization of State-Owned Enterprises and New Forms of State Ownership." *Houston Journal of International Law* 18 (1): 1–57.

_____. 1993. "Civil Law and the Transformation of State Property in the Post-Soviet Economy." *Pacific Basin Law Journal* 12: 131–202.

Baldwin, Carliss, and Kim Clark. 1991. "Capabilities and Capital Investment: New Perspectives on Capital Budgeting." Washington, DC: Council on Competitiveness.

Baldwin, William. 1967. *The Structure of the Defense Market, 1955–64*. Durham, NC: Duke University Press.

Ball, Nicole. 1986. "Converting the Workforce: Defence Industry Conversion in Industrialized Countries." *International Labour Review* 125(4): 401–421.

Bandow, Doug. 1997. "Ethanol Keeps ADM Drunk on Tax Dollars." Washington, DC: Cato Institute.

Banfield, Edward. 1964. "Supplement: Note on Conceptual Scheme." In Martin Meyerson and Edward Banfield, eds., *Politics, Planning and the Public Interest*. New York: The Free Press.

Barnekov, Timothy, and Daniel Rich. 1989. "Privatism and the Limits of Local Economic Development Policy." *Urban Affairs Quarterly* 25(2): 212–238.

Baron, David, and David Besanko. 1987. "Monitoring, Moral Hazard, Informational Asymmetries and Risk-Sharing in Procurement Contracting." *RAND Journal of Economics* 18: 509–532.

Bartik, Timothy. 1991. *Who Benefits from State and Local Economic Development*. Kalamazoo, MI: Upjohn Institute.

Bean, Gerard. 1995. *Fiduciary Obligations and Joint Ventures*. Oxford: Clarendon Press.

Beck, Ulrich. 1992. *Risk Society: Towards a New Modernity*. London: Sage Publications.

Beesley, Michael, and Thomas Evans. 1978. *Corporate Social Responsibility*. London: Croom Helm.

Bellah, Robert. 1977. Foreword to *Reflections on Fieldwork in Morocco*, by Paul Rabinow. Berkeley: University of California Press.

Benenson, Bob. 1990. "A 'Safety Net' for Defense Transition?" *Congressional Quarterly*, January 13: 89.

Beran, Harry. 1987. *Consent Theory of Political Obligation*. New York: Croom Helm.

Berger, Phillip, and Eli Ofek. 1996. "Bustup Takeovers of Value-Destroying Diversified Firms." *Journal of Finance* 51: 1175–1200.

Berk, Gerald. 1994. *Alternative Tracks: The Constitution of American Industrial Order, 1865–1917*. Baltimore: Johns Hopkins University Press.

Berle, Adolph, and Gardiner Means. 1932. *The Modern Corporation and Private Property*. New York: MacMillan.

Biddle, Wayne. 1985a. "General Dynamics Faces Cost Query." *New York Times*, March 24.

_____. 1985b. "Dynamics' Brief Stay in the Pentagon Doghouse." *New York Times*, August 15.

Birkler, John, et al. 1994. *The U.S. Submarine Production Base: An Analysis of Cost, Schedule and Risk for Selected Force Structures*. Santa Monica, CA: RAND.

Bischak, Greg. 1993. "The Obstacles to Real Security: Military Corporatism and the Cold War State." In Kevin Cassidy and Greg Bischak, eds., *Real Security: Converting the Defense Economy and Building Peace.* Albany: SUNY Press.

Bischak, Greg, Michael Oden, and Chris Evans-Klock. 1995. "The Technology Reinvestment Project: The Limits of Dual-Use Technology Policy." Washington, DC: National Commission for Economic Conversion and Disarmament.

Black, Bernard, and Ranier Kraakman. 1996. "A Self-Enforcing Model of Corporate Law." *Harvard Law Review* 109: 1011–1982.

Blair, Margaret. 1996. *Wealth Creation and Wealth Sharing: A Colloquium on Corporate Governance and Investment in Human Capital.* Washington, DC: Brookings Institution.

_____. 1995. *Ownership and Control: Rethinking Corporate Governance for the Twenty-First Century.* Washington, DC: Brookings Institution.

Blair, Margaret, ed. 1993. *The Deal Decade: What Takeovers and Leveraged Buyouts Mean for Corporate Governance.* Washington, DC: Brookings Institution.

Block, Fred. 1987. *Revising State Theory: Essays in Politics and Postindustrialism.* Philadelphia: Temple University Press.

Bloomberg Financial. 1996. Stock Quotes. www.bloomberg.com.

Bluestone, Barry, and Irving Bluestone. 1992. *Negotiating the Future: A Labor Perspective on American Business.* New York: Basic Books.

Bluestone, Barry, and Bennett Harrison. 1982. *The Deindustrialization of America.* New York: Basic Books

Boardman, Anthony, and Aidan Vining. 1991. "The Behavior of Mixed Enterprises." *Research in Law and Economics* 14: 22–53.

Borrus, Amy. 1993. "Defense Stocks Are Going Great." *Business Week,* September 20: 88.

Borrus, Michael. 1992. "Investing on the Frontier: How the U.S. Can Reclaim High-Technology Leadership." *The American Prospect,* Fall: 79–87.

Borrus, Michael, and John Zysman. 1992. "Industrial Competitiveness and American National Security." In Wayne Sandholtz, et al., eds., *The Highest Stakes: The Economic Foundations of the Next Security System.* New York: Oxford University Press.

Bowles, Samuel, and Herbert Gintis. 1988. "Contested Exchange: Political Economy and Modern Economic Theory." *American Economic Review* 78: 145–160.

Bowles, Samuel, David Gordon, and Thomas Weiskopf. 1990. *After the Wasteland: A Democratic Economy for the Year 2000.* Armonk, NY: M. E. Sharpe.

Bowman, Scott. 1996. *The Modern Corporation and American Political Thought.* University Park, PA: Penn State University Press.

Branson, Douglas. 1995. "The Death of Contractarianism and the Vindication of Structure and Authority in Corporate Governance and Corporate Law." In Lawrence Mitchell, ed., *Progressive Corporate Law.* Boulder: Westview.

Bratton, William. 1989. "The 'Nexus of Contracts' Corporation: A Critical Appraisal." *Cornell Law Review* 74 : 407–465.

Brecher, Jeremy, and Tim Costello. 1990. *Building Bridges: The Emerging Grassroots Coalition of Labor and Community.* New York: Monthly Review.

Brenner, Brian. 1992. "General Dynamics Takes a Tomahawk to Itself." *Business Week,* June 22: 36.

Breyer, Steven. 1982. *Regulation and its Reform*. Cambridge, MA: Harvard University Press.

Brudney, Victor. 1985. "Corporate Governance, Agency Costs and the Rhetoric of Contract." *Columbia Law Review* 85: 1403–1444.

Burnett, William, and William Kovacic. 1989. "Reform of the U.S. Weapons Acquisition Process: Competition, Teaming Agreements and Dual Sourcing." *Yale Journal on Regulation* 6: 249–317.

Butler, Henry. 1989. "The Contractual Theory of the Corporation." *George Mason Law Review* 11: 99–123.

Butler, Henry, and Larry Ribstein. 1989. "Symposium: The Contract Clause and the Corporation." *Brooklyn Law Review* 55: 767–801.

Butler, Stuart. 1985. *Privatizing Federal Spending*. New York: Universe Books.

Call to Action. 1995. *Handbook on Alternative Use for Local Labor Unions*. Cambridge, MA: Northeast Citizen Action Resource Center.

_____. 1994. *A Primer on Defense Conversion and Economic Rejuvenation*. Cambridge, MA: Northeast Citizen Action Resource Center.

Carbone, Gerald. 1993. "The Knife Cuts Deeper at E.B." *Providence Journal*, July 13: D1.

Carver, Martin. 1989. "The Second Pillar of Prosperity: The International Security Economy and the Reconstruction of Industry and State Relations in the United States." Master's thesis, Cornell University.

Cassata, Donna. 1995. "Swords-to-Plowshares Program Faces Uncertain Future." *Congressional Quarterly*, February 25: 620–624.

Center for Security Policy. 1995. "U.S. Still Needs a Top-Flight Undersea Warfare Capability and the Robust Industrial Base It Requires." Note No. 95-P39, June 26.

Chandler, Alfred. 1977. *The Visible Hand: The Managerial Revolution in American Business*. Cambridge, MA: Belknap Press.

Christopherson, Susan. 1997. "The Institutional Dimension in Comparative Perspective." Paper prepared for the U.S. Department of Labor, Bureau of International Affairs.

_____. 1993. "Market Rules and Territorial Outcomes: The Case of the United States." *International Journal of Urban and Regional Research* 17: 274–288.

Christopherson, Susan, and Rachel Weber. 1994. "Defense Conversion: Assessing Clinton's New Agenda." Paper prepared for the Association of Collegiate Schools of Planning annual meeting, Phoenix, AZ, October.

Clark, Gordon. 1995. "Sunk Costs: A Framework for Economic Geography." *Transactions of the Institute of British Geographers* 20: 204–223.

_____. 1994. "Strategy and Structure: Corporate Restructuring and the Scope and Characteristics of Sunk Costs." *Environment and Planning A* 26: 9–32.

_____. 1993. *Pensions and Corporate Restructuring in American Industry*. Baltimore: Johns Hopkins University Press.

_____. 1992. "The Problematic Status of Corporate Regulation in the United States: Toward a New Moral Order." *Environment and Planning A* 24: 705–725.

Clark, Gordon, and Neil Wrigley. 1995. "Exit and Sunk Costs." Unpublished manuscript, July.

Clark, Robert. 1991. "Agency Costs versus Fiduciary Duties." In John Pratt and Richard Zeckhauser, eds., *Principals and Agents: The Structure of Business.* Boston: Harvard Business School Press.

Clinton, Bill, and Albert Gore, Jr. 1993. *Technology for America's Economic Growth, A New Direction to Build Economic Strength.* Washington, DC: GPO.

Coase, Ronald. 1994. "The Institutional Structure of Production." In Ronald Coase, ed., *Essays on Economics and Economists.* Chicago: University of Chicago Press.

_____. 1960. "The Problem of Social Costs." *Journal of Law and Economics* 3: 1–44.

_____. 1937. "The Nature of the Firm." *Economica* 4: 386–405.

Coburn, George. 1988. "How Contractors Can Minimize the Risk of Becoming 'Federal Actors.'" *Public Contract Law Journal* 17: 361–387.

Coffee, John. 1991. "Liquidity versus Control: The Institutional Investor as Corporate Monitor." *Columbia Law Review* 91: 1277–1343.

_____. 1988. "Shareholders versus Managers: The Strain in the Corporate Web." In John Coffee, et al., eds., *Knights, Raiders, and Targets: The Impact of the Hostile Takeover.* New York: Oxford University Press.

Cohen, Linda, and Roger Noll. 1991. *The Technology Pork Barrel.* Washington, DC: Brookings Institution.

Cohen, Morris. 1927. "Property and Sovereignty." *Cornell Law Review* 13: 8–53.

Coles, Robert. 1997. *Doing Documentary Work.* New York: Oxford University Press.

Commons, John. 1957. *The Legal Foundations of Capitalism.* Madison: University of Wisconsin Press.

Connecticut Center for Economic Analysis. 1993. "Defense Spending Cuts in New London County: An Economic Impact Study." Storrs: University of Connecticut.

Connecticut Department of Economic and Community Development. 1996. *The Connecticut Economic Digest* 1(2).

Connecticut Department of Economic Development. 1992. "Defense Subcontracting in Connecticut: Survey Results." Hartford: DED.

Connecticut Department of Labor. 1993. "Planning Guide: Economic Statistics." Hartford: Department of Labor.

Cooper, Julian. 1994. "Transformation of Russia's Defense Industry." *Jane's Intelligence Review*, October 1.

Council on Economic Priorities. 1986. *Rating America's Corporate Conscience.* Reading, MA: Addison-Wesley.

Crotty, James. 1992. "Neoclassical and Keynesian Approaches to the Theory of Investment." *Journal of Post-Keynesian Economics* 14(4): 483–496.

Crystal, Graef. 1992. "Chairman of the Bucks." *Washington Post Magazine*, April 5: 11–15.

Cyert, Richard, and James March. 1963. *A Behavioral Theory of the Firm.* Englewood Cliffs, NJ: Prentice-Hall.

Dan-Cohen, Meir. 1986. *Rights, Persons and Organizations: A Legal Theory for Bureaucratic Society.* Berkeley: University of California Press.

Daniels, Ronald. 1993. "Stakeholders and Takeovers: Can Contractarianism Be Compassionate?" *University of Toronto Law Review* 43: 315–351.

Davis, Gerald, and Suzanne Stout. 1992. "Organization Theory and the Market for Corporate Control: A Dynamic Analysis of the Characteristics of Large Takeover Targets, 1980–1990." *Administrative Science Quarterly* 37: 606–633.

Defense Conversion Commission. 1992. *Adjusting to the Drawdown*. Washington, DC: GPO.

Defense Week. 1995. "Dual-Use Program to Fill Top Panels with Pentagon People," June 12.

Demott, Deborah. 1989. "Beyond Metaphor: An Analysis of Fiduciary Obligation." *Duke Law Journal* 1988: 879–924.

_____. 1988. "Limiting Director's Liability." *Washington University Law Quarterly* 66: 295–322.

Denis, David, Diane Denis, and Atulya Sarin. 1997. "Agency Problems, Equity Ownership and Corporate Diversification." *Journal of Finance* 52(2): 135–160.

Denny, Jeffrey. 1992. "Who Needs Enemies? Why Congress Won't Slash the Military Budget." *Common Cause Magazine*, Summer.

DeSouza, Patrick. 1985. "Regulating Fraud in Military Procurement: A Legal Process Model." *Yale Law Journal* 95: 390–413.

Dewey, John. 1939. *Theory of Valuation*. Chicago: University of Chicago Press.

_____. 1926. "The Historic Background of Corporate Legal Personality." *Yale Law Journal* 35: 655–693.

Dial, Jay, and Kevin Murphy. 1995. "Incentives, Downsizing and Value Creation at General Dynamics." *Journal of Financial Economics* 37: 261–314.

Donahue, John. 1989. *The Privatization Decision: Public Ends, Private Means*. New York: Basic Books.

_____. 1987. "Private Agents, Public Acts: The Architecture of Accountability." Ph.D. dissertation, Harvard University.

Donaldson, Gordon. 1994. *Corporate Restructuring: Managing the Change Process from Within*. Boston: Harvard Business School Press.

Drucker, Peter. 1993. *Post-Capitalist Society*. New York: Harper and Row.

Dumas, Lloyd. 1977. "Economic Conversion, Productive Efficiency and Social Welfare." *Journal of Sociology and Social Welfare* 4(3–4): 567–596.

Duncan, Francis. 1990. *Rickover and the Nuclear Navy*. Annapolis, MD: Naval Institute Press.

Easterbrook, Frank, and Daniel Fischel. 1993. "Contract and Fiduciary Duty." *Journal of Law and Economics* 36: 425–446.

_____. 1991. *The Economic Structure of Corporate Law*. Cambridge, MA: Harvard University Press.

Eccles, Thomas, and Henry Marcus. 1992. "Integrating Design and Production: A Case Study of the Naval Submarine Program." *International Journal of Production Economics* 28: 107–126.

The Economist. 1997. "A Shrinking Arms Market," November 22: 20.

Eggertsson, Thrain. 1990. *Economic Behavior and Institutions*. New York: Cambridge University Press.

Eisenberg, Melvin. 1976. *The Structure of the Corporation: A Legal Analysis*. Boston: Little, Brown.

Eisinger, Peter. 1995. *The Rise of the Entrepreneurial State*. Madison: University of Wisconsin Press.

Electric Boat. 1996. "The History of Electric Boat." Groton, CT. Photocopy.

Ellerman, David. 1992. *Property and Contract in Economics*. Cambridge, MA: Blackwell.

Ellis, James. 1991a. "More Instant Cash than a Lottery." *Business Week*, May 20: 42.

_____. 1991b. "Layoffs on the Line, Bonuses in the Executive Suite." *Business Week*, October 21: 34.

Ergas, Henry. 1986. "Does Technology Policy Matter?" Brussels: Centre for European Policy Studies.

Ettlinger, Nancy. 1992. "The Peace Dividend and Defense Conversion in the Context of Corporate Restructuring." *Growth and Change* 24: 107–126.

Etzioni, Amitai. 1988. *The Moral Dimension: Toward a New Economics*. New York: Free Press.

Evangelista, Matthew. 1988. *Innovation and the Arms Race*. Ithaca: Cornell University Press.

Evans, Peter. 1995. *Embedded Autonomy: States and Industrial Transformation*. Princeton: Princeton University Press.

Fama, Eugene. 1990. "Efficient Capital Markets: A Review of Theory and Empirical Work." *Journal of Finance* 25: 383–417.

_____. 1980. "Agency Problems and the Theory of the Firm." *Journal of Political Economy* 88: 288–307.

Federation of American Scientists. 1993. *Arms Sales Monitor* 21 (July).

Feinman, Jay, and Peter Gabel. 1990. "Contract Law as Ideology." In David Kairys, ed., *The Politics of Law*. New York: Pantheon Books.

Field, James. 1993. *Economic Profit in U.S. Government Defense Contractors*. Ph.D. dissertation, Harvard University.

Finnegan, Philip. 1990. "Investor Group's Increasing Clout Worries Industry: Execs Face Pressure to Increase Short-Term Profit, Skimp on Research." *Defense News*, June 11.

Fisher, William, Martin Horwitz, and Thomas Reed, eds. 1993. *American Legal Realism*. New York: Oxford University Press.

Fixer, Paul, and Robert Poole. 1987. "Status of State and Local Privatization." In S. Hanke, ed., *Prospects for Privatization*. New York: Academy of Political Science.

Fligstein, Neil. 1990. *The Transformation of Corporate Control*. Cambridge, MA: Harvard University Press.

Fligstein, Neil, and Peter Brantley. 1992. "Bank Control, Owner Control or Organizational Dynamics: Who Controls the Modern Corporation?" *American Journal of Sociology* 98: 280–307.

Fox, J. Ronald. 1974. *Arming America*. Cambridge: Harvard University Press.

Fox, J. Ronald, and James Field. 1988. *The Defense Management Challenge: Weapons Acquisition*. Boston: Harvard Business School Press.

Frank, Allan. 1985. "Revenge Is a Dish . . ." *Forbes*, July 15: 98.

Franklin, Roger. 1986. *The Defender: The Story of General Dynamics*. New York: Harper and Row.

French, Howard. 1994. "'Give It Back,' Union Urges UTC Execs." *(Norwich) Journal Inquirer*, March 24: A1.

Frickel, Scott. 1996. "Engineering Heterogeneous Accounts: The Case of the Submarine Thermal Reactor Mark I." *Science, Technology and Human Values* 21(1): 28–53.

Friedberg, Aaron. 1992. "Why Didn't the United States Become a Garrison State?" *International Security* 16(4): 109–143.

Friedman, Milton. 1970. "The Social Responsibility of Business Is to Increase Its Profits." *New York Times*, September 13.

Friedman, Norman. 1994. *U.S. Submarines Since 1945*. Annapolis, MD: Naval Institute Press.

Froomkin, A. Michael. 1995. "Reinventing the Government Corporation." *University of Illinois Law Review* 1995: 543–634.

Frug, Gerald. 1980. "The City as a Legal Concept." *Harvard Law Review* 93: 1059–1154.

Furubotn, Eirik. 1974. *The Economics of Property Rights*. Cambridge, MA: Ballinger Press.

Galbraith, John Kenneth. 1969. *How to Control the Military*. New York: Signet Press.

Gansler, Jacques. 1995. *Defense Conversion*. Cambridge, MA: MIT Press.

_____. 1991. *Affording Defense*. Cambridge, MA: MIT Press.

_____. 1980. *The Defense Industry*. Cambridge, MA: MIT Press.

General Dynamics. 1993. Press Release, July 15.

_____. 1985–1996. Annual Reports and Proxy Statements. Falls Church, VA.

"General Dynamics Sees 1990 Earnings, Cash Flow under Pressure." *Aerospace Daily*, March 14, 1990.

Gerth, Jeff. 1985a. "Pentagon Cuts Some Payments." *New York Times*, April 11: 22.

_____. 1985b. "U.S. Weapons Makers Ring Up Healthy Profits." *New York Times*, April 9: 23.

_____. 1985c. "Legislation Would End Rule." *New York Times*, March 18: 18.

_____. 1985d. "Pentagon Study Explores Profits for Contractors." *New York Times*, March 18: 18.

_____. 1985e. "Dynamics' Deferral of U.S. Income Taxes." *New York Times*, February 1: 27.

Giddens, Anthony. 1984. *The Constitution of Society: Outline of the Theory of Structuration*. Cambridge, UK: Polity Press.

Gilpin, Kenneth. 1994. "Reshaping the Arms Industry: Top Officials Share Skill and Vision." *Los Angeles Times*, August 31: D5.

Goldberg, Victor. 1976. "Regulation and Administered Contracts." *Bell Journal of Economics* 7: 426–452.

Goldstein, Don. 1995. "Financial Structure and Corporate Behavior in Japan and the U.S.: Insulation vs. Integration with Speculative Pressures." Unpublished manuscript, Allegheny College.

Goodman, Adam. 1991. "Dynamic Force Execs: General Dynamics on a Survival Mission." *St. Louis Post-Dispatch*, June 2.

Goodman, Sherri Wasserman. 1988. "Legal Dilemmas in the Weapons Acquisition Process: The Procurement of the SSN-688 Submarine." *Yale Law and Policy Review* 6: 393–427.

Goodwin, Jacob. 1985. *Brotherhood of Arms: General Dynamics and the Business of Defending America*. New York: Times Books.

Gordon, David. 1996. *Fat and Mean: The Corporate Squeeze on Working America and the Myth of Managerial Downsizing*. New York: Martin Kessler Books.

Goyal, Vidhan, Kenneth Lehn, and Stanko Racic. 1993. "Investment Opportunities, Corporate Finance, and Compensation Policy in the U.S. Defense Industry." Unpublished manuscript, University of Pittsburgh.

Graham, Cosmo, and Tony Prosser. 1988. "Golden Shares: Industrial Policy by Stealth?" *Public Law* 1988: 413–431.

Granovetter, Mark. 1985. "Economic Action and Social Structure: The Problem of Embeddedness." *American Journal of Sociology* 91: 481–510.

Green, Brian. 1995. "Defense Budget Gets a Boost." *Air Force Magazine*, August: 13.

Greer, Willis, and Shu Liao. 1986. "An Analysis of Risk and Return in the Defense Market: Its Impact on Weapon System Competition." *Management Science* 32(10): 1259–1273.

Habermas, Jurgen. 1973. *Legitimation Crisis*. Boston: Beacon Press.

Haddock, David , Jonathan Macey, and Fred McChesney. 1987. "Property Rights in Assets and Resistance to Tender Offers." *University of Virginia Law Review* 73: 701–746.

Hale, Robert. 1923. "Coercion and Distribution in a Supposedly Non-Coercive State." *Political Science Quarterly* 38: 470–502.

Hall, Peter. 1986. *Governing the Economy: The Politics of State Intervention in Britain and France*. New York: Oxford University Press.

Hamilton, Robert. 1996a. "Fidelity Stake in G.D. Tops 10 Percent." *The New London Day*, September 12: C1.

_____. 1996b. "600 Get Pink Slips from E.B." *New London Day*, August 3: C1.

_____. 1996c. "100 E.B. Retirees Sue over Buyout." *New London Day*, July 18: C1.

_____. 1996d. "Safety Question Means New Hatches for Seawolf." *New London Day,* April 20: B2.

_____. 1996e. "Emotions Running High at Electric Boat as Longtime Shipbuilders Say Goodbye." *New London Day*, March 30: B1.

_____. 1996f. "General Dynamics Top Brass Would Receive Millions under Severance Plan." *New London Day*, March 29: D1.

_____. 1996g. "E.B. Leads $22 Million High-Tech Design Plan." *New London Day*, March 22: C1.

_____. 1996h. "E.B. Wins $1.5 Billion Design Deal." *New London Day*, January 30: A1.

_____. 1996i. "G.D. Earnings Rise." *New London Day*, January 25: C1.

_____. 1996j. "E.B. Will Lay Off 1500 This Year." *New London Day*, January 19: A1.

_____. 1996k. "E.B. Losing as Repair Work Goes to Kittery." *New London Day*, January 1: C1.

_____. 1995a. "G.D. Wins Decision in Navy Dispute." *New London Day*, December 21: A1.

_____. 1995b. "Navy Says Sub Fleet Will Cost $71 Billion." *New London Day*, December 20: D1.

_____. 1995c. "E.B. Heads for More Autonomy." *New London Day*, December 17: C1.

_____. 1995d. "E.B., Now a Division, to Become Wholly Owned Subsidiary of G.D." *New London Day*, December 15: C1.

_____. 1995e. "Top 3 Execs Earn $20 Million at E.B. Parent Firm." *New London Day*, November 17: C1.

_____. 1995f. "G.D.'s Stock Is Up." *New London Day*, August 30: A1.

_____. 1995g. "G.D. Buys Bath Shipyard." *New London Day*, August 18: A1.

_____. 1995h. "Union Gives a Big 'Yes' to E.B. Contract." *New London Day*, July 8: A1.

_____. 1995i. "E.B., Union Agree on a Three-Year Contract, No Pay Raises." *New London Day*, July 3: A1.

_____. 1995j. "Seawolf Issue Not Affecting G.D. Stock." *New London Day*, May 26: C1.

_____. 1995k. "E.B. Trims Middle Management." *New London Day*, May 4: C1.

_____. 1995l. "Merger Could Shift Destroyer Work." *New London Day*, April 29: C1.

Hanley, Christine. 1993. "Labor Told to Push for Conversion." *New London Day*, June 19: A9.

Harden, Ian. 1992. *The Contracting State*. London: Open University Press.

Harrison, Bennett. 1995. *Lean and Mean: The Changing Landscape of Corporate Power in the Age of Flexibility*. New York: Basic Books.

Harrison, Bennett, and Barry Bluestone. 1988. *The Great U-Turn: Corporate Restructuring and the Polarizing of America*. New York: Basic Books.

Hart, Oliver, and John Moore. 1990. "Property Rights and the Nature of the Firm." *Journal of Political Economy* 98: 1119–1158.

Hartog, Hendrik. 1983. *Public Property and Private Power: The Corporation of the City of New York, 1730–1870*. Chapel Hill: University of North Carolina Press.

Hartung, William. 1996. *Welfare for Weapons Dealers: The Hidden Costs of the Arms Trade*. New York: World Policy Institute.

_____. 1994. *And Weapons for All*. New York: Harper Collins.

Hartz, Louis. 1955. *The Liberal Tradition in America*. New York: Harcourt, Brace and World.

Hatcher, General Julian. 1948. *The Book of the Garand*. Washington, DC: Infantry Journal Press.

Hayden, Lisa. 1994a. "E.B. Gives 133 Pink Slips to Workers." *New London Day*, April 26: C2.

_____. 1994b. "Labor Probe Continues at E.B." *New London Day*, March 25: C1.

Hayes, Robert, and William Abernathy. 1980. "Managing Our Way to Economic Decline." *Harvard Business Review* 58: 66–77.

Hawkins, Keith, and John Thomas. 1984. *Enforcing Regulation*. Boston: Kluwer.

Henwood, Doug. 1997. *Wall Street*. New York: Verso Press.

Herman, Edward. 1981. *Corporate Control, Corporate Power*. New York: Cambridge University Press.

Hill, Catherine, et al. 1993. "Converting the Military Industrial Economy: The Experience of Six Communities." In Kevin Cassidy and Greg Bischak, eds., *Real*

Security: Converting the Defense Economy and Building Peace. Albany: SUNY Press.

Hite, Gailen, James Owers, and Ronald Rogers. 1985. "The Market for Interfirm Asset Sales: Partial Sell-offs and Total Liquidations." *Journal of Financial Economics* 19: 229–252.

Hodgson, Geoffrey. 1988. *Economics and Institutions.* Cambridge, UK: Polity Press.

Holley, Irving. 1964. *Buying Aircraft: Materiel Procurement for the Army Air Forces.* Washington, DC: Office of the Chief of Military History.

Hooks, Gregory. 1992. *Forging the Military-Industrial Complex.* Urbana: University of Illinois Press.

Hooks, Gregory, and Leonard Bloomquist. 1992. "The Legacy of World War II for Regional Growth and Decline: The Cumulative Effects of Wartime Investments on U.S. Manufacturing, 1947–1972." *Social Forces* 71: 303–337.

Horrock, Nicholas, and James O'Shea. 1985. "Firms Build Immunity to Regulation." *Chicago Tribune*, December 22.

Horwitz, Morton. 1992. *The Transformation of American Law, 1870–1960.* New York: Oxford University Press.

Hovenkamp, Herbert. 1991. *Enterprise and American Law, 1836–1937.* Cambridge, MA: Harvard University Press.

Hu, Henry. 1990. "Risk, Time and Fiduciary Principles in Corporate Investment." *UCLA Law Review* 38: 277–389.

Huntington, Samuel. 1967. *The Soldier and the State: The Theory and Politics of Civil-Military Relations.* Cambridge, MA: Belknap.

Hurst, James Willard. 1970. *The Legitimacy of the Business Corporation in the Law of the United States, 1780–1970.* Charlottesville: University of Virginia Press.

Hutchinson, Allen, ed. 1989. *Critical Legal Studies.* Totowa, NJ: Rowman and Littlefield.

Hutton, Will. 1995. *The State We're In.* London: Jonathan Cape.

Hyde, Alan. 1982. "Beyond Collective Bargaining: The Politicization of Labor Relations under Government Contract." *University of Wisconsin Law Review* 1982: 1–41.

Jacobs, Michael. 1991. *Short-Term America: The Causes and Cures of Business Myopia.* Boston: Harvard Business School Press.

Jacobson, Ken. 1995. "Flamm Claims Dual-Use Accepted Throughout DOD," *Defense Week*, July 17.

Jefferson, David, and Andrew Pasztor. 1990. "Pentagon Audits Show Contractors Owe U.S. Hundreds of Millions in A-12 Job." *Wall Street Journal*, December 19.

Jensen, Michael. 1989. "The Eclipse of the Public Corporation." *Harvard Business Review*: 61–83.

Jensen, Michael, and William Meckling. 1976. "Theory of the Firm: Managerial Behavior, Agency Costs and Ownership Structure." *Journal of Financial Economics* 3: 305–360.

Jensen, Michael, and Kevin Murphy. 1990. "Performance Pay and Top Management Incentives." *Journal of Political Economy* 98: 225–264.

Johnston, Paul. 1988. "Of Public Work and Labor Struggle." *Berkeley Journal of Sociology* 33: 37–71.

Kadish, Sanford. 1964. "Some Observations on the Use of Command Sanctions in Enforcing Economic Regulation." *University of Chicago Law Review* 30: 436–482.

Kaldor, Mary. 1981. *The Baroque Arsenal*. New York: Hill and Wang.

Kaminski, Paul. 1996. "Report on Payment of Restructuring Costs under Defense Contracts." Washington, DC: U.S. Department of Defense, June.

_____. 1995. Interview. *Government Executive,* August.

Kaplan, Karen. 1995a. "Shipyard's Purchase Buoys E.B." *New London Day*, August 19: C1.

_____. 1995b. "Bonuses, 'Adjustments' in E.B. Pact." *New London Day*, July 4: C2.

Kapstein, Ethan. 1992. *Defense and Dependence in a Global Economy*. Washington, DC: Congressional Quarterly, Inc.

Katzenstein, Peter, ed. 1996. *The Culture of National Security*. New York: Columbia University Press.

_____. 1984. *Corporatism and Change: Austria, Switzerland and the Politics of Industry*. Ithaca: Cornell University Press.

Kaufman, Allen. 1996. "In the Procurement Officer We Trust: Constitutional Norms, Air Force Procurement and Industrial Organization, 1938–1948." Cambridge, MA: Defense and Arms Control Studies Program, MIT.

Kaufman, William, and John Steinbruner. 1991. *Decisions for Defense: Prospects for a New Order*. Washington, DC: The Brookings Institution.

Keating, Chris, and Michael Remez. 1995. "Thames Dredging Approved." *Hartford Courant*, July 7: A3.

Kelley, Maryellen, and Todd Watkins. 1995. "In from the Cold: Prospects for Conversion of the Defense Industrial Base." *Science* 268: 525–532.

Kennedy, Duncan. 1982. "The Stages of Decline of the Public/Private Distinction." *University of Pennsylvania Law Review* 130: 1349–1357.

Kester, W. Carl. 1990. "Governance, Contracting and Investment Time Horizons." Washington, DC: Council on Competitiveness.

Kettl, Donald. 1993. *Sharing Power: Public Governance and Private Markets*. Washington, DC: Brookings Institution.

King, Desmond. 1995. *Actively Seeking Work? The Politics of Unemployment and Welfare Policy in the U.S. and Great Britain*. Chicago: University of Chicago Press.

Klare, Karl. 1988. "Workplace Democracy and Market Reconstruction: An Agenda for Legal Reform." *Catholic University Law Review* 38: 1–48.

_____. 1982. "The Public/Private Distinction in Labor Law." *University of Pennsylvania Law Review* 130: 1358–1422.

Kleinman, Robert. 1989. "The Shareholder Gains from Leveraged Cash-outs." In Joel Stern, G. Bennett Stewart, and Donald Chew, eds., *Corporate Restructuring and Executive Compensation*. Cambridge, MA: Ballinger Press.

Knight, Frank. 1971. *Risk, Uncertainty and Profit*. Chicago: University of Chicago Press.

Knight-Ridder News Service. 1985. "Tax Loophole a Boon to Arms Makers," September 27.

Koistinen, Paul. 1980. *The Military-Industrial Complex*. New York: Praeger.

Korb, Lawrence. 1996. "Merger Mania: Should the Pentagon Pay for Defense Industry Restructuring?" *Brookings Review* 14: 22–25.

Kosiak, Steven. 1997. "Analysis of the Fiscal Year 1998 Defense Budget Request." Washington, DC: Center for Strategic and Budgetary Assessments.

Kovacic, William. 1991. "Merger Policy in a Declining Defense Industry." *Antitrust Bulletin* 36(3), September 22.

_____. 1990a. "Regulatory Controls as Barriers to Entry in Government Procurement." Paper presented at Association for Public Policy and Management conference, October.

_____. 1990b. "The Sorcerer's Apprentice: Public Regulation of the Weapons Acquisition Process." In Robert Higgs, ed., *Arms, Politics and the Economy*. New York: Holmes and Meier.

Krepinevich, Andrew. 1996. "A New Navy for a New Era." Washington, DC: Center for Strategic and Budgetary Assessments.

Kurth, James. 1973. "Aerospace Production Lines and American Defense Spending." In S. Rosen, ed., *Testing the Theory of the Military-Industrial Complex*. Lexington, MA: Lexington Books.

Kuznetsov, Yevgeny, ed. 1996. "Learning to Restructure: Studies of Transformation in the Russian Defense Industry." Paper written for the Bonn International Center for Conversion, June.

Lasswell, Harold. 1994. *Essays on the Garrison State*. Jay Stanley, ed. New Brunswick, NJ: Transaction Publications.

Lazonick, William. 1992. "Controlling the Market for Corporate Control: The Historical Significance of Managerial Capitalism." *Industrial and Corporate Change* 1: 445–488.

_____. 1990. "Organizational Capabilities in American Industry: The Rise and Decline of Managerial Capitalism." In Howard Gospel, ed., *Industrial Training and Technological Innovation*. London: Routledge.

LeRoy, Greg, et al. 1994. *No More Candy Store: States and Cities Making Job Subsidies Accountable*. Chicago: Federation for Industrial Renewal and Retention.

Lessure, Carol. 1994. "President Clinton's Defense Transition Program: FY 1995 Budget Request and Five-Year Funding Plan." Washington, DC: Defense Budget Project.

Lindblom, Charles. 1977. *Politics and Markets*. New York: Basic Books.

Logistics Management Institute. 1993. *Impacts of Defense Spending Cuts on Industry Sectors, Occupational Groups, and Localities*. Washington, DC: LMI.

Lorsch, Jay, and Elizabeth MacIver. 1991. "Corporate Governance and Investment Time Horizons." Washington, DC: Council on Competitiveness.

Lovering, John, and Louise Curran. 1996. "The Integration of Europe and the Disintegration of the European Defence Industry: Implications of Economic Governance without Government." Unpublished manuscript.

Lowi, Theodore. 1969. *The End of Liberalism*. New York: Norton.

Lundquist, Jerrold. 1992. "Shrinking Fast and Smart in the Defense Industry." *Harvard Business Review* 70(6): 74–79.

Macey, Jonathan. 1989. "Externalities, Firm-Specific Investments and the Legal Treatment of Fundamental Corporate Changes." *Duke Law Journal* 1989: 173–201.

_____. 1988. "Public Choice Theory: The Theory of the Firm and the Theory of Market Exchange." *Cornell Law Review* 74: 43–61.

MacIntyre, Robert, and Robert Folen. 1984. *Corporate Income Taxes in the Reagan Years*. Washington, DC: Citizens for Tax Justice.

MacKenzie, Donald. 1990. *Inventing Accuracy*. Cambridge, MA: MIT Press.

MacNeil, Ian. 1978. "Contracts: Adjustment of Long-term Economic Relations under Classical, Neoclassical and Relational Contract Law." *Northwestern University Law Review* 72: 854–910.

Maine Economic Conversion Project. 1994. "Conversion Efforts in New England." Portland: MECP.

Manne, Henry. 1965. "Mergers and the Market for Corporate Control." *Journal of Political Economy* 73: 110–120.

Markusen, Ann. 1997a. "The Post–Cold War Persistence of Defense Specialized Firms." Gerald Susman, ed., *Defense Diversification*. Oxford: Elsevier Science.

_____. 1997b. "The Economics of Defense Industry Mergers and Divestitures." *Economic Affairs*.

_____. 1985a. *The Economic and Regional Consequence of Military Innovation*. University of California, Berkeley: Institute of Urban and Regional Development.

_____. 1985b. *Profit Cycles, Oligopoly and Regional Development*. Cambridge, MA: MIT Press.

Markusen, Ann, and Sean Costigan, eds. 1999. *Arming the Future*. New York: Council on Foreign Relations Press.

Markusen, Ann, and Laura Powers. 1999. "A Just Transition? Lessons from Defense Worker Adjustment in the 1990s." Technical Report. Washington, DC: Economic Policy Institute.

Markusen, Ann, and Joel Yudken. 1992. *Dismantling the Cold War Economy*. New York: Basic Books.

Markusen, Ann, et al. 1991. *The Rise of the Gunbelt*. New York: Oxford University Press.

Marris, Peter. 1996. *The Politics of Uncertainty*. London: Routledge.

Marshall, Robert, Michael Meurer, and Jean-Francois Richard. 1991. "The Private Attorney Meets Public Contract Law." *Hofstra Law Review* 20: 1–45.

Martin, John, and John Kensinger. 1990. *Exploring the Controversy over Corporate Restructuring*. Morristown, NJ: Financial Executives Research Foundation.

Massey, Doreen, and Richard Meegan. 1982. *Anatomy of Job Loss*. London: Methuen.

Mata, Jay. 1991. "Sunk Costs and Entry by Small and Large Plants." In P. Geroksi and J. Schwalbach, eds., *Entry and Market Contestability*. Oxford: Blackwell.

Mayer, Kenneth. 1991. *The Political Economy of Defense Contracting*. New Haven: Yale University Press.

Mayer, Kenneth, and Anne Khademian. 1996. "Bringing Politics Back In: Defense Policy and the Theoretical Study of Institutions and Processes." *Public Administration Review* 56(2): 180–190.

McCain, John. 1995. Letter to the Editor. *Washington Post*, October 25: A16.

McCartney, Robert. 1991a. "A Most Unusual Executive Bonus Plan." *Washington Post*, October 21: A1.

_____. 1991b. "Defense Firm's Execs Reap Bonus Bonanza." *Washington Post*, October 9: A1.

McConnell, Grant. 1967. *Private Power and American Democracy*. New York: Knopf.

McCubbins, Matthew, et al. 1989. "Structure and Process, Politics and Policy: Administrative Arrangements and the Political Control of Agencies." *University of Virginia Law Review* 70: 431–482.

McNaugher, Thomas. 1989. *New Weapons, Old Politics*. Washington, DC: Brookings Institution.

Meadows, Sandra. 1996. "Defense Acquisition: Merger Players Shift into Overdrive." *National Defense*, February: 37.

Melman, Seymour. 1983. *Profits without Production*. New York: Knopf.

_____. 1974. *The Permanent War Economy*. New York: Simon and Schuster.

_____. 1971. *Pentagon Capitalism*. New York: McGraw Hill.

Mendelsohn, Everett, Merritt Roe Smith, and Peter Weingart, eds. 1988. *Science, Technology and the Military*. Boston: Kluwer Press.

Mensch, Elizabeth. 1982. "The Colonial Origins of Liberal Property." *Buffalo Law Review* 31.

Meyer, John, and W. Richard Scott. 1983. *Organizational Environments: Ritual and Rationality*. Beverly Hills, CA: Sage.

Midwest Center for Labor Research. 1996. "Social Cost Analysis of the Impact of Mass Layoffs of Electric Boat Shipyard Workers on New London County, Connecticut and Washington County, Rhode Island." Chicago: MCLR.

"Mike Armstrong's Leap of Faith." 1992. *Business Week*, March 9: 58–59.

Miller, Judith. 1993. General Counsel of the Department of Defense, June 13. Unpublished letter.

Millon, David. 1991. "Redefining Corporate Law." *Indiana Law Review* 24(2): 223–277.

_____. 1990. "Theories of the Corporation." *Duke Law Journal* 1990: 201–262.

Mintz, John. 1994a. "Muscular or Moribund: It's a Matter of Opinion When It Comes to General Dynamics." *Washington Post*, December 26: 1.

_____. 1994b. "Pentagon Assailed on Merger Aid." *Washington Post*, July 28: 3.

_____. 1993. "Aspin Sees Military Promoting Clinton Industrial Policy." *Washington Post*, September 3: 11.

Misheloff, Jane. 1994. "Economic Competitiveness and the Future of the Military Industrial Base." *Journal of Strategic Studies* 17: 209–237.

Mitchell, Lawrence, ed. 1995. *Progressive Corporate Law*. Boulder: Westview.

Modligliani, Franco, and Merton Miller. 1958. "The Cost of Capital, Corporation Finance and the Theory of Investment." *American Economic Review* 48: 261–295.

Moe, Ronald. 1987. "Exploring the Limits of Privatization." *Public Administration Review* 47(6): 453–460.

Moe, Terry. 1984. "The New Economics of Organization." *American Journal of Political Science* 28: 739–777.

Mohr, Charles. 1985. "Bill Seeks to End Interest Subsidies to Military Contractors." *New York Times*, January 31: B12.

Moore, Stephen, and Dean Stencil. 1995. "Ending Corporate Welfare as We Know It." Washington, DC: Cato Institute.

Moran, Peg. 1996. "Report to the Manufacturing Cluster Group." Norwich, CT: Corporation for Regional Economic Development, September 17.

Morgenson, Gretchen. 1999. "In Efforts to Please Investors, Reports Too Good to Be True." *New York Times,* December 21: A1.

Morocco, John. 1992. "House Panel Seeks to Boost Pentagon Manufacturing Technology Program." *Aviation Week and Space Technology,* June 1: 52.

Morrison, David. 1993. "Eat or Be Eaten." *National Journal,* March 6: 559.

Morton. 1965. *Public Contracts and Private Wages.* Washington, DC: Brookings Institution.

Moss, Kary. 1995. "The Privatizing of Corporate Wealth." *Fordham Urban Law Journal* 23: 101–153.

Mowery, David, and Rose Marie Ham. 1995. "Enduring Dilemmas in U.S. Technology Policy." *California Management Review* 37(4): 89–129.

Mowery, David, and Nathan Rosenberg. 1993. "The U.S. National Innovation System." In Richard Nelson, ed., *National Innovation Systems.* New York: Oxford University Press.

Mueller, Elizabeth, et al. 1994. "Retraining for What? Displaced Defense Workers Come Up Against EDWAA." New Brunswick, NJ: Project on Regional and Industrial Economics, Rutgers University.

Nagy, Barbara. 1994. "Turner Says E.B. Must Alter Course." *New London Day,* January 20: D1.

_____. 1993. "At E.B. Much Work Is Grinding to a Halt." *New London Day,* October 10: A9.

_____. 1991. "Navy Issues Revised Solicitation for Seawolf." *New London Day,* August 15: C1.

National League of Cities. 1992. *Local Officials Guide to Defense Economic Adjustment.* Washington, DC: NLC.

Neikirk, William. 1994. "Defense Conversion Grants: Smart Cash or Corporate Pork?" *Chicago Tribune,* February 27: 1.

Nelson, Richard. 1988. "Institutions Supporting Technical Change in the United States." In Giavonni Dosi, et al., eds., *Technical Change and Economic Theory.* New York: Pinter Publishers.

"Newport News Ship Suit Likely to Set New Precedent," *Defense Daily,* May 31, 1991.

Nilsson, Cheryl. 1994. "Defense Contractor Recovery of Clean-Up Costs at Contractor Owned and Operated Facilities." *Air Force Law Review* 38: 1–61.

North, Douglass. 1981. *Structure and Change in Economic History.* New York: Norton.

O'Connor, Marleen. 1993. "How Should We Talk about Fiduciary Duty?" *George Washington Law Review* 61: 954–983.

_____. 1991. "Restructuring the Corporation's Nexus of Contracts: Recognizing a Fiduciary Duty to Protect Displaced Workers." *North Carolina Law Review* 69: 1189–1260.

Oden, Michael. 1999. "Cashing-in, Cashing-out and Converting: Restructuring the Defense Industrial Base in the 1990s." In Ann Markusen and Sean Costigan, eds., *Arming the Future: A Defense Industry for the 21st Century.* New York: Council on Foreign Relations Press.

_____. 1994. "The Microeconomics of Defense-Serving Organizations: Implications for Conversion and Adjustment." Paper presented at Allied Social Science Association meeting, Boston, January.

Oden, Michael, and Greg Bischak. 1995. *Coming in from the Cold: Arms Industry Restructuring and Economic Conversion Policies in the U.S., 1989–1993*. Geneva: International Labor Organization.

Oden, Michael, et al. 1993. "Changing the Future: Converting the St. Louis Economy." New Brunswick, NJ: Project on Regional and Industrial Economics, Rutgers University.

Offe, Claus. 1984. *Contradictions of the Welfare State*. Cambridge, MA: MIT Press.

"Once Mighty Shipyard Battens Hatches." *Norwich Bulletin*, March 13, 1994: 1.

Orlans, Harold. 1967. *Contracting for Atoms*. Washington, DC: Brookings Institution.

O'Shea, James. 1985. "Defense Firms Score Direct Hit on Tax Law." *Chicago Tribune*, August 25: C1–C3.

Packard, David. 1986. *An Interim Report to the President by the Blue Ribbon Commission on Defense Management*. Washington, DC: U.S. Department of Defense, February 28.

Pages, Erik. 1995. "The Future of the U.S. Defense Industry: Smaller Markets, Bigger Companies, and Closed Doors." *SAIS Review*, Winter-Spring: 135–151.

_____. 1993. "Special Report: Next Steps in Business Conversion." Washington, DC: Business Executives for National Security.

Pazniokas, Mark. 1992. "Weicker Tax Break Aids Just 1 Company." *Hartford Courant*, February 11: B1.

Pearlstein, Steve. 1993. "General Dynamics CEO to Step Down; Anders Supervised Downsizing, Turnaround of Defense Company." *Washington Post*, March 19: A1.

_____. 1991. "Hard Sell for U.S. Arms: Weapons Makers Feel Same Competitive Pressures as Other Global Industries." *Washington Post*, April 7: H1.

Peck, Merton, and Frederic Scherer. 1962. *The Weapons Acquisition Process: An Economic Analysis*. Boston: Harvard Business School.

Peppard, Don. 1995. "In the Shadow of Foxwoods: Some Effects of Casino Development in Southeastern Connecticut." *Economic Development Review* 13: 44–46.

Perry, Nancy. 1993. "General Dynamics' Selling Strategy." *Fortune*, January 11: 56–57.

Pezard, Alice. 1995. "The Golden Share of Privatized Companies." *Brooklyn Journal of International Law* 21: 85–95.

Pfeffer, Jeffrey, and Gerald Salancik. 1978. *The External Control of Organizations: A Resource Dependence Perspective*. New York: Harper and Row.

Philpott, Nick. 1995. "G.D. Is Mum to Shareholders on Bath Plan." *The New London Day*, May 4: C1.

Pilling, Donald. 1989. *Competition in Defense Procurement*. Washington, DC: Brookings Institution.

Polanyi, Karl. 1944. *The Great Transformation*. Boston: Beacon Press.

Porter, Michael. 1992. *Capital Choices: Changing the Way America Invests in Industry*. Washington, DC: Council on Competitiveness.

Pratt, John, and Richard Zeckhauser. 1991. *Principals and Agents: The Structure of Business*. 2d edition. Cambridge: Harvard Business School Press.

Price Waterhouse and Co. 1976. *1976 Survey of Financial Reporting and Accounting Practices of Government Contractors*.

Rabinow, Paul. 1977. *Reflections on Fieldwork in Morocco.* Berkeley: University of California Press.

Rajan, Raghuram, and Luigi Zingales. 1996. "Power in a Theory of the Firm." Unpublished manuscript, University of Chicago.

Ravenscraft, David, and Frederic Scherer. 1987. *Mergers, Sell-Offs, and Economic Efficiency.* Washington, DC: Brookings Institution.

RAND. 1970. "A Preliminary Analysis of Contractual Outcomes for Nine Air Force Systems Command Contracts." Santa Monica: RAND.

Rawls, John. 1971. *Theory of Justice.* Cambridge, MA: Belknap Press.

Reder, Alan. 1994. *In Pursuit of Principle and Profit.* New York: Putnam.

Regan, Edward. 1988. "GOVERNMENT INC: Creating Accountability for Economic Development Programs." New York: Government Finance Research Center of Government Finance Officers Association 25.

Reich, Robert, and John Donahue. 1985. *New Deals: The Chrysler Revival and the American System.* New York: Times Books.

Remez, Michael, and Frances Grandy Taylor. 1992. "Executive Salaries Spark Anger, Debate." *Hartford Courant,* March 8: A1.

Renner, Michael. 1993. "Environmental Dimensions of Disarmament and Conversion." In Kevin Cassidy and Gregory Bischak, eds., *Real Security.* Albany: SUNY Press.

Reppy, Judith. 1988. "Technology and Trade: Does Military R&D Make a Difference?" In Philip Gummett and Judith Reppy, eds., *The Relations between Defence and Civilian Technologies.* Dordrecht, the Netherlands: Kluwer Academic Publishers.

_____. 1999. "Dual-Use Technology: Back to the Future?" In Ann Markusen and Sean Costigan, eds., *Arming the Future.* New York: Council on Foreign Relations Press.

Rice, Berkeley. 1971. *The C-5A Scandal.* Boston: Houghton-Mifflin.

Robinson, Melissa. 1996. "Even with a Third Seawolf, the State's Defense Industry Will Keep Losing Jobs." *New London Day,* May 12: A4.

Rodengen, Jeffrey. 1994. *The Legend of Electric Boat.* Fort Lauderdale, FL: Write Stuff Syndicate.

Roe, Mark. 1994. *Strong Managers, Weak Owners: The Political Roots of American Corporate Finance.* Princeton: Princeton University Press.

_____. 1990. "Political and Legal Restraints on Ownership and Control of Public Companies." *Journal of Financial Economics* 27: 7–41.

Rogerson, William. 1990. "Quality versus Quantity in Military Procurement." *American Economic Review* 80: 83–110.

Romano, Roberta. 1984. "Metapolitics and Corporate Law Reform." *Stanford Law Review* 36: 923–1016.

Rose, Frederic. 1993. "Peace, Labor and Environmental Coalitions: Class Culture and Democratic Change." Ph.D. dissertation, Cornell University.

Rose-Ackerman, Susan. 1988. "Inalienability and the Theory of Property Rights." *Columbia Law Review* 85: 931–974.

Runzel, Neil. 1994. Letter to the Editor. *Navy News & Undersea Technology,* June 13: 3.

Samuels, Richard. 1994. *Rich Nation, Strong Army: National Security and Ideology in the Technical Transformation of Japan.* Ithaca: Cornell University Press.

Sandel, Michael. 1996. *Democracy's Discontent.* Cambridge, MA: Belknap.

Sandler, Todd, and Keith Hartley. 1995. *The Economics of Defence*. London: Cambridge University Press.

Sapolsky, Harvey. 1990. *Science and the Navy: The History of the Office of Naval Research*. Princeton: Princeton University Press.

Sapolsky, Harvey, and Eugene Gholz. 1999. "Private Arsenals: America's Post–Cold War Burden." In Ann Markusen and Sean Costigan, eds., *Arming the Future: A Defense Industry for the 21st Century*. New York: Council on Foreign Relations Press.

Sapolsky, Harvey, Eugene Gholz, and Ethan McKinney. 1996. "The Quest for Weapons Acquisition Reform." Cambridge, MA: Defense and Arms Control Studies Program, MIT.

Savage, Jon. 1994. "Clinton Following Reagan, Bush in Defense Job Policy." *St. Louis Post-Dispatch*, November 17: 5B.

Savas, Emanuel. 1987. *Privatizing the Public Sector*. Chatham, NJ: Chatham Publishing.

Saxenian, Anna Lee. 1995. *Regional Advantage: Culture and Competition in Silicon Valley and Route 128*. Cambridge, MA: Harvard University Press.

Schauer, Frederick. 1991. *Playing by the Rules: A Philosophical Examination of Rule-Based Decision Making*. New York: Clarendon Press.

Scheppele, Kim, and Jeremy Waldron. 1991. "Contractarian Methods in Political and Legal Evaluation." *Yale Journal of Law and Humanities* 3: 195–242.

Scherer, Frederic. 1964. *The Weapons Acquisition Process: Economic Incentives*. Boston: Harvard Business School Press.

Schine, Erik. 1994. "Cuts Won't Cut It Anymore." *Business Week*, January 10: 72.

Schlesinger, Tom. 1987. "Labor, Automation and Regional Development." In John Tirman, ed., *The Militarization of High Technology*. Boston: Ballinger Press.

Schmitter, Philippe, and Gerhard Lembruch. 1979. *Trends Toward Corporatist Intermediation*. Beverly Hills, CA: Sage.

Schmookler, Jacob. 1966. *Invention and Economic Growth*. Cambridge, MA: Harvard University Press.

Schoeni, Robert, and Michael Dardia. 1996. *Wage Losses and Displaced Workers*. Santa Monica, CA: RAND.

School for Workers and the National Commission for Economic Conversion and Disarmament. 1993. *Defense Industry Conversion: Strategies for Job Redevelopment*. Washington, DC: NCECD.

Schultze, Charles. 1968. *The Politics and Economics of Public Spending*. Washington, DC: Brookings Institution.

Schweickart, David. 1980. *Capitalism or Worker Control?* New York: Praeger.

Sclove, Richard. 1995. *Democracy and Technology*. New York: Guilford Press.

Scott, W. Richard, and John Meyer. 1994. *Institutional Environments and Organizations*. Thousand Oaks, CA: Sage.

Selznick, Philip. 1992. *The Moral Commonwealth*. Berkeley: University of California Press.

"Senate Democrats Mobilize for Defense Conversion." *Navy News & Undersea Technology*, April 9, 1990: 5.

Sennott, Charles. 1996. "Armed for Support: The Selling of U.S. Weapons." *Boston Sunday Globe Special Report*, February 11.

Sharrock, Tim. 1995. "U.S. Shipyards Split over Plan to Implement OECD Ban." *Journal of Commerce*, May 26: 14.

Siegel, Lenny, et al. 1991. *The U.S. Military's Toxic Legacy*. Boston: National Toxic Campaign Fund.

Simon, Herbert. 1958. *Administrative Behavior*. New York: MacMillan.

Simon, William. 1993. "What Difference Does It Make whether Corporate Managers Have Public Responsibilities?" *Washington and Lee Law Review* 50: 1673–1696.

_____. 1991. "Social-Republican Property." *UCLA Law Review* 38: 1335–1413.

_____. 1990. "Contract Versus Politics in Corporation Doctrine." In David Kairys, ed., *The Politics of Law*. New York: Pantheon.

Singer, Joseph. 1988a. "Legal Realism Now." *California Law Review* 76: 465–544.

_____. 1988b. "The Reliance Interest in Property." *Stanford Law Review* 40: 611–751.

Sklar, Martin. 1988. *The Corporate Reconstruction of American Capitalism, 1890–1916*. New York: Cambridge University Press.

Skowroneck, Stephen. 1982. *Building the New American State: The Expansion of National Administrative Capacities, 1877–1920*. New York: Cambridge University Press.

Slaughter, Sheila, and Gary Rhoades. 1996. "The Emergence of a Competitiveness Research and Development Policy Coalition and the Commercialization of Academic Science and Technology." *Science, Technology, and Human Values* 21(3): 303–339.

Smith, Chris. 1996. *Congressional Record*. 104th Congress, 2nd session, Volume 142, Part 87: 6345–6349.

Smith, Lee. 1993. "Coping with the Defense Build-Down." *Fortune*, June 29: 68.

Smith, Merritt Roe. 1980. *Harper's Ferry Armory and the New Technology: The Challenge of Change*. Ithaca: Cornell University Press.

_____. 1985. *Military Enterprise and Technological Change*. Cambridge, MA: M.I.T. Press.

Spar, Deborah, and Raymond Vernon. 1991. *Iron Triangles and Revolving Doors: Cases in U.S. Foreign Economic Policy*. New York: Praeger.

Spinardi, Graham. 1994. *From Polaris to Trident: The Development of U.S. Fleet Ballistic Missile Technology*. New York: Cambridge University Press.

Spivak, Miranda. 1993. "New Deal in Washington: Establishing National Industrial Policy." *Hartford Courant*, March 1: A1.

Starr, Paul. 1988. "The Meaning of Privatization." *Yale Law and Policy Review* 6: 6–41.

Stigler, George. 1971. "The Theory of Economic Regulation." *Bell Journal of Economics* 2: 3–31.

Stigler, George, and Claire Friedland. 1971. "Profits of Defense Contractors." *American Economic Review* 61: 233–251.

Stone, Christopher. 1975. *Where the Law Ends: The Social Control of Corporate Behavior*. New York: Harper and Row.

Stone, Katherine. 1993. "Policing Employment Contracts Within the Nexus of Contracts Firm." *University of Toronto Law Review* 43: 353–387.

_____. 1988. "Labor and Corporate Structure: Changing Conceptions and Emerging Possibilities." *University of Chicago Law Review* 55: 73–173.

Stowsky, Jay. 1999. "The History and Politics of the Pentagon's Dual-Use Strategy." In Ann Markusen and Sean Costigan, eds., *Arming the Future.* New York: Council on Foreign Relations Press.

Stowsky, Jay, and Burgess Laird. 1992. "Conversion to Competitiveness: Making the Most Out of the National Labs." *American Prospect,* Fall: 91–98.

Strack, Blake, and Claude Welch. 1993. "Laissez-Faire Follies; The Politics of Peacetime Conversion." *Society* 30 (4): 4–10.

Strother, Barbara. 1996. "Living and Dying by Submarines: The Submerging and Resurfacing of a Local Economy." Master's thesis, University of Oklahoma.

Stroud, Michael. 1991. "Lockheed's Tellep Rejoices in Simmons' Exit." *Investor Daily,* March 27.

Sunstein, Cass. 1985. "Interest Groups in American Public Law." *Stanford Law Review* 38: 29–101.

TECHCONN. 1993. *TECHCONN Report to Board of Advisors.* Norwich, CT, June 21.

Tilly, Charles. 1990. *Coercion, Capital and European States, A.D. 990–1990.* Cambridge, MA: Blackwell.

Todd, Daniel. 1991. *Industrial Dislocation: The Case of Global Shipbuilding.* London: Routledge.

Tomanelli, Steven. 1995. "Rights and Obligations Concerning Government-Furnished Property." *Public Contract Law Journal* 24: 413–452.

_____. 1993. "The Duty to Eliminate Competitive Advantage Arising from Contractor Possession of GFP." *Military Law Review* 142: 141–163.

Trebilcock, Michael. 1993. *An Exploration of the Limits of Freedom of Contract.* Cambridge, MA: Harvard University Press.

Tuhus, Melinda. 1995. "Housing the Seawolf: River's Role Debated." *Sunday New York Times,* September 10, Section 13: 12.

Tyler, Patrick. 1986. *Running Critical: The Silent War, Rickover and General Dynamics.* New York: Harper and Row.

Tyson, Laura D'Andrea. 1992. *Who's Bashing Whom? Trade Conflict in High-Tech Industries.* Washington, DC: Institute for International Economics.

Uchitelle, Louis. 1995. "Defense Industry Migrating." *New London Day,* April 23: E1.

U.S. Conference of Mayors. 1988. *A Shift in Military Spending to America's Cities.* Lansing, MI: Employment Research Associates.

U.S. Congress Office of Technology Assessment. 1991. *Global Arms Trade: Commerce in Advanced Military Technology and Weapons.* Washington, DC: GPO.

_____. 1991. *Redesigning Defense: Planning the Transition to the Future U.S. Defense Industrial Base.* Washington, DC: GPO.

U.S. Congressional Budget Office. 1993. "Reemploying Defense Workers: Current Experiences and Policy Alternatives." Washington, DC: CBO.

U.S. Department of Defense. 1996. *National Defense Budget Estimates for FY 1997.* Washington, DC: Office of the Comptroller.

_____. 1995. *Dual Use Technology: A Defense Strategy for Affordable, Leading-Edge Technology.* Washington, DC: Department of Defense.

_____. 1993. "Top 100 Prime Contract Awards." Washington, DC: Directorate for Information, Operations and Research.

_____. 1989. "Prime Contract Awards by Region and State." Washington, DC: Directorate for Information, Operations and Research.

_____. 1976. *Profit '76: Summary Report*. Washington, DC: Office of the Assistant Secretary of Defense Installations and Logistics.

U.S. General Accounting Office. 1997. *Defense Industry Trends: Spending, Industrial Productivity, and Competition*, GAO/BEMD-97-3. Washington, DC: GAO.

_____. 1996. *Defense Contractor Restructuring: First Application of Cost and Savings Regulations*, GAO/NSIAD-96-80. Washington, DC: GAO, April.

_____. 1995a. *Defense Contractors: Pay, Benefits, and Restructuring during Defense Downsizing*, GAO/NSIAD-96-19BR. Washington, DC: GAO, October.

_____. 1995b. *Defense Restructuring Costs*, GAO/NSIAD-95-106. Washington, DC: GAO, August.

_____. 1995c. *Defense Downsizing: Selected Contractor Business Unit Reductions*, GAO/NSIAD-95-114. Washington, DC: GAO, May.

_____. 1994a. *Defense Conversion: Capital Conditions Have Improved for Small- and Medium-Sized Firms*, GAO/NSIAD-94-224. Washington, DC: GAO, July.

_____ 1994b. *Navy Ships: Seawolf Cost Increases and Schedule Delays Continue*, GAO/NSIAD-94-201 BR. Washington, DC: GAO, June.

_____. 1993. *Problems Continue to Plague the Seawolf Submarine Program*, GAO/NSIAD-93-171. Washington, DC: GAO, August.

_____. 1988a. *Department of Defense's Management of Government Property Furnished to Defense Contractor*, GAO/T-NSIAD-88-19. Washington, DC: GAO.

_____. 1988b. *Navy Contracting: Cost Overruns and Claims on Navy Shipbuilding Contracts, Report to the Chairman, Subcommittee on Defense, House Committee on Appropriations*, GAO/NSIAD-88-15. Washington, DC: GAO.

_____. 1986a. *Government Contracting: Assessment of the Study of Defense Contractor Profitability*. Washington, DC: GAO.

_____. 1986b. *Contractors Should Further Restrict Use of Completed Contract Method*, GAO/GGD-86-34. Washington, DC: GAO.

_____. 1985a. *Defense Industrial Base: Department of Defense's Manufacturing Technology Program Needs Systematic Evaluation*, B-201974. Washington, DC: GAO.

_____. 1985b. *Investigation by the Department of Justice into Navy Shipbuilding Claims*, GAO/GGD-85-70 B-216322. Washington, DC: GAO.

_____. 1980. *Better Navy Management of Shipbuilding Contracts Could Save Millions of Dollars*, PSAD-80-18. Washington, DC: GAO, January.

U.S. House. 1995. Subcommittee on National Security. *Hearing before Committee on Appropriations*. 107th Congress, 1st Session, April 5.

_____. 1982. Joint Economic Committee. *Hearings on Economics of Defense Policy*. 97th Congress, 2nd Session, January 28.

_____. 1966. Subcommittee on Department of Defense Appropriations. *Hearings on Department of Defense Appropriations Act of 1967*. 89th Congress, 2d Session, Part 6.

U.S. Senate. 1988. Committee on Governmental Affairs. *Government-Furnished Property: Provided to Department of Defense Contractors*. 100th Congress, 2nd Session.

Useem, Michael. 1993. *Executive Defense: Shareholder Power and Corporate Reorganization*. Cambridge, MA: Harvard University Press.

_____. 1984. *Large Corporations and the Rise of Business Political Activity in the U.S. and U.K.* New York: Oxford University Press.

Vartabedian, Ralph. 1994. "Martin Wins U.S. Concessions." *Los Angeles Times,* March 24: D3.

_____. 1990. "Under the Gun: Arms and Fraud." *Los Angeles Times,* May 9: A1.

Velocci, Anthony. 1997. "Index Points to Weakness in U.S. Market Response." *Aviation Week and Space Technology,* June 9: 50–57.

_____ 1996a. "U.S. Industry in Vigorous Fight against Proposed Policy Reversal." *Aviation Week and Space Technology,* July 22: 30–31.

_____. 1996b. "Loral Buy Challenges Lockheed-Martin Skills." *Aviation Week and Space Technology,* January 15: 22–23.

_____. 1995. "Profit Wave Uncovers Nagging Paradoxes." *Aviation Week and Space Technology,* May 29: 36–38.

_____. 1994. "Defense Firms Show Financial Prowess." *Aviation Week and Space Technology,* May 30: 40–47.

Wainwright, Hilary. 1994. *Arguments for a New Left.* Oxford: Blackwell.

Wainright, Hilary, and Dave Elliott. 1982. *The Lucas Plan: A New Trade Unionism in the Making.* London: Allison and Busby.

Walker, William, Mac Graham, and Bernard Harbor. 1988. "From Components to Integrated Systems." In Philip Gummett and Judith Reppy, eds., *The Relations between Defence and Civil Technologies.* Dordrecht, the Netherlands: Kluwer Academic Publishers.

Walzer, Michael. 1983. *Spheres of Justice.* New York: Basic Books.

Wayne, Leslie. 1994. "Have Shareholder Activists Lost Their Edge?" *New York Times,* January 30.

_____. 1989. "Arms Makers Gird for Peace." *New York Times,* December 17, Sec. 3, Late Edition: 1.

Weber, Max. 1978. *Economy and Society.* Edited by Gunther Ross and Claus Wittich. Berkeley: University of California Press.

Weber, Rachel. 2000. "Why Economic Development Subsidies Don't Create Jobs: A Legal Analysis of Corporate Incentive Structures." *The Urban Lawyer* 32 (1): 97–120.

Weida, William, and Frank Gertschner. 1987. *The Political Economy of Defense.* Boulder: Westview.

Weir, Margaret, 1992. *Politics and Jobs.* Princeton: Princeton University Press.

Weisman, Robert. 1994. "General Dynamics to Pay $3.3 Million Settlement." *Hartford Courant,* August 3: B1

_____. 1993a. "E.B. Backs Away from Civilian Market." *Hartford Courant,* September 19: 22.

_____. 1993b. "E.B. Parent Hears Calls for Consolidation." *Hartford Courant,* May 6: 1.

_____. 1992a. "Analysts Firing Linked to General Dynamics." *Hartford Courant,* December 20: 11.

_____. 1992b. "Stock Purchase Has Analysts Predicting Breakup of E.B. Parent." *Hartford Courant,* July 24: 1.

_____. 1992c. "General Dynamics to Begin Buyback." *Hartford Courant,* June 9: 1.

_____. 1991a. "After Heady Days, Electric Boat and Pratt and Whitney Fall into Turmoil." *Hartford Courant*, August 3: 1.

_____. 1991b. "Seawolf: Tiny Cracks, but Huge Overruns and Delays." *Hartford Courant*, August 2: 1.

Weisman, Robert, and John Fitzgerald. 1991. "Defiant Navy Offers Seawolf Terms." *Hartford Courant*, August 15: 1.

Wheeler, James, and Edmund Outslay. 1986. "The Phantom Federal Income Taxes of General Dynamics Corporation." *The Accounting Review* 61(4): 760–774.

White, George. 1991. "Investor Ends Lockheed Fight at Cost of $30 Million." *New York Times*, March 19: A1.

Williamson, Oliver. 1985. *The Economic Institutions of Capitalism*. New York: Free Press.

_____. 1975. *Markets and Hierarchies*. New York: Free Press.

Wilson, Randy. 1993. "Making Peace Practical." *In These Times*, July 12: 19–22.

Wrubel, Robert. 1992. "Crown Agents." *Financial World*, June 9: 26.

Yeager, Holly. 1996. "'Payoffs for Layoffs' Targeted." *New London Day*, July 7: C2.

Yudken, Joel. 1993. "Economic Development, Technology and Defense Conversion." In Kevin Cassidy and Greg Bischak, eds., *Real Security: Converting the Defense Economy and Building Peace*. Albany: SUNY Press.

Zeckhauser, Richard, and John Pound. 1990. "Are Large Shareholders Effective Monitors?" In R. Glenn Hubbard, ed., *Asymmetric Information, Corporate Finance and Investment*. Chicago: University of Chicago Press.

Zysman, John. 1983. *Government, Markets and Growth*. Ithaca: Cornell University Press.

Index